Outdoor Life

Narrow Escapes and Wilderness Adventures

by Ben East

Published by **OUTDOOR LIFE BOOKS**

Distributed in the trade by **STACKPOLE BOOKS**

LIBRARY OF CONGRESS CATALOG CARD NUMBER 60-8093

ISBN 0-943822-14-9

Tribute to Ben East Edition: 1982

PRINTED IN THE UNITED STATES OF AMERICA

Foreword to the 1982 Edition

BY Bill Rae, Former Editor-In-Chief, OUTDOOR LIFE

Ben East, now in semiretirement, is many things: photographer, lecturer, and conservationist of national renown. More than all of these, however, he is a writer — an editor's writer — and never better than when turning his hand to a yarn of high adventure, close-call, or hardship in the outdoors. With never a thought for his own safety, if it came to that.

I was his editor at *Outdoor Life* for 22 years and published a great number of the 1,200 stories he has written.

I had occasion many a time to thank my stars for having this paragon of field men on tap whenever an exciting ordeal came to light anywhere within a radius of 5,000 miles or so of his home in Holly, Michigan. Once he got on the job, I automatically checked off another exciting story for *Outoor Life*.

Contents

Foreword . . . v

Introduction . . . ix

Frozen Terror . . . 1

She-Bear in the Night . . . 19

Devil of the Laurel Hells . . . 27

Between Life and Death . . . 39

The Bitter Night . . . 55

A Very Tough Bear . . . 67

Hell in Cold Water . . . 81

Handgun versus a Brownie . . . 95

Night without Fire . . . 107

The Cruel Cold . . . 123

Arrow for a Grizzly . . . 137

Squall of Content . . . 149

The Widow Maker . . . 161

Search for a Boy . . . 179

Foot Race with a Grizzly . . . 197

Strike of Death . . . 209

The Circuit Rider . . . 223

Arrow in the Night . . . 239

Lost for Forty Days . . . 253

The Desperate Search . . . 281

The Bad Actors of Africa . . . 295

Introduction

THIS BOOK is dedicated with profound admiration to the people whose ordeals are described in its pages. My thanks, first of all, for their permission to include their stories here.

This is a collection of stories about humans who suffered pain and fear, hunger, freezing and exhaustion; ordinary persons confronting the ultimate, frightened but swallowing their fear, knowing the odds but refusing to die.

With the exception of one, these stories describe narrow escapes that happened in connection with hunting and fishing, which are certainly not regarded as dangerous pastimes and are engaged in safely by many millions each year. Every now and then, however, because of an error in judgement or behavior on the part of the sportsman himself, or through unusual and unforeseen circumstances beyond his control, danger confronts him in one form or another, suddenly and without warning. These are the chronicles of twenty-odd men and a woman and a boy to whom that happened.

They were not heroes, not extraordinary in any way, not specially trained, fitted or equipped for what befell them. They were like you who read this book or like your hunting and fishing companions. All possessed one common attribute—a fierce, unquenchable will to live, just as you and I do. And without exception, when danger breathed down their necks, when things got tough, when the stakes were living and dying, they rose simply and unpretentiously to heroic levels, they showed unflinching courage and fortitude, they endured what they had to and fought back with brave and stubborn determination. It's good to know that common men behave that way at such times.

How did these stories come to be written? In the more than twenty years I worked as a freelance outdoor writer and, since 1946, as a staff editor of *Outdoor Life* magazine, stories of exceptional adventure and close calls by hunters and fishermen have held a particular fascination for me. This is partly because stories of this kind are not common, more because of their inherent interest and the qualities of courage and resourcefulness they so often reveal. I have tracked down and investigated many of them. These twenty-one are the best of the lot, those that stood up to scrutiny and seemed worth putting on paper.

All of them were written originally for *Outdoor Life*. Some were recorded by the men themselves, some I wrote as they were related to me, others I pieced together from diaries, letters and similar material. In all cases I did editorial work on them and had firsthand knowledge of the events they recount.

I think the reader will be likely to ask one question. Did these things really happen?

I believe I can answer that. I know these people personally. In all cases where the circumstances were not already known to me, I checked their stories carefully before *Outdoor Life* published them. I examined newspaper accounts, hospital records, letters written by friends or members of the families, or I gathered conclusive evidence as to the truthfulness of the men themselves. I give you my word that these adventures happened as they are related here.

I should like to make one further point. There is no sermon on safety between these covers. Nevertheless, the reader will find suggestions and rules of common sense that, if followed by hunters, fishermen and outdoorsmen generally, may do much to save others from what these men endured. Hunters who have been lost know how to avoid being lost again. Once struck by a venomous snake, the victim is eager to tell you how to shun such an ordeal. Those who have faced enraged and dangerous game animals have sound advice for others in a similar situation. Such things are told in these pages. They are worth remembering.

Ben East

Holly, Michigan

Narrow

Escapes and

Wilderness

Adventures

Frozen Terror

LEWIS SWEET tramped across the rock-strewn, snowy beach of Crane Island with two companions on that bitterly cold Tuesday morning in January, 1929. Lew didn't know that before the week was up his name would be on the lips of people and on the front pages of newspapers across the country. Nor did he guess, as he pushed on toward the rough shore ice and the lake-trout grounds beyond, that he was walking that beach for the last time in his life on two good feet.

The three men were planning to spend the day fishing through the ice off Crane Island in their lightproof shanties. As they reached the fishing area, Lew waved good-bye to his friends and headed for his shanty. He would kindle a fire of dry cedar in the tiny stove, sit and dangle a wooden decoy in the clear, green water beneath the ice in the hope of luring a prowling trout up to within reach of his heavy, seven-tined spear. If he was lucky he would take four or five good fish by midafternoon. Then he could still drive the 30 miles to his home in the village of Alanson in time for supper.

The Crane Island winter fishing grounds lay west of Waugoshance Point, at the extreme northwest tip of Michigan's mitten-shaped lower peninsula. The point is a long, narrow tongue of sand, sparsely wooded, roadless and wild, running out into the lake at the western end of the Straits of Mackinac. Crane Island marks land's end. Both the island and the Point were unpeopled. Between them on the open ice of Lake Michigan, a mile offshore, Lew and the other fishermen had their darkhouses.

Fishing was slow that morning. It was close to noon before the heavy bulk of a trout slid into sight under the hole where Lew was keeping vigil and stalking his decoy. Maneuvering the wooden minnow away, he eased his spear noiselessly through the water. The trout moved ahead a foot or two, deliberate and cautious. As it came to rest directly beneath him, eying the slow-swimming decoy with a mixture of hunger and wariness, Lew drove the spear down with a hard, sure thrust.

The handle was a steel rod between eight and ten feet long, but it was attached to the roof of the shanty by 50 feet of stout line. After he felt the barbed tines go deep into the fish, Lew let go of the handle and the heavy spear swiftly forced the impaled, twisting trout bottomward to the reef 30 feet below the ice. Let the two of 'em fight it out down there.

The fish ceased struggling after a couple of minutes, so Lew hauled it up on the line. When he opened the shanty door and backed out to disengage the trout from the spear, he noticed that the wind was rising and that the air was full of snow. The day was turning blustery. Have to watch the ice on a day like that, Lew reflected. Could break loose along the shore and go adrift. The wind, however, was still blowing from the west. Lew knew that so long as it didn't change direction there was no danger.

About an hour after he had taken the first trout, the two men fishing with him stopped by.

"We're goin' in, Lew," one of them hailed. "The wind is haulin' around nor'east. It don't look good. Better come along."

Lew stuck his head out the door of his shanty and squinted skyward, studying the weather.

"Be all right for a spell, I guess," he answered. "The ice'll hold unless it blows harder than this. I want one more fish."

He waved and shut the door, and they went on.

It was only 30 minutes later that Lew, alone now, suddenly heard the crunch and rumble of breaking ice off to the east.

The grinding, groaning noise, coming closer, rolled across the field like thunder. The vibration caused the darkhouse to shake as if a train were passing.

Lew had done enough winter fishing on the Big Lake to know the terrible portent of that sound. He flung open the shanty door, grabbed his ax and trout, and raced out across the ice for the snow-clouded timber of Crane Island.

Halfway to the beach he saw what he dreaded—a narrow

vein of black zigzagging across the white of the ice field. When he reached the band of open water, it was only ten feet across, but it widened perceptibly while he watched it, wondering if he dared risk plunging in. But he knew the chance was too great to take. He was a good swimmer, but the water would be numbingly cold. He reckoned, too, on the sucking undertow set up by 100,000 tons of ice driving lakeward with the wind. Even if he crossed the few yards of water successfully, he would have little hope of crawling up onto the smooth shelf of ice on the far side.

He stood there spellbound, watching the black channel grow to 20 feet, then to 100. At last, when he could barely see across it through the swirling snowstorm, he turned and walked grimly back to his darkhouse.

There was a supply of firewood to last through the after-noon and night, and although he wanted desperately to take advantage of a fire and shelter, he knew better. His only chance lay in remaining out on the open floe, watching the ice for cracks and breaks, staying alert for the eventual break-up of the entire field.

Resolutely turning his back on the darkhouse, Lew moved to the center of the drifting floe and set to building up a low wall of snow to break the wind. It was slow work with no tool but his ax, and he hadn't been at it long when he heard a pistol-sharp report rip across the ice. He looked up to see his shanty settling into a yawning black crack. While he watched it, the broken floe crunched and ground back against the main field, completely crushing the frail darkhouse. Half an hour later the ice swallowed up, one after the other, the two shanties of his companions. Now his last hopes of warmth and shelter were gone. Live or die, he would have to see it through on the open ice with nothing between him and the wind, save his snowwall. With grim determination, he went back to building it.

He realized that his chances weren't very good. Unless the ice field grounded on Hog or Garden Island, at a place where he could get to the beach, some 60 miles of open water lay ahead between him and the west shore of the lake. There was little hope, however, that the floe would hold together that distance, not with a winter gale churning up the lake. Lew knew that even a sheet of ice three miles across and two feet thick, buffeted by wind and pounding waves, can stay intact only so long. But even if the field did hold together, there was little chance that the wind would stay steady in one quarter long enough to drive him straight across. It was blowing from due east now, but before morning it would more likely go back into the northeast. If he was still alive by that time, he would be out in midlake beyond Beaver, High and the other outlying islands. And there, with a northeast storm behind him, he would drift more than 100 miles without sighting land.

In midafternoon hope welled up in him for a little while. The drift was carrying him toward Waugoshance Light, a lighthouse abandoned and dismantled years before. It looked for a time as if he would ground against its foot, but then the currents shifted the direction of the ice field a couple of degrees. When he went past he was only a hundred yards or so away.

Waugoshance was an empty place without fuel or food, no more than a broken crib of rock and concrete and a gaunt, windowless shell of rusted steel. But it was a pinpoint of land there in the vast, gray lake. It meant escape from the icy water all around, and it spelled survival, for a few hours at least. Almost within reach of the landmark, Lew looked hungrily at the squat, red tower which first drifted by and then receded, with heart-breaking finality, into the swirling storm.

At that time, although Lew had no way of knowing it, a search incorporating the rescue resources of the entire state was being marshalled and organized. The two men who had fished with him that morning had still been on Crane Island when the ice had broken away. They had stayed on, concerned and uneasy, watching the weather, waiting to make sure Lew made it back to the beach before they left the area. Later, even through the blinding snow, they had seen the unmistakable black streak of icy water grow wider and wider as the floe went adrift. They knew Lew was still out there somewhere on the ice. Losing no more time, they piled into their car and raced for the hamlet of Cross Village, ten miles to the south on the high bluffs of Sturgeon Bay.

Actually there was little the Cross Villagers or anybody else could do at the moment; however, word of Lewis Sweet's plight was flashed south to downstate cities and relayed across the nation. One of the most intense, and fruitless, searches for a lost man in Michigan's history was under way.

The situation was a dramatic but familiar one: puny man pitted against the elements. A flyspeck of humanity was out there alone, somewhere in an endless waste of ice and water, beset by snow and gale, numb and half frozen, trying to stave off death hour after hour as best he could. No one who heard the story was unmoved. Millions sat by their firesides that winter night, wondering about Lewis Sweet, drifting unsheltered in the bitter darkness.

The blinding snowstorm continued throughout that night and it was still snowing Wednesday morning. During the forenoon, however, the storm blew itself out, and then every available searcher in northern Michigan went into action.

There was too much ice in the north end of Lake Michigan to use boats for the search. It had to be made from the air and on foot along the shore of Waugoshance Point and around Crane Island, south into Sturgeon Bay and on the frozen beaches of the islands that lay farther out in the lake.

Coast Guard crews and civilian volunteers joined forces. Men walked the beaches, clambering over rough hummocks of shore ice, looking for tracks, a thread of smoke, the remnants of fire—any sign at all that Lew had made land. Other men scanned the ice fields and the outlying islands of Garden, Hog and Hat from the air. Pilots plotted 2,000 square miles of lake and ice into strips and grids and flew them systematically, one by one, searching for a black dot that might be a man huddled on a drifting floe.

Lewis Sweet, who Tuesday morning was hardly known to anyone beyond the limits of Alanson, had overnight become an object of nationwide concern. Men, 1,000 miles from the ice of Lake Michigan, were buying their local papers to learn the latest news about the lost fisherman. The reports were all the same—little by little, hour by hour, hope ebbed among the searchers. No man could survive long on the open ice. Time spun out, a day, two, then three days, and still no trace of Lew had been found. By Friday night hope was just about dead. How could any man endure so many hours of cold and storm without shelter, fire or food? On Saturday, the last day of the search, those who remained in it were looking only for an immobile, dark spot on the beach—a frozen body scoured bare of snow by the wind. At dusk that day even the feeble hope of making that find had died out. Reluctantly, the searchers abandoned the rescue operation.

Nobody was wondering any more whether Lewis Sweet would be rescued, or how. Instead they asked themselves whether his body would be found on some lonely beach when spring came, or if the manner of his dying would ever be known.

But Lew had not died.

Twice more on Tuesday after passing Waugoshance Light he had believed that he would escape the lake before dark. The first time was when Hat Island loomed up through the storm, a timbered dot on a gray sea that smoked with snow. The floe seemed to be bearing directly down on it.

He knew no one lived on Hat and that he would find no cabin or other shelter there. But there was plenty of dry wood for a fire and he had his big trout for food. He could get along all right until the storm was over and, when the weather cleared, some way would be found to rescue him. But even while he was anticipating the immense relief of being able to trade the drifting ice floe for solid ground and of knowing he was not going to die, he saw that the course of the field was taking him clear of the island. Bitterly, he resigned himself to a night of drifting.

The next time it had been the much bigger Hog Island, which also offered no shelter, that seemed to lie in his path. But again the wind and currents played their tricks and he was carried past, little more than a stone's throw from the beach. As if to tantalize him deliberately, a solitary gull, a holdover from the big flock that had bred there in summer, flew out from the ice hummocks heaped along the shore, alighted on his floe, and then, after a few minutes, casually soared back to the island.

"This is the first time in my life I wish I had wings!" Lew muttered to himself.

That night was pretty bad. The storm mounted into a raging blizzard. As the winter darkness was coming down, the section of ice where Lew had built his snow shelter suddenly broke away from the main field. There in the dusk, he heard the splintering noise, saw the crack start to widen only a few yards away. He gathered up his fish and his precious ax and ran for a place where the pressure of the wind still held together the two masses of ice which were grinding against each other. Even there the crevice opened ahead of him as he reached it, but it was only a couple of feet wide and he was able to jump across to the temporary safety of the big floe.

Again he set to work to build a shelter with blocks of snow. When it was finished he lay down behind it to escape the bitter wind. But the cold started to numb him after a few minutes, and he got to his feet and raced back and forth across the ice to get his blood going again.

He spent the rest of the night that way, lying briefly behind a snow wall for shelter, then forcing himself to his feet once more to fight off the fatigue and drowsiness that he knew would finish him if he gave in to it.

He was out in the open lake now, miles from any lee shore, where the storm had a chance to vent its full fury on the ice field. Before midnight the field broke in two near him again, compelling him to abandon his snow shelter once more in order to stay with the main floe. Again he had the presence of mind to take his ax and trout along. The same thing happened once more after that, in the small hours of the morning.

Toward daybreak the cold grew more intense. And now the storm played a strange and cruel prank. The wind hauled into the southwest, reversing the drift of the ice field and sending it back almost the way it had come, toward the distant north shore of Lake Michigan. In the darkness, however, Lew was not immediately aware of the shift.

9

The ice was staying together better than he anticipated. As near as he could estimate—and daylight was to confirm his guess—the field was still some two miles across, marked by breaks and cracks but not disintegrating.

The huge floe went aground an hour before daybreak, without warning. There was a sudden crunching thunder of sound and the edge of the ice rose out of the water directly ahead of Lew, curled back upon itself like the nose of a giant toboggan and came crashing down in an avalanche of two-ton blocks. The entire field shuddered and shook and seemed about to splinter into fragments. Lew ran for his life.

It took the two-mile field five to ten minutes to lose its momentum and come to rest on the reef that had stopped it. When the splintering, grinding noise finally subsided, Lew went cautiously back in the predawn dark to learn what had happened. He had no idea where he was on the lake or what obstacle the floe had encountered. He was not even sure from which direction the wind was blowing. To his astonishment, he found that he had been brought up at the foot of White Shoals Lighthouse, one of Lake Michigan's most isolated lights, which rises from a concrete crib bedded on a submerged reef more than a dozen miles from the nearest land. The floe had slid aground on the reef and the heavy crib sheared into it like a giant plow until it finally stopped moving.

Lew was close to temporary safety at last. Just 22 feet away, up the vertical concrete face of the crib, lay shelter, fuel and food. Only 22 feet, four times his own height. But it might as well have been 22 miles. For the entire crib above the water line was encased in ice a foot thick, formed by freezing spray, and the steel ladder bedded in the concrete wall showed only as a bulge on the smooth, sheer face of the ice.

Lew located the ladder in the gray light of that stormy winter morning and went to work with his ax. He chopped away the ice as high as he could reach, standing on the floe, freeing the rungs one at a time. Then he stepped up on the first one, hung on with one hand and went on chopping with the other, chipping and worrying at the flinty sheath that enclosed the rest of the ladder.

Three hours after he had cut the first chip of ice away he was three rungs away from the top. Three steps, less than a yard—but he knew he wasn't going to make it! His hands had lost all feeling more than two hours before. They were so badly frozen now that he could no longer keep a grip on either the ladder or the ax, which he dropped half a dozen times, clambering awkwardly down after it, then mounting wearily up the rungs again. The first couple of times it hadn't been so bad but the climb had become more difficult each time after that. Now he realized he was through. His feet were wooden stumps on which he could no longer trust his weight. He had to look to make sure his fingers were hooked around a steel rung. The next time he dropped the ax he wouldn't be able to come back up the ladder. He took a few short, ineffectual strokes and the ax went clattering to the ice below. He climbed stiffly down and huddled on a block of ice to rest.

It's hard to give up and die of cold and hunger with food and warmth only 20 feet away. Lew refused to accept the idea. There had to be some way up to the top.

Hunched there on his block of ice, out of sight of land, with ice and water all around and the wind driving snow into his clothing at every buttonhole, an idea came to him. He could build a ramp of ice blocks up to the top of the crib.

The material lay waiting. It had piled up when the edge

of the floe had shattered against the base of the light. It would have taken ten men to move some of the blocks, but some were small enough for Lew to lift. Frozen hands or no, he went to work.

Three hours later he finished the job and, crawling and dragging himself, thrust himself over the icy, treacherous lip of the crib.

Any man in his right mind could have seen that Lewis Sweet's situation was still a critical one. White Shoals Light had been closed weeks before, at the end of the lake's navigable season. Lew, with frozen hands and feet, was alone on a concrete island 100 feet square, in midlake where a January blizzard was blowing itself out—and not a living soul had the faintest inkling he was there or that he was alive. It was hardly a time for celebrating, but in his 50 some years he had never known a more triumphant moment.

The lighthouse crew had left the door unlocked when they departed for the winter, except for a heavy screen that posed no barrier to a man with an ax. After his hours on the ice and his ordeal at the foot of the crib, the lost man found paradise.

There was bacon, rice, dried fruit, flour, tea and other supplies in abundance. There were three small kerosene stoves and plenty of fuel for them. There were matches. There was everything to keep a man alive for weeks, maybe until spring.

At the moment Lew had no interest in food. He was too worn out to eat. He wanted only to sleep. So he cut the shoes off his frozen feet, thawed his feet and hands as best he could over one of the oil stoves and fell into a bed in the living quarters of the light.

He slept nearly 24 hours. When he awoke Thursday morning, he cooked the first meal he had eaten since his breakfast at home 48 hours before. It put new life into him, and he sat down to take careful stock of his situation.

The weather had cleared and he could see the timbered shore of the lake both to the north and south, beckoning, taunting him, a dozen miles away. Off in the southeast he could even see the low shape of Crane Island where he had been set adrift. But between him and the land, in any direction, lay those miles of water, dotted with fields of drifting ice. From the tower of the light, Lake Michigan was a curious patchwork of color. It looked like a vast white field, veined and netted with gray-green. That network of darker color would be open leads and channels separating the ice fields. Unless there came a night of severe cold without wind or sea to close all that open water, Lew knew he would have to remain a prisoner on the tiny concrete island.

Had it not been for his frozen hands and feet, that would not have worried him greatly. But he knew that unless he got medical attention soon he was in for serious trouble. There was a fair chance the lake might not freeze all the way across to shore the rest of the winter. It wasn't a nice predicament, but he was safe for the present, and he wouldn't worry about it. He would take one thing at a time.

He was doing exactly that shortly after noon on Thursday, sitting beside his oil fire opening bloody blisters on his feet, when he heard the thrumming roar of a plane outside.

Instinctively he knew it was a rescue craft sent out to search for him, and bounding up on his crippled feet, he rushed to the nearest window.

But the windows were covered with heavy screen to protect them from wind and weather. No chance to wave or signal there. The door opening out on the crib, by which he had gained entrance to the light, was two or three flights below the living quarters. No time to get down there. There was a nearer exit in the lens room at the top of the tower, one flight up.

The pilot of the plane had gone out of his way to have a look at White Shoals. He didn't really hope to find any trace of the lost man there, so he saw no reason to linger. Two or three hundred feet above the lake, he tipped the plane into a steep bank and roared once around the light. Seeing nothing but a ridge of ice and snow piled in jumbled disorder the length of the reef, he leveled off and headed for his home field for a fresh supply of gas to carry him out on another flight.

While the pilot made that one swift circle of the light, Lew was hobbling up the iron stairs as fast as his swollen, painful feet would carry him. But he was too late. When he reached the lens room and stepped out through the door, the plane was already far out over the lake, disappearing swiftly to the south.

Most men would have lost heart then and there, but Lew had been through too much to give up at that point. Back in the living quarters he sat down and went stoically on with the job of administering first aid to his feet.

"It don't hurt to freeze," he related later with a dry grin, "but it sure hurts like hell to thaw out!"

Before the day was over another plane, or the same one on a return flight, roared over White Shoals. But the pilot didn't even bother to circle that time and Lew didn't even make the stairs. He watched helplessly from a screened window as the plane became a speck in the sky and finally vanished.

Lew was convinced then that if he was going to get back to shore he would have to do it on his own. It was plain that nobody guessed his whereabouts, or seriously considered the empty lighthouse a possibility.

There was no way for Lew to put the light into operation. Its powerful beam would certainly have attracted attention at that season. But after dark that night he tried another way to signal the mainland. He rigged a crude flare, a ball of oil-soaked waste on a length of wire, and went out on the balcony of the lens room and swung it back and forth, hoping its feeble red spark might be seen by someone on shore. As he stood there, he could see the bright lights of Cross Village winking from the high bluff twenty miles away at the south end of Sturgeon Bay. How they seemed to mock him! After a long while he gave up for the night.

On Friday morning Lew hung out crude signal flags—towels and clothing—on the chance that another plane might pass, but none came near the light that day. The hours dragged by. Fresh blisters kept swelling up on Lew's feet and he opened and drained them as fast as they appeared. He cooked and ate three good meals, and at nightfall he climbed back to the lens room, went outside in the bitter wind and swung his oil-rag beacon again for a long time. He did that twice more during the night, sending the faint signal winking through the dark. But it could hardly have been seen two miles away, let alone across all the ice and water that separated him from land.

The lake still held him a prisoner Saturday, but that night he began to believe that his escape from the lighthouse was at hand. The wind fell, the night was starlit and still and very cold. When he awoke on Sunday morning there was no open water in sight. The leads and channels were covered with new ice as far as he could see. And it was ice that would bear a man's weight.

Whether he would encounter open patches of water before he reached shore there was no way to guess. He couldn't worry

15

about that now. Lew knew that his time was running out; the search for him had certainly been given up by this time. This was his last chance, and he would have to gamble on it. His feet were in terrible shape; in another day or two it would be too late for him to travel. If he didn't get away from White Shoals today, he would never leave it alive. His feet were too swollen for shoes, but he had found plenty of heavy woolen socks in the lighthouse. He pulled on three or four pairs, and contrived to get into the heavy rubbers he had been wearing over his shoes when he was blown out into the lake on Tuesday.

When he climbed painfully down from the crib that crisp Sunday morning and started his slow trek over the ice toward Crane Island, he took along two items: his ax and the frozen trout he had speared five days before. If he succeeded in reaching shore they meant fire and food. More important, however, they had become symbols of his fierce, steadfast determination to stay alive. So long as he kept them with him he was able to believe that he would not freeze or starve.

Now an odd thing happened, one of those ironic quirks that seem to be destiny's special delight at such times. At the very hour when Lew was climbing down from the lighthouse and moving off across the ice, three searchers were setting out from the headquarters of Wilderness State Park, ten miles east of Crane Island to have a final look for his body.

They had decided to search the ice-fringed beach of Waugoshance Point one more time. They carried no binoculars that morning. The three men had left them behind deliberately to eliminate useless weight, certain they would have no need for them. Had they had a pair along as they snowshoed down the shore and searched around the ice hummocks on the sandy beach of the point, and had they turned them a single time in the direction of White Shoals Light, a far-off gray sliver rising out of the frozen lake, they could not possibly have failed to pick up the tiny black figure of a man crawling at snail's pace over the ice.

Had they spotted him the searchers could have had him ashore shortly after noon that day and in a hospital by nightfall. By that time Lew needed medical attention so urgently that he would spend the ten weeks following his rescue in a hospital where surgeons amputated all his fingers and toes and where his frozen hands and feet slowly healed.

But the hospital was still two days away. Toward noon the three searchers trudged back from their fruitless search, never suspecting how close they had come to a dramatic rescue of the man who had been sought during the five days of the most intensive mass search in the history of that lonely section of Michigan.

Lew crept over the ice all day. His progress was slow. Inside the heavy socks he could feel fresh blisters swelling on his feet. The blisters puffed up until he was literally rolling on them as he walked. Again and again he went ahead a few steps, sat down and rested, got up and doggedly drove himself on. At times he had to crawl on all fours.

He detoured around places where the new ice looked unsafe. Late in the afternoon he passed the end of Crane Island, at about the spot where he had been set adrift. Land was within reach at last and night was coming on, but he did not go ashore. He had set his sights on Cross Village as the nearest source of help, and he knew he could make better time on the open ice than along the rocky beach of Sturgeon Bay.

Late that day, Lew realized that his mind was faltering for the first time. He kept becoming confused and found it hard to keep his course. At dark he stumbled into a deserted shanty on the shore of the bay, where fishermen sometimes spent a night. He was still seven miles short of his goal.

The shanty meant shelter for the night and in it he found firewood and a rusty stove, but no supplies except coffee and a can of frozen milk. He was still carrying his trout, but he was too weak now to thaw and cook it. With great effort he succeeded in making coffee. It braced him and he lay down on the bunk to sleep.

Before morning he was violently ill with nausea and cramps, perhaps from lack of food or from the frozen milk he had used with the coffee. At daybreak he tried to drive himself on toward Cross Village, but he was too sick and weak to stand. He lay helpless in the shanty all day Monday and through Monday night, eating nothing.

Tuesday morning he summoned his little remaining strength to start south once more, hobbling and crawling over the rough ice of Sturgeon Bay. It was a long trek, but he made it. Near noon of that day, almost a week to the hour from the time the wind had set him adrift on his ice floe, he stumbled up the steep bluff at Cross Village and called to a passing Indian for help.

Alone and unaided, Lewis Sweet had come home from the lake. When the Indian ran to help him only then did Lew put down the two things he was carrying—the battered ax that had been dulled against the iron ladder of White Shoals light, and the big lake trout that had frozen hard as granite.

She-Bear in the Night

HARRY LANCE made his bed on the bank of the Saaok River on Alaska's Chicagof Island that August night in 1931. Deciding not to make a fire, he laid his .30/40 Krag on the ground beside him, rolled up in his blanket, fought mosquitoes awhile, and drifted into sleep as soon as darkness fell.

He was to discover that he had made his bed at the crossing of two of the most heavily used brown-bear trails in Alaska.

Some time later he was awakened abruptly. He came out of sleep sitting bolt upright, startled and scared, gripping the Krag with both hands, certain there was something near him, yet without the slightest idea what it was. He could hear only the familiar sounds of fast water tumbling over rocks down in the river, and the far-off honking of a small flock of wild geese passing high overhead. The night was pitch black; Harry could see nothing at all. Yet the feeling persisted that he was being watched at close range, and, in view of the fact that this was bear territory, he couldn't help but think that the watcher might be an Alaska brownie.

The biggest carnivore left on earth, the brown bear fascinated Harry, and from the time he was old enough to read about them the idea of photographing them had seemed to him the most exciting adventure imaginable.

When the Philadelphia Academy of Natural Sciences sent him to Alaska with the Atterbury Expedition in the spring of 1931 to do the expedition's collecting and taxidermy work, he naturally considered the post as an opportunity to fulfill his lifelong ambition.

The expedition had spent the spring and early summer in the fog and mists of the Bering Sea, collecting seals, sea lions and a variety of sea-birds. Early August found the Pribilof Islands and their teeming horde of fur seals far astern, as the party headed toward the Alaskan Panhandle, where they were to take a group of mountain goats. Now, Harry told himself, he would get his bear pictures.

When they reached Chicagof Island, they found the sand bars and river banks there trampled by brown bears. Huge tracks crisscrossed the sand flats where the brownies had converged on the streams for their annual feast of salmon. At frequent intervals along the banks, the tall grass was tramped down in beds the size of dinner tables, and partially eaten salmon littered the bars. But for five days nobody actually saw a bear.

Harry was frantic. Here he was in as good brown-bear country as he could ever hope to find, yet his chances for pictures seemed to be slipping away. At last in desperation, he went to the expedition leader and asked permission to spend a night ashore. He said he wanted to hike inland, away from the beach, sleep in the open, and be on hand at daybreak when the bears came to the Saaok to feed.

His superior was reluctant, but the young taxidermist finally received grudging consent. About seven that evening, two other members of the party rowed him to the beach in a dory and pulled away with a few parting wisecracks about man-eating brown bears and a crazy taxidermist who was going to "stuff 'em a new way." Harry admitted later that when he realized he was on his own he felt a little uneasy.

Adjusting his hip boots and pack, he started up the Saaok. Thick tangles of devil's-club, the curse of Alaskan foot travel, made walking impossible on the banks, so he took to the middle of the stream and waded. He made slow progress, but he kept going. More than an hour later, some two miles upriver, he spotted the sort of place he was looking for: a little opening covered by a thick bed of soft moss, with a clear view for some distance up and down the stream. He moved back ten yards or so from the river bank, kicked off his boots and pants and, to protect himself against the mosquitoes, rolled up in his blanket.

He lay for a long time debating the question of a fire. Common sense dictated that he build one for safety's sake, but there were also good arguments on the other side. A fire would be likely to scare off any bear that came along. Also the expedition's time on Chicagof was nearly up now. If he didn't get the pictures he wanted this time, he probably wouldn't get them at all. He had waited a long time for this chance. He decided to risk doing without the fire.

He had been in the blanket about an hour, the long Alaskan twilight was beginning to fade, making it too dark for pictures, when he heard a commotion in the river about 30 yards away. He grabbed the Krag and sat up, and there in the stream, head cocked to one side as it watched for salmon, was a brown giant that looked to Harry like a full ton of bear. While he watched, the brownie lunged for a fish, missed and grunted loudly.

It came on, wading slowly downstream in his direction, closer and closer, until it was only 30 feet away. Lifting its head and sniffing in sudden suspicion, it turned and looked directly at Harry.

It was a long, hard look. Just how long the bear and the man stared at each other, ten paces apart, Harry couldn't say for sure. In the fading light he watched, fascinated, as the bear twisted its snout inquisitively from side to side, while beads of water coursed down its face and dripped from its muzzle.

The bear made the first move. It swung back into the river with a disdainful snort, and moved on downstream, continuing its fishing without so much as a backward glance.

For a few minutes Harry gave serious thought to pulling out and going back to the ship. After all, the bear was terribly big, and it had come far too close for comfort. But Harry still wanted the pictures he had come for, and he dreaded the ridicule of the rest of the party. They would never believe his story. They would be sure Harry had simply lost his nerve. So in the end he decided to stick it out.

He concluded that he had been right after all in not building a fire. He had just had proof that a brown bear was willing to live and let live. The big fellow had come within 30 feet, seen him clearly, and gone its way without showing any desire to pick a fight. He was as safe here as he would be back on shipboard, Harry told himself, and as dusk deepened into darkness he fell asleep.

Then, near midnight, he found himself wide awake, staring into the dark, every hair on his head standing the wrong way.

He kicked the blanket aside and got to his feet. Suddenly a stick cracked off to his right. As he whirled in that direction, he heard something move on his left. His heart pounded and, for a few terrifying seconds, he stood fingering the safety on the rifle, convinced he was surrounded by bears.

Then the night was still again except for the murmur and clatter of the stream. Had he imagined the noises? His nerves were just beginning to steady down when something furry and warm brushed against his right foot.

As he yanked his foot aside, the frightened squalls of a pair of bear cubs split the night apart. There was one on either side of him. Instantly, from the river, he heard the answering bellow of the she-bear, half growl, half roar, one of the most blood-chilling noises man has ever heard.

She came splashing through the stream and hit the near bank with a loud clatter of rocks, growling and bawling in full-throated rage. Harry knew he was in for it. He could see nothing, but as nearly as he could judge the bear was only 50 feet away and coming like an express train.

His mind raced, weighing one alternative after another in fractions of a second. Should he run for the river? Try rolling back into the underbrush behind him? Climb a tree? Risk a shot at the sound of the charging bear? But he knew none of these actions could save him. So he stood and waited while she rushed him, holding the Krag out in front of him, pointing it in the direction of the sound. He even had time to damn himself for not building a fire.

With a scream of rage and hate, she crashed into the muzzle of the rifle and Harry yanked the trigger. As the shot exploded, loud in the night, the gun was sent flying out of his hands and he was knocked flat to the ground. Snorting, sobbing, grumbling, the bear put a heavy paw on his shoulder, ground him down hard into the moss and stood over him, holding him there.

Her blood, streaming down into his face, felt like warm water poured from a pitcher, and from her coughing and labored breathing he felt sure she was lung shot. He remembered the cases of bear attack he had heard and read about. Other men had escaped by feigning death, so he lay limp and motionless. He recalled afterward praying that she would kill him outright rather than work him over with her claws. At the time death seemed better than the prospect of crippling injuries.

Although he was still conscious, he was not aware that the bear had taken her foot off his shoulder until he heard her thrashing in the underbrush a few feet away. She was making a terrible racket, coughing, growling and popping her teeth. The instant he realized he was free, Harry rolled over and groped frantically on the ground for his rifle.

He located it at last, about 15 feet from the spot where the bear had knocked him down, but his relief at regaining the Krag was short-lived. There seemed to be something wrong with the gun. The bolt was jammed and he couldn't eject the empty cartridge. Slow, agonizing seconds ticked off, while the bear struggled and choked and growled a few yards away, before Harry discovered that the rifle was all right after all. His right hand seemed to lack the strength to work the bolt. He felt the hand with his left one, and found it was swollen and bleeding profusely. He realized then that he had been clawed or bitten on the hand. He felt no pain.

With his uninjured hand he bolted a fresh cartridge into the chamber. Then he fumbled around on the ground until he found his boots, drew them on and backed away into the river.

In his haste he didn't bother about his pants. All he had in mind was to get away from the snarling bear as fast as he could. But before he had waded 50 yards downstream, Harry realized how great an error he had made. Without his pants he had no belt or suspenders to hold up his hip boots. They kept filling with water in the deep holes, then slipping down around his knees when he reached shallower places. That made hard going, but Harry would not have gone back after his pants for the heaviest poke of gold that ever came out of Alaska.

The trip back to the beach was a nightmare. He had to

wade the stream all the way, since the devil's-club on shore was too much to cope with in the darkness. He had to climb over scores of windfalls, slow and hazardous work without a light. The treacherous footing of the bottom caused him to slip and stumble again and again, and he fell repeatedly in the cold water. Every few steps he yelled at the top of his voice to let every bear on the river know he was coming. When the yelling became monotonous, he resorted to singing hymns.

"I picked some good ones, too," he told the expedition later, "and I sang 'em loud."

At last he found himself clear of windfalls and the river seemed to be widening out. He waded on, stepped into a deep hole, got a mouthful of water, which to his consternation was salty. He had walked out into the bay. He turned, angled off to one side, and a minute later was standing on the beach. Climbing a low rise, he saw the masthead light of the expedition ship shining through the trees.

He shouted and fired the Krag until he aroused someone on board. A dory was lowered and made its way toward him. When it grated on the beach and he climbed in, the men at the oars could hardly believe their eyes. He was a sorry sight, dripping wet, scratched and bruised, boots dangling around trouserless legs, hair matted with bear blood, and his right hand looking like an inflated rubber glove.

His only injury was the bite on the hand. The bear's teeth had gone all the way through from back to palm, but luckily they had missed bone.

At daybreak a party went up the river to collect the gear Harry had left behind. Pictures or no pictures, he didn't want to go with them or to see that spot again.

The party searched a long time, but could find no trace of

the cubs. The bear, however, was lying dead only ten yards from Harry's blanket. Although his shot had sent a 180-grain softpoint through her lungs, she had died slowly. In her final struggle for life, she had clawed and torn up a patch of brush and turf half as big as a living room rug, until the ground looked as if it had been combed with great steel rakes. Harry owed his life to the fact that she had walked a few steps away from him before she went down. No man within her reach could have survived that terrible death mauling. If the bear had stayed with her paw on Harry's shoulder and then fallen on him, the rescue party would have found a dead bear and a dead man.

Devil of the Laurel Hells

MOST MEN who have hunted the European wild boar agree that it is the toughest and meanest game animal on the North American continent. Since 1939, Paul Moore, a staff photographer for the Tennessee Conservation Department, has been of that opinion.

The wild boar, when cornered or enraged, literally has no fear. He has the strength of a hog, as well as its cussedness and meanness. Nimble as a deer and almost as fast, the boar is possessed of a temper as hair-triggered and vicious as any bear's. He is long-winded in the chase and terrible in battle. In a class by himself, he is a quarry and a trophy worth whatever he costs in time, heart-breaking effort and risks to dogs or men.

Found in the tangled fastnesses of the Unicoi Mountains in eastern Tennessee and western North Carolina, the European wild boar is actually a relatively new immigrant from the forests of Germany and Russia. (The southern mountain people have nicknamed him "Roosian" to distinguish him from their half-domesticated native razorbacks.) In 1912, a small herd was brought to this country and released in a 600-acre enclosure near Hooper Bald in North Carolina. Later, around 1920, this herd escaped and crossed over into Tennessee. The wild boar is now one of the most important game animals of that state.

There is only one other denizen of those mountains that comes near to being the equal of the wild boar. That is the black bear. But experienced hunters say that pound for pound the bear is actually no match for the boar. A bear fights wickedly, but not with the hog's blind, deadly rage, the "I'll get you and I don't give a damn what happens to me" brand of courage.

A pack of good dogs can hold a bear at bay, but not a wild boar. He will back in against a rock or log so that his rear is protected and fight off a pack of dogs—a stalling action he keeps up until he is rested and ready to run again. When he makes up his mind to break bay, he charges out through a ring of dogs with the speed of a thunderbolt, heedless of the odds, chopping and slashing with his long, keen tusks. Indeed, any hound that stands in his way or makes the mistake of fighting it out at close quarters with a boar usually gets cut to ribbons.

The wild hog won't pick a quarrel with a man if it can be avoided. Under normal circumstances, he's wary and retiring, and if one lets him alone he's willing to do the same by the hunter. But the wild boar tolerates no liberties, and he's a devil when aroused. Fortunately for them, hunters ordinarily only have contact with a boar when his fury is directed toward a pack of dogs.

Paul Moore was to discover, however, that the distraction provided by a pack of dogs is no guarantee to man of protection from an enraged boar.

He and Val Solyom, a Conservation Department game technician from Nashville, were hunting in the wild and rugged country above Tellico Plains, a little town in the southeastern part of Tennessee—an area widely reputed to be the wild boar capital of this continent. Ben Ellis, who at the time was owner of the most famous pack of boar dogs in the mountains, was guiding them.

Val Solyom was the hunter of the party, armed with an 8 mm. Mauser. Paul carried nothing more formidable than a

4x5 Speed Graphic camera. It was his ambition to get some good photographs of a boar at bay fighting off hounds. No one had done it up to that time. He had already gone out on 30 boar hunts in the attempt to get such pictures for the department. Despite a grueling routine of day-after-day climbing and racing through mountain thickets, however, one thing or another had always prevented Paul from getting his pictures. Each time he had reported back empty-handed. This hunt with Val was to be his thirty-first try.

After leaving the car, the three men headed into the rough country along the Bald River. Ben had with him four of his best dogs: Lead and Old Red, plus two mongrels notorious for their savage infighting. The men started with the dogs on leash; however, when less than a mile from the car, they found fresh hog sign and turned the pack loose.

Lead and Red struck at once, and then all four dogs were off, cold trailing straight up a steep ridge and making the mountains ring with their hair-raising music. The men clambered up the ridge behind them, doing their best to keep the dogs within hearing.

Following hounds on a boar track is a tough job. The wild hog instinctively keeps to the roughest and most broken country. If there is a rock-strewn slope covered with a tangled mat of laurel, he will make for it. If there is a rhododendron hell along a branch in which the big laurel and dog hobble are so thick a man can barely claw his way through on all fours, the boar will invariably plunge into it. In such surroundings, the agility and endurance of the boar are really astounding. All in all, keeping up with dogs on a hot boar trail is something even the most seasoned mountain hunter can hardly hope to do.

The three men panted along after the pack, up one ridge

and down into a valley, then up again and down the far side of a second ridge. But even though the men raced, the dogs were slowly pulling away from them. The track was still cold.

"That's a boar," Ben panted as they came into a timbered cove at the foot of the second ridge. "Ain't no sow gonna travel that way. They ain't even got him up yet."

They were struggling up a third ridge, fighting their way through sawbrier and pulling themselves up with the aid of brush and saplings, when they heard the dogs opening on a hot trail from the far side of the crest. They knew that the dogs had driven the boar from his daytime bed.

The rolling trail music the men had heard up to that time was nothing compared with the wild and frenzied clamor now breaking from the canine throats as the four dogs drank in the first hot reek of wild hog. Their bawling sounded insane with eagerness; it rolled back like savage bugle notes. But it faded fast. Within a minute, the men knew that they couldn't hope to keep the pack in hearing. They found their way onto the crest of the ridge with Ben in the lead, but when they topped out, breathless and drenched with sweat, the echo of the last dog's music had faded into silence. They had no way to tell in which direction the chase had gone.

"They've run him plumb out of the country," Ben said.

"Where'll they be likely to wind up?" Val asked.

"Ain't so sure they'll wind up," Ben grunted. "That ain't no shoat they're followin'. They can likely catch him, but it's gonna take a powerful lot of dog to hold him!"

"Where do you figure he's headed?" Paul asked.

"Into the upper Tellico country, if he don't change his mind. But you know how a hawg is."

Paul did know. During 30 hunts he had had plenty of

opportunity to learn that it is futile to try to predict the actions of a wild boar. Just when the hunter thinks he knows what the hog is going to do, the animal invariably seems to take exactly the opposite course.

They loped down the ridge at a half trot. Then for the next three hours they combed the roadless wilderness between the Bald and the upper Tellico, following ridges, stopping time after time in coves and gaps to listen, hoping to pick up a far-off thread of hound music. But the search was in vain. The boar obviously had done as Ellis had predicted: led the dogs out of the country. Try as they might they couldn't re-establish contact with the pack. At noon Ben gave up.

"We might as well circle back to the car and eat lunch," he said. "Hit's a fur piece back there. If we don't hear no more from the dogs, after we eat we'll drive up the Tellico as far as the road goes and circle back on the Bald. That hawg might go right back where we started him!"

It was, as Ben had said, a far piece back to the car, but they made it at last and sat down at the roadside for lunch. It was while they were eating that they caught from far up on a ridge the sound of the dogs. They were a long way off. Their baying was no more than a low throbbing, a faint drumbeat, carried across the ridges by the cool wind. The dogs, however, were driving hard and coming straight for the road; their baying grew and swelled until it was loud and clear. Dropping their lunches, Paul dived for his camera and Val grabbed his Mauser.

"They ain't bayed that hawg yet," Ben declared. "They've run him all this while without catchin' him. You're gonna see quite a boar if you set eyes on that fellow!"

The dogs came bawling down off the ridge, nearer and nearer, heading for a point less than a quarter mile down the road. All three men ran to intercept them. When the pack was almost to the road, the boar suddenly broke out of the laurel.

It came into sight above the road, on top of a ten-foot bank. As it jumped down clumsily, Paul noted that the hog was a gray-black, ugly looking brute. It pivoted and raced away up the middle of the road at a speed that came close to matching a whitetail's. The three men saw that the boar was not as big as they had hoped. A really big boar will weigh in excess of 300 pounds. Ben guessed this one's weight at about 200. When they had a chance to verify the guess later on, they found he had been close.

The three men had mapped their campaign in advance. They had decided that their best chance of getting close-ups of a hog at bay would be by crippling it. In that way the dogs could hold the hog while Paul closed in. Val was carrying the Mauser, Ben a .45 Colt automatic. They had agreed that who-ever did the shooting would do his best to slow the hog down but not kill it.

The boar raced up the road for 100 yards, with lead kick-ing up dust all around it. Val finally scored. Not until the ad-venture was over did they have a chance to learn the nature of the damage his bullet had inflicted. It had traveled the length of the boar's back, just under the skin, plowing a shallow scratch. The wound set the boar wild. It stopped in its tracks and whipped its head from side to side in blind rage, snapping and slashing at its own shoulders. Then it turned and plunged down the bank into the swiftly-flowing water of Bald River. At the same instant the hounds broke onto the road. Seeing their quarry below, they redoubled their clamour.

The boar went through the river as if it were a creek a foot deep, while the dogs followed, yammering at its heels. As they disappeared into a tangled green hell of rhododendron and sawbrier on the far bank, the three men waded into the river. The water was chest deep, icy cold and running like a millrace. In their excitement, they barely felt the chill. Somehow Paul managed to keep his camera dry while trying to keep from slipping on the big, slick boulders.

Now the rolling trail song of the dogs changed to angry, excited barking and snapping as they brought the boar to bay. They caught it on a steep slope 200 yards above the river in a thicket that was so dense the men could hardly force their way into it.

After he had pushed his way to the center of the tangle where he was within a few yards of the action, Paul realized there was no hope of getting the pictures he wanted in such a place. He did, however, get a glimpse of an eye and an ear of the boar through the tangle before, in a savage rush through the ring of dogs, the enraged hog broke bay. As it was charging out, both Ben and Val poured out some more lead, which missed its target. It was impossible to get a good shot in that dense cover.

Now the boar began to fight a running battle up the steep slope during which it was never more than a few yards ahead of the dogs, and the three men were never very far behind them. Twice more the hog came to bay, making brief stands to fight the pack off. Each time it broke and ran as the hunters crowded in, preventing Paul from gettting any pictures. Val and Ben got in a shot or two at each stand but still without effect. In the back of Paul's mind the thought took form that they were all stretching their luck pretty far. If they kept inching in on a thoroughly enraged and crippled boar, they might eventually have trouble in spite of all the dogs were doing to divert the hog's attention.

But Paul never voiced his growing doubt; nobody would have backed off at that point, even had they known what was about to happen.

Then as the hog broke away from the dogs once more, Val shouted out disturbing news.

"I'm out of shells! I'm going down to the car to get some."

Ben, clawing through the brush ahead, stopped long enough to answer.

"Don't stop to pick no p'simmons!" he yelled. "We may need you. I shot my last one five minutes ago!"

At this turn of events, Paul became convinced there was going to be trouble.

The boar made its stand in a little opening in a laurel thicket, about 50 feet by 30. It had gained 100 yards or so on the men before the dogs overtook it, forcing it to come to bay. Ben reached the place first and called Paul in. Paul broke out of the laurel at the upper end of the little clearing, less than ten yards above the hog and the dogs.

The boar had backed in against a stump to stand off the pack. It was winded, but there was plenty of fight left in it. The wicked looking brute was chopping and slashing at the dogs with its long tusks, while froth drooled from its jaws and blood oozed down its side from the back wound. The dogs had the hog well cornered. They were all bleeding from minor cuts, however, and none of them wanted any really close dealings with it now that they had caught it. Even the mongrels that were famous for their courage at close quarters were cautious of the deadly tusks.

"Will he stayed bayed?" Paul asked Ben in a low voice.

"Reckon he'll stay for a spell this time. He's plumb tuckered out."

The packsack Paul had on his back was bothering him, so he slipped out of it. Since it was too dark in the laurel and rhododendron for daylight pictures, he rigged a flashgun on the camera and slipped a bulb into place, taking his time, confident the boar would not break bay this time. When the camera was ready, he worked carefully down toward the hog, moving in close for a picture.

When he was only a few yards away, Paul focused on a perfect action shot: the four dogs were bunched in a tight ring in front of the hog, barking in his face; the boar, eyeing them sullenly and savagely, was waiting his chance to do real damage. As the white glare of the flashbulb lighted the dark crannies under the laurel, Paul knew that he had the hunting picture of a lifetime. But the hog gave him little time to gloat.

The flash of the bulb was all that the boar needed. It came out through the ring of hounds as if they were toy dogs and they scattered and let the hog go. It was headed straight away from Paul, uphill in Ben's direction.

Paul said later he had never seen anything more grim or more business-like than the hog's charge. It had got its eye on Ben. It seemed as though the boar had made up its mind that Ben was the cause of all its troubles; it plowed up the hill like a small bulldozer, straight for the guide. When the hog was almost on him, Ben swung up into a low tree. Even so, the boar managed to clip one of his boot heels with a tusk as it lunged at him. The instant it realized Ben was beyond reach, the boar spun around in its tracks and charged hellbent for Paul.

Paul hadn't moved since the hog broke bay. There was no tree within his reach. He had deliberately stood still; it seemed the safest and wisest course in view of the steep slope and poor footing. Any hope, however, that the enraged boar would overlook him was quickly shattered. Paul said afterward that the boar's charge was the most terrifying thing that ever happened to him. Every detail of that experience etched itself clearly and indelibly on his memory: the black hulk of the boar's shoulders, its red pig eyes, its curved tusks and its lumbering run.

It was Old Red's intervention that probably saved Paul's life. When the hog was no more than three or four yards away, the hound flashed in from nowhere, actually jumped over the boar's head and, as he was sailing over, took a good big nip out of that ugly snout.

The hog didn't stop or turn aside, but the deadly accuracy of its charge was upset. It veered slightly off course instead of heading square into the man's belly.

Paul realized in a flash that he had a chance. The hog was going to hit him, but not with a head-on blow. Using the only weapon he had, Paul swung his heavy camera with all his strength, belting the boar over the nose just as it reared and lunged at him.

The blow turned aside a tusk that would have ripped the photographer open like a sack of meal. Instead, the hog's shoulder caught him at the waist. The blow knocked Paul sprawling, and he landed flat on his back in the brush and leaves, shaken and the most frightened man in Tennessee. The momentum of the boar's charge carried it across a fallen log, and it didn't turn back to attack again. The dogs were swarming all over the hog by that time. It lunged 50 feet down the slope and backed its hind quarters in under a boulder that was as high as a man. There the boar came to bay once more.

As the dogs closed in Lead got too close. The powerful jaws of the boar snapped down on the hound's neck and shoulders. The dog's long wailing howl told Ben that one of his hounds was in serious trouble.

Ben went past Paul like a tornado, running for the rock where the boar was holding the dog in its vise-like jaws. As he scrambled up over the boulder, he pulled his long-bladed hunting knife from its sheath. Lead's howling was now an unbroken wail of agony and terror; Ben was not the kind of dog man to let such an appeal for help as that go unanswered.

Watching, Paul could hardly believe his eyes. Clambering over the rock, Ben dropped astride the boar's back as squarely as a cowboy mounting an outlaw horse in a rodeo chute. As his knife flashed down, Lead's howling stopped. No butcher had ever stuck a farmyard pig more accurately and neatly; Ben had put the knife in the boar's throat up to the hilt. The wound

37

caused the hog to break its grip on the dog. The boar wheeled to meet this new threat.

Ben, who was now on the ground, dodged aside, grabbed the hound's legs and yanked him to safety. The other dogs were piling in and doing their share, as Val came panting into the arena. The hog was sagging by that time, and one shot from the Mauser finished the job.

When the three men took inventory, they found that their casualties were amazingly light—but heartbreaking nonetheless.

Ben hadn't been hurt at all, and Paul had just been shaken up. None of the dogs had suffered more than flesh cuts, even Lead. Ben was relieved to find that his daring had saved the dog from being injured seriously. But the camera, which lay on the ground where it had fallen after Paul had used it to club the hog, was smashed beyond repair. Only the lens and shutter were worth salvaging. The film holder had been knocked off, and the film on which he had made his perfect action shot lay upturned to the light. The picture he had gone on 31 wild-boar hunts to get was as worthless as a sheet of blotting paper.

Paul was pretty glum over having lost the picture of a lifetime; however, as he thought about it afterward, the terrible memory of the boar charging across the little opening in the laurel made him realize he was lucky to be alive.

Between Life and Death

FOREST YOUNG and his hunting partner, Marty Cordes, spent the last half of September, 1955, hunting moose north of Haines in Alaska's Chilkat Valley, where they lived and worked as construction men. The first ten days they had no real luck. Young wounded a bull the second day out and followed the blood trail, but the heavy rain that was falling eventually washed out the trail. For a straight week after that they did not lay eyes on a moose with horns, so finally they loaded their gear in the canoe and outboarded ten miles farther up the Chilkat River to moose country that had never failed them in the past. There was a vacant cabin near the river they had used before. They would have gone there sooner, but figured the area might be too crowded with hunters.

There was no cause, however, for complaint on that score. They had things to themselves, and the first day they saw enough moose sign to convince them they had come to the right place. It was only an hour after they started out the second morning, in a patch of willow-grown muskeg about two miles from camp, that they came on two bulls and several cows feeding together. The bulls were good ones. The men dumped both of them.

They spent the balance of that day dressing their two moose and packing part of the meat to camp. The rest of the meat and the two hides were cached in trees, out of reach of bears. Browns and grizzlies were plentiful in the area; the men knew that any meat left where bears could get at it would be almost sure to disappear during the night.

The following morning, which was the last day of September, they packed in enough additional meat to make a canoe load and Marty cranked up the outboard and took off for Haines. Forest made several more trips to bring in meat during that afternoon and the next forenoon. By the time Marty got back from town late Saturday afternoon, Forest had everything in camp except the hide of Marty's moose. That was still stretched about a dozen feet off the ground in the branches of a birch at the spot where they had made the kill.

Sunday morning Marty said that he wanted to pick up a mess of grouse for a stew. Forest agreed to bring in the moose hide. Both men planned to be back in the cabin about an hour before noon, ready to break camp and head for home with the hides and the balance of the meat.

When Forest arrived at the site of the kill, he found that bears had taken over. The ground looked as if someone had gone over it with a garden rake. There were two neat mounds of grass and moss near-by. Forest knew that the bears had covered up the uneaten portions of the moose entrails. That cache of the bears should have been a warning to him that they would be coming back.

Marty's moose hide was still up in the birch, unmolested. Forest walked over to the tree and threw his packboard down. As he glanced up, he saw movement in the brush about 300 feet away. Taking a closer look, he was able to make out the backs and heads of two bears over the top of the brush. They were about 30 feet apart.

They didn't scare him. Although he was sure from their color and shape that they were grizzlies, any bear he had ever met had lit out as soon as it discovered him. These would, too. As he watched them, however, they suddenly disappeared from sight. The next thing Forest knew one was coming headlong at him through the thicket. Although he couldn't see the bear, he could see the brush moving. The bear was smashing through the brush, making such a commotion that it was easy for Forest to trace its course.

He still wasn't scared. He jumped up and down and waved his arms, yelling to frighten the grizzly off. Then he suddenly realized that this was one bear that wasn't going to be bluffed. It was still coming hellbent.

Forest wasn't carrying a gun, or even a hunting knife. He had gone lightly equipped for the job of packing the 80-pound green moose hide into camp. Quickly sizing up the situation, he jumped for a branch of the birch and started up the tree, hand over hand. But before he had climbed his own height, the grizzly broke out of the brush and came swarming at him.

The bear didn't fool around. It sank its teeth into the back of Forest's right leg just above the knee and pulled him down with one savage yank. He landed on his back, and they tussled for a few seconds. Young wound up sitting up, with the bear's left front leg across both of his, pinning him to the ground. Then the bear grabbed him by the inside of the thigh, just below the crotch, and took a deep, deliberate bite, tearing away a strip of flesh. Forest saw his blood spurt out. He braced himself with his left arm and pummeled the grizzly in the face with his other fist, but the bear paid no more attention to this than it would have to a fly buzzing around its head.

The first moments of the ordeal were pure terror. The bear's face was less than a foot away from Forest's. The grizzly had a big burly head, with long, stiff, gray guard hairs standing

41

out all over its face. Its eyes were red with hate, and its muzzle was screwed up in a sullen mask. It slobbered as it chewed. The bear went on shredding his clothing, skin and flesh. Every second Forest expected the bear to grab him by the throat and finish him off with one shake. His woolen trousers and heavy underwear were no protection against the grizzly's claws and teeth. He felt the bear grind cloth into flesh with each bite. With horror he realized the bear could tear his legs off and he wouldn't be able to do a thing about it. He punched the grizzly in the face until he broke his hand. The silvertip wasn't fazed a bit.

"I read once that a merciful numbness comes over a man being mauled by a big carnivore," he said to Marty later. "Maybe that happens in some cases, but it certainly didn't in mine. I was anything but numb. I could feel every bite he took, and it hurt like hell!"

He never knew how long he was pinned down by the bear. Maybe a minute, maybe only a few seconds, but it seemed half an eternity. Suddenly it flashed through Forest's mind that his only clear hope for survival was to play dead. He flopped over on his back and side, making himself go limp.

The bear instantly stopped chewing. Instead, it merely stood over its victim, continuing to pin him down with one leg. Forest tried not to breathe. In spite of all his will power, however, and the knowledge that his life hung in the balance, the pain was too intense. He involuntarily emitted a low groan. At that the grizzly grabbed him again, as a cat grabs a mouse. Forest felt another stab of excruciating pain as the long yellow teeth sank deeper into his flesh than before. They slashed through the right side of his scrotum and ripped loose a flap of skin and muscle that exposed his bladder. The pain was awful.

42

Forest lay inert and let the grizzly continue to tear at him. It took another bite or two and dropped him for the second time.

Then Forest must have inadvertently moved again, or else the bear just decided to make sure of finishing him. It nailed him once more, this time by the back below the right shoulder, and with a lunging bite ripped three ribs loose from the spine and tore a hole that reached all the way into the chest cavity. If the bite had been placed a little lower, in the kidney area, it would have been fatal.

This time Forest didn't fight back, move or groan. He knew now it was a case of play dead or be dead. The grizzly dropped the limp body; Forest heard the bear walk away. He couldn't see it without turning his head, which he didn't dare risk, so he just lay motionless and hoped it wouldn't come back.

Suddenly, however, he felt the muskeg shake under him and heard heavy feet pounding in. The silvertip was making a queer sort of panting noise, not a bawl and not a growl. Forest braced himself for another mauling, but the bear didn't touch him. He could see its feet and lower legs were only a yard from his face. The bear just stood there looking him over for a minute or so. Then, apparently satisfied, it turned and walked slowly away.

About five minutes later the bear repeated the performance, approaching the man at a panting run, standing over him without molesting him, and then walking off. Forest decided his possum act was working.

For what seemed an interminable length of time, Forest continued to play dead. He couldn't see or hear the bear. All this time it was becoming increasingly difficult to breathe because of the open hole in his back. Forest realized that he was going to strangle unless he turned over on his face and let his nose and mouth drain. He kept still as long as he could, then counting on the bear's having gone for keeps, he slowly and painfully managed to roll over. The movement and the sound provoked no reaction; he began to hope that the worst of his troubles were past.

Quite a while later he thought he heard faint sounds coming from the moose leavings, 100 feet away, but when he held his breath to listen the noise seemed to stop. That happened three or four times. Forest didn't know what to think. Then he felt the muskeg quake under him once more and heard that familiar, terrifying panting. No noise out of the pit of hell itself could have sounded worse to the tortured man.

The bear must have sensed from Forest's position that he had moved. It let out a murderous roar and tore into him again, grabbing him by the buttocks. The grizzly spanned Forest's entire rear with its jaws, and bit through to the bone. Then it took a deeper bite as if attempting to sever his body in two. Picking him up off the ground, it shook him until he thought his back would break or his head snap off his body. Forest had seen bears kill salmon that way, shattering the spine with one flirt of their jaws. It seemed inevitable that the same thing was going to happen to him. But then the grizzly dropped him as abruptly as it had seized him, turned away and lumbered off. He heard the heavy footfalls fade. It was quiet again.

The bear had dropped him face down, so he was in no danger of choking, but he was in pain beyond all description. The bear had torn the flesh away from the inside of his legs, ripped both buttocks, mangled his right hand, torn one rib entirely out and left two others protruding through the skin, punched a big hole into his lung cavity and chewed at him from head to knees.

"There is no way to tell you what the agony was like," he said later.

In addition to the pain, Forest was also plagued by the cold water from the muskeg seeping through his clothing.

Forest couldn't stand the pain. He wasn't even granted the mercy of passing out. He decided to prod fate—to kill himself.

He was convinced he was going to die anyway. He couldn't see a chance of getting out alive by himself, hurt as he was. Forest realized it would be hours before Marty would find him lying in the muskeg. Other men badly mauled by bears had killed themselves; now in his mind, clouded by pain, he understood the logic of their action.

It must have taken him half an hour to work his good hand down into the pocket where his small jackknife was lodged. With great difficulty, he managed to extract the weapon. Then he moved his arms up in front of his head, opened the knife and made a deep slash in his left wrist, trying for the big artery. No blood appeared. Hardly feeling the pain from the knife cut over the red flashes of agony that were stabbing all through his body, he slashed again. The third slash exposed the wrist tendons, but still no blood appeared.

It didn't occur to Forest that he might have missed the artery. He took it for granted that he had already lost so much blood that there was none left to flow. That meant he couldn't bleed himself to death through the wrist. If he cut the tendons and then by some miracle survived, he knew he would have a crippled hand the rest of his life. He was willing to kill himself, but not to chance a crippled hand, so he gave up that scheme. Insane from torture? Maybe.

The next idea that came to him, born of pain and desperation, was even more horrible: to find and cut his jugular vein with the knife. He knew that would afford a mercifully quick death. He instinctively knew that he musn't fumble, lest he run the risk of severing his windpipe and thus suffer the added torture of being strangled. He laid the fingers of his good hand against his throat, feeling for the pulse that would mark the location of the big vein, but he couldn't find it. This exertion was almost too much for him. He slumped back and rested. As he was starting to probe again for the vein, he heard Marty off in the brush calling him.

Marty shuddered as he examined the torn body of his partner. His first thought was to try packing him the two miles back to camp. When he started to lift Forest, however, the injured man screamed in agony. Marty had to discard that scheme. The pain was more than Forest could endure. They agreed there was only one alternative. Marty would have to go all the way to Haines for help. While he was gone, Forest would have to take his chances. It wasn't a pleasant prospect.

Before leaving for Haines, Marty made a fast trip to camp and brought back a sleeping bag and an air mattress, a shotgun and shells, cigarettes, a water bottle, food, matches, and a gas lantern. He eased Forest into the bag, and then hung most of his outer clothing on bushes overhead to keep off the rain that was now falling in a cold drizzle. He laid the shotgun beside Forest, lighted the gas lantern and set it down within reach.

"I'll make the fastest trip any man ever made to Haines." Marty promised.

"I'll be here when you get back," Forest told him, but he was far from sure.

It was now midafternoon. The bear had jumped Forest about a quarter past ten in the morning. He was sure of the time, since he had looked at his watch just before he came in

46

sight of the moose hide in the tree. He couldn't expect Marty back before midnight; it was two miles to camp, and a round trip of 30 miles by outboard and 60 by truck to Haines and back. It would also take Marty a little while to round up a rescue party. A glacial river running through very steep country, the Chilkat is quick to flood but also quick to drop. At the time it was at low stage. Forest knew that Marty, without a fast current, would have a slow run. The upstream trip back would take longer than usual, since Marty would be navigating in the dark and probably be bringing at least two extra passengers. Forest knew he would have to wait at least eight hours for help to arrive, perhaps longer. He wasn't sure he could hang on that long. Even if he could, there was still the grizzly to worry about. Forest didn't think it had left the neighborhood.

An hour or so after Marty left, Forest's spirits began to rise. The pain lessened, and he was warming up. He began to think that maybe he was going to make it after all. Soon after that the afternoon light began to fade. Dusk was coming. Everything had been quiet and peaceable for hours. He had almost stopped worrying about the bear, but he fought off the impulse to doze. Then suddenly the muskeg began to shake under him, and once more he heard the snuffling, panting noise that marked the grizzly's approach.

His arms were inside the sleeping bag and his face was covered with the top of it. He didn't move or even breathe. He heard the bear stop a few feet away, let out a blood-chilling roar, and then turn and run off. Forest shuddered with relief. He concluded that Marty's clothes draped over the brush, the glowing gas lantern and the appearance of the bag had caused the bear to bolt.

After about half an hour of dread and fear Forest was

beginning to relax when he heard a new noise on his right, something rustling in the brush. His arms were out of the sleeping bag now, and his face uncovered. His hand was on the shotgun. Twisting his head toward the right, he saw, about 15 feet away, a small bear cub standing in the gathering twilight. The idea flashed through his mind that this cub might belong to the bear that had attacked him. But then Forest knew that couldn't be. He had been mauled by a grizzly; this cub looked like a young black.

Whatever bear it belonged to, Forest was sure the old lady wasn't far off, and he didn't want the cub to bring her down on him. It took a few steps toward the man, watching him with lively curiosity; he didn't know quite what to do. If he scared it and it squalled, he would surely be in for more trouble. He tried a loud, sharp hiss. That did it. The cub swapped ends and ran without squalling. Five minutes later, however, Forest heard another rustling at the edge of the brush. It was back . . . with a twin. He hissed again, and the two of them scrammed. But they were too curious to stay away. With impish persistence, the two little black cubs came back, and for half an hour they kept Forest on pins and needles. Circling around him, they took turns footing in for a look, but neither ever came closer than about 15 feet. Forest lay quiet, frantically trying to think of a scheme that would drive them off for keeps. He expected the she-bear to come ambling along any minute to investigate what her cubs had found. Eventually, however, they lost interest in Forest and retreated into the brush. All was quiet again.

It was close to full dark when the flame of the gas lantern grew dimmer and then went out. Under normal circumstances that would have been a minor annoyance; however, it was a terrifying experience for Forest. Now he had no protection at all against the night. He couldn't control his fear; it grew to the borders of panic as he thought of the grizzly possibly returning. Then, just as he feared, he heard the frightening, panting noise off in the brush.

The bear wasn't rushing him this time. It was approaching slowly, stalking toward his head from an angle that would make it impossible for Forest to see it. He figured that the grizzly was cautious after the earlier encounter with the lantern. Once it discovered the light was no longer there, he figured the bear would jump him.

In desperation, he raised the shotgun, pointed it in the direction of the noise, elevated the barrel so the shot would pass over the bear. When he pulled the trigger, a red stab of flame flashed from the muzzle. The kick jolted him from head to foot. The blast of the shot ripped the quiet of the night apart. The noise and flash must have scared the bear witless. Forest heard a strangled roar, then the crackling of brush and the pounding of a heavy animal running off. The man was left again with the stillness of the night.

It wasn't long, however, before he heard noise from bears back at the moose remains, a combination of growling and gnawing. That horrible noise went on for three or four hours. During that time, his fear gradually subsided. Forest began to feel that, with any kind of luck, Marty and the rescue party were going to find him alive after all. Sometime later the bears left off feeding and quiet returned.

But that was short-lived. The savage grizzly hadn't forgotten Forest. About an hour before midnight he heard once more the panting that signaled its approach, which this time was from his left. The bear was walking in cautiously; Forest brought the shotgun into position with the barrel laid across his body, and got set to shoot. He knew the risk involved if the shot should only wound, rather than kill the grizzly; however, it was better than lying there and letting it get at him again. He couldn't take another going over. He decided to let the bear come within ten feet. If it approached that close, he would know it meant business. At that range, even in the dark, he would be able to make out its outline; he would give it both barrels together, square in the face. That might drive the bear off, even if it failed to kill.

When the grizzly sounded as though it was about 25 feet away, it stopped. Forest could hear it panting and snuffling, and then it circled him and started to prowl in from the other side. He trained the gun and waited, but the grizzly didn't come any closer. Apparently something about the setup bothered the grizzly. Maybe it remembered the shotgun blast. After ten minutes or so of nosing around, it moved off. Forest didn't know it, but his bear troubles were over.

Around midnight still awake and alert, Forest caught the far-off thrum of Marty's outboard. He had never heard a more welcome sound. It grew louder and nearer. When it died away abruptly, he knew the rescue party would soon be heading for him on foot.

By this time the rainy night was pitch black. Forest was afraid they might have trouble finding him in the brush, so he took half a dozen matches out of his pocket and held them in his hand, ready for striking as soon as he heard the men approaching. He lay there in the sleeping bag, hanging onto the matches and waiting for what seemed hours. It was actually only about 30 minutes. While he was waiting, he heard again the sound of a distant outboard. His hopes sank pretty low. Forest thought the rescuers had turned back; he was too far gone to figure out that a second boat, still a long way off, was feeling its way up the Chilkat.

A little later he couldn't believe his ears when he heard voices in the brush close by. He struck all the matches at once.

"There he is! There's a light!" somebody said.

Flashlights winked toward him through the darkness. Half a minute later Forest was looking up into the faces of Marty and two companions. He took the first easy breath he had drawn since the bear had first grabbed him. They laid a stretcher on the ground beside the sleeping bag. He asked the time. It was nearly one in the morning. The ordeal had lasted 14½ hours. That's a long time to lie helpless, waiting for a grizzly to finish you off.

The two men Marty had brought back with him were Carl Heinmiller and Walt Dueman. Heinmiller was a retired Army major, who had lost three fingers and an eye in the South Pacific during World War II. Despite his handicaps, he was the top first-aid man around Haines. Heinmiller immediately set to work giving Forest a shot of penicillin and then one of morphine. After that the three of them eased him onto the stretcher. While carrying him back to the cabin, they lost the trail in the darkness. It took them three and a half hours to get through the brush and timber. The pain from his injuries, plus the jolting from the stretcher ride, were pretty bad; however, the morphine, which was dulling Forest's consciousness, helped. Actually the trip was about as tough for the rescuers as it was for him.

The grizzly didn't seem to want to give up. The men heard it bawl in the distance twice on their way back to camp. They thought it was trailing them; each time the bear bawled the sound seemed just as close to them. They imagined that it was sullen and quarrelsome but not willing to jump so large a party.

When the rescuers reached the cabin, they found a second rescue party of three men waiting. Their boat was the one Forest had heard away off down the Chilkat. They had reached the camp just before the stretcher bearers arrived with their burden. They decided to get some sleep, knowing that nothing further could be done for Forest until the next day.

Shortly after eight in the morning, Dr. Robert Schuler reached the cabin. Although a resident of Juneau, he had been in Haines the evening before when Marty brought in the word about Forest. The doctor started for the cabin at daylight by airboat with John Fox. They hadn't dared to tackle the river in the dark, but once it was light the fast airboat got them to the cabin in 45 minutes. It had taken Marty four hours, and the other boat party almost eight. The Chilkat is tough to run at night.

By the time the doctor was attending to Forest, machinery of a full-scale rescue, utilizing Alaskan and Canadian volunteers and equipment, was in motion. At midmorning a big helicopter from the RCAF base at Whitehorse, 100 miles away, settled down in the little clearing in front of the cabin. The 'copter had been torn down for overhaul the day before; however, when word of the mishap reached the base late in the evening, the repair crew worked all night to get it back together and in shape to undertake the rescue.

The whirly-bird was big enough to carry a five-man rescue crew, including a doctor and nurse, plus a complete supply of drugs and plasma. The medics, however, didn't waste time treating Forest at the camp; he was a critical hospital case by that time. They bundled him aboard, and he was air-lifted to Haines. During the short hop, he received transfusions. A Coast Guard PBY flew him from Haines to Juneau, where he was taken by ambulance to St. Anne's Hospital. Just 27 hours after the bear nabbed him, Forest was on the operating table being patched up by a Juneau surgeon, Dr. Cass Carter.

Surgical attention was long overdue. Forest had more than a hundred tooth marks on the front of his body, from his shoulders to his knees, plus countless other cuts and gashes in his back and side. Several ribs were broken and one had been torn out. Dr. Carter had to remove part of two; the end of one had pressed in against a lung, which fortunately had not been punctured. The surgeon cut and sewed and patched for three hours. During surgery, it was necessary to give Forest additional blood transfusions. After operating, the doctor said he wouldn't have believed that any man who had been injured as seriously as Forest could have stayed alive more than six hours without medical help.

Forest's life hung by a thread for days. With time, however, his name was removed from the critical list. He was in the hospital from October 3 to December 10. When released, he was 30 pounds underweight, but he soon gained it back. The mauling left him short three ribs and marked by some ugly scars. His right hand was permanently banged up and the third finger was half an inch shorter than it had been, but Forest still had the use of the hand. Within a year he had recovered almost completely and was back on the job.

Following his return to work, Forest and Dr. Carter, who was an enthusiatic big-game hunter, and Marty built a hunting cabin in the same area in which Forest had been attacked. That fall the three of them hunted there. Doc Carter and Forest both accounted for a moose. Forest killed his only about 400 yards from the place where the bear had mauled him.

The hunters were to discover that grizzlies were still in

the area. When Carter shot his moose, he only had time to dress it out and cover it with a tarp before nightfall. The men had been told that if they built a low fence of sticks around a kill it would keep bears off, so they tried it. When they went back the next morning, however, the fence had been knocked down, the tarp pulled away, and the moose head dragged off to one side. In a patch of sand, they found a round depression, which had been made by the fat rump of a big bear as it sat beside the kill and sized things up. From the size of the tracks and the shape of the claw marks, they knew the outlaw was a silvertip. Apparently the noise of their airboat or their approach had spooked the grizzly. It had left without feeding on the moose at all. Forest wondered if it was the same grizzly he had tangled with. He guessed he would never know. They packed the meat to the cabin without further delay. Although they saw no more of the bear, they kept a close grip on their rifles while moving the meat.

In fact, Forest never went into the woods a minute during this trip without his rifle, and he'll probably never be in the woods again without one, at least not as long as he lives in that part of the country. While he was hunting moose he was also watching for that big grizzly with stiff gray whiskers all over its face, always waiting for the chance to even the score. Although Forest never got that chance, it's a safe bet that no bear will ever catch him with his guard down again.

The Bitter Night

THERE WAS never anything along the upper Mississippi like the Armistice Day storm of 1940.

It started out as a mild, cloudy November morning, with the temperature between 50 and 60. Men went to work in their shirt sleeves. Even the duck hunters were in their shirt sleeves. The wind picked up as the day went along, but there was nothing to get excited about until late afternoon. Then, with little warning, a full-scale prairie blizzard screamed in out of the northwest.

By dark the air was smoking with gale-driven snow, and the thermometer had plunged almost to zero. The bitter winds of hell blew all that night. The weather experts said afterward the winds at times had reached 80 miles an hour. The storm laid a track of death and destruction across half a dozen states. It pounded ships to pieces on the Great Lakes, blocked roads, isolated towns, paralyzed cities, buried cars so deep their tops could not be seen. It marooned hundreds on the highways and caused a crack streamliner to roll into Minneapolis 27 hours late. And when the following morning broke, wintry and gray, 20 duck hunters lay scattered in stiff, grotesque poses where they had frozen to death on the mud bars, sand spits and willow-grown islands of the Mississippi bottoms, between Red Wing, Minnesota, and La Crosse, Wisconsin.

Ray Sherin was among the luckier ones. He spent the endless hours of that terrible night huddled with two companions under an overturned skiff on a mud bar, wet from head to foot, without fire or heavy clothing, his cotton pants frozen to his legs. Only the body warmth of the men who lay on either side of him kept him alive. The storm cost him six weeks of agony in a hospital and half of his left foot. But at least he survived.

Ray was a boy of 14 at the time, attending high school in his home town of Winona, Minnesota. School let out at eleven that morning because it was Armistice Day and Ray scurried home, planning an afternoon of duck hunting.

The wind was fairly fresh by that time, and his mother was uneasy. "The storm warnings are up," she told him while she was getting his lunch. But he had grown up in Winona and knew the river, and at his age bad weather held no dread for him. It only meant good shooting. Ducks had been scarce all fall. Maybe a blow would bring 'em down. So he hurried through lunch and went on with his arrangements, impatient to be in a blind.

He had expected to hunt alone but, while he was loading his gear in the car, a cousin, Bob Stephens, showed up with a partner, Cal Wieczorek. They decided to join him. Bob was 20, Cal about 19.

The three of them drove to the Prairie Island spillway, at the lower end of the Winona pool, where Ray's dad kept his boat, a 16-footer pointed at both ends, with a home-made bracket at the stern for an outboard. They had decided to hunt at a place known as the Firing Line, along the border of the Upper Mississippi Wildlife Refuge three or four miles upstream. Hunters lined up there to intercept ducks flying in and out of the refuge, and in stormy weather the pass shooting was exceptionally good. This looked like the right kind of day.

The wind was blowing half a gale now and was beginning to have a bite. Ominous dark clouds raced overhead and scuds of cold rain pelted down. The signs all pointed to a perfect afternoon to bag ducks. They also pointed to trouble but, along with scores of older and more experienced hunters, the boys were too wrapped up in the prospects of good shooting to take heed.

They clamped a balky, old three-horse outboard onto the boat, cranked the motor and headed out into the choppy seas of the pool. Since the three of them were a heavy load for the skiff, it made slow headway against the wind.

They didn't give it a thought at the time, but they could hardly have been more poorly prepared for what was coming. Ray was wearing cotton pants and shirt, a cotton jacket, lighter than a hunting coat, cotton socks, and overshoes over a pair of leather shoes. Except for their hip boots, Bob and Cal were dressed about the same as Ray. Cal and Ray had gloves; Bob didn't. He did have a heavy raincoat, however, and that item probably made the difference between living and dying for Ray.

Among them, they had one paper folder of matches and no pocket knife. Ray was carrying a 16-gauge single-barrel Winchester, the other two had pumps. Because they intended to pass shoot, they had taken no decoys.

Backed up by a series of low dams, the Mississippi is a big river in that section, two to three miles wide, where the flooding of its bottoms forms open lakes, meandering channels, small islands, bars and rush beds. Threading through this maze, the skiff wallowed in the heavy waters. It took the boys an hour and a half to make the three or four miles to the Firing Line. The sky was full of ducks, flying in a way that would have warned them something was wrong had the three paid any attention. The birds were barreling across the bottoms in crazy skeins, riding the wind, turning and twisting at less than treetop height. It was plain they didn't like the looks of the weather. Before the afternoon was over Ray actually swung at a big greenhead with his gun as it hung just above his head, almost stationary, trying to fight its way into the gale.

When they finally got to the Firing Line they found it too crowded to suit them. The blinds there were only about 25 yards apart, and each one was occupied. Ducks were rocketing back and forth over the marsh, and the shooting was a ragged but steady barrage. The boys decided to move on and find a spot where they could have things a little more to themselves.

By the time they found it, on a willow-covered island with a big rush bed out in front, they were beginning to lose interest in shooting. The wind was booming down off the high bluffs to the west with sleet and fine snow in its teeth, howling like a banshee. They hunkered in the willows for the better part of an hour, killed three or four ducks and then decided that they had had enough. The cold was bone-chilling by that time, their hands were so stiff they could hardly handle their guns, and they were starting to worry about getting back to the landing.

Two strangers who came by just then in a little duck boat made no secret of the fact that they were scared. That settled it for the three boys. But going home would not be easy. None of them knew exactly where they were, and when they tried to shove away from the shore of the island the seas threatened to swamp the skiff. They finally dragged it across to the lee side where they managed to get it afloat and the motor started. But before they had gone 200 yards, they ran aground on a mud bar, which they couldn't go around because of the wind and seas. They dragged the boat across the bar and started on again.

They repeated that operation three or four times before they found themselves at the edge of a big, open slough. It didn't look familiar, and then they had to admit they were lost. It was almost dark now and the air was so full of snow they couldn't see a hundred feet around them. They couldn't even look into the wind. The storm cut their eyeballs like a sandblast. And in front of them the slough was a welter of dirty, gray, foaming water in which it didn't seem likely the skiff could survive more than a minute or two.

While they stood debating what to do, another boat loomed out of the stormy dusk, loaded down with four hunters. Two were boys only a little older than Ray; one was in his home room at school. The other two were grown men. They said that they had hunted on the river bottom all their lives and that they knew the way back to Prairie Island. When they said that they believed they could make it without swamping, the three boys decided to follow them.

But something was wrong with the outboard now, and Ray couldn't get it started. Bob and Cal rowed, handicapped by cold-numbed hands, while Ray tinkered with the motor. They managed to keep the other boat in sight for a few minutes. Then, pitching and rolling in great seas, it disappeared, and they didn't see it again. When their frantic yells brought no answer, they realized they were on their own once again. It was days before they were to learn what happened to the other party: The skiff capsized, and three of the hunters died, standing in the icy water, not knowing which way to wade to land. By some miracle one of the boys lived through the night and rescue parties found him on a near by island at daybreak.

A few minutes after they lost the other boat, the storm washed the three ashore on a sand spit grown with grass and rushes. Bob and Cal leaped clear as they grounded and escaped a wetting. Ray wasn't so lucky. In the stern of the skiff, still working on the outboard, he was in the path of a six-foot sea that smashed over the boat almost the instant it touched bottom. The wave drenched him from head to heels.

The shock of that icy dunking was beyond description. He clawed his way out of the swamped boat as the wind cut into him like a braided whip. When he tried to get to his feet his legs wouldn't hold him up. He crawled across the mud on all fours until he was beyond reach of the waves, and lay there, too cold and weak to care what happened next.

Cal and Bob dragged the boat up on dry land, dumped the water out of it and propped it up on one side with the motor to make a shelter. When Ray crawled under it, his pants and jacket crackled. His clothing had frozen stiff in those few minutes while he lay exposed to the wind.

The boys still had only a vague idea of their location, but they knew that large, open lakes lay between them and any landing, water they could not cross in the puny, disabled skiff. They didn't talk much about it. They didn't need to. There was only one alternative. Live or die, they would have to spend the night where they were.

Bob and Cal did everything they could to help Ray. First they gathered armfuls of dead rushes and spread them under the boat to keep Ray out of the wet mud. Then they began a desperate search for firewood, but there was not so much as a scrub willow on the sand spit. They finally found a few pieces of water-logged driftwood, the poorest sort of fuel, and heaped them into a little pyramid in front of the boat. Then they

turned the motor up to drain gas on the wood, but the screaming wind seemed to whip the gas into nowhere as fast as it ran
out of the tank. When it was gone they struck one match after
another without getting a spark of fire.

When the last match flared and died in the darkness, they
crawled under the boat with Ray and lay down on the wet
rushes, one on either side of him. They covered themselves

with their hunting coats and spread Bob's raincoat on top. The
raincoat kept the worst of the wind out and possibly saved
Ray from freezing.

They had little sense of time and did little talking. Bob
spoke only two or three times during the night, expressing concern about the anxiety his father and mother must be feeling.

The wet boy lay shivering in his icy clothes for what

seemed like hours, with his hands wedged between his thighs, since that seemed to be the warmest place on his body. He prayed to himself. He didn't think much about dying. He believed they would somehow get through the night and in the morning find their way home. He realized finally that he had lost all feeling in his feet. They were wooden stumps, no longer a part of him. He must have been sleeping for short periods, for afterward he recalled waking up and feeling warm for a minute or two before starting to shiver again.

The thing he remembered best was the unending scream of the wind. It never stopped for a second. It raged across the bar, searching under the overturned boat, wailing, screeching, terribly alive, terribly cold.

Sometime in the night Bob recalled that he had two apples and a couple of sandwiches in the pocket of his hunting coat. They were frozen as hard as rocks, but the three gnawed at them and they seemed to make them feel warmer.

Two or three times the sound of distant gunshots reached them, and once they thought they heard faint, far-off yells for help. Their own guns, however, were so crusted with ice by that time they could not fire them, and it was useless to try to shout in reply against such a wind.

They knew, of course, that they were not the only hunters lost there on the river bottoms. Others were enduring the same brand of torture. They felt sure there must be rescuers trying to reach them, but they didn't think anybody would succeed while the storm was raging.

It was not until days later that they learned all that happened that bitter night. Rescue efforts had got under way at dark, and men fought the storm and seas all night long in rowboats and skiffs and powerboats. Some even waded the sloughs in boots to bring lost men to shore. It was not a night for small craft, and no one ever knew how many boats were overturned, swamped or driven back in the darkness. But each time a boat was driven back a bigger boat took over and the search went on, hour after hour, heedless of the wind, the cold and the snow. The story of the heroic things that were done along the upper Mississippi that night would fill a book.

For the hunters waiting to be rescued the night was an awful and unbelievable ordeal. Some lived, some died. One party huddled on a marshy island beside a fire they started with dead grass and then fed with more than 40 cedar decoys, using gas from an outboard to rekindle the blaze each time it died down. Another group marched and jumped and sparred around a fire built from their boats. Still another found a patch of timber, got a fire going and then shot dead branches off trees for fuel.

They were the lucky ones. Others did not fare as well. Two died under an overturned boat 400 yards from a blazing bonfire, blinded by the storm, never even knowing that the fire was there. Two more reached shore along a railroad embankment, left their boat, crawled halfway up the bank, fell and froze to death, too weak to walk out to safety. Others gave up, lay down where they were in the willows and rushes without fire or shelter and died. A few drowned. Most of the victims froze. Even when the last of the living were rescued, the grim search for bodies still went on. It was three days before all the missing were accounted for and the final toll of 20 dead was tallied up.

Toward morning the air cleared enough so that Bob and Cal and Ray caught glimpses of light on the Winona dam, two or three miles away. The lights glimmered through the driving snow, tantalizing and mocking the boys who at least knew now in which direction they should go when daylight came. It was about that time that Bob remarked that his hands were frozen, and he supposed he would lose them. He said it quietly, as if it didn't really matter.

At first light the wind seemed to lose its gale force. It was still blowing hard but after studying the lake in the gray dawn of the cheerless morning they decided the skiff might weather the seas.

They were in bad shape. Cal and Bob could barely stand and Ray couldn't get to his feet without help. Their hands were stiff and useless. The spit where they had spent the night was rimmed now with a 50-foot belt of ice that made launching the boat a tough job. But they didn't have much choice. They couldn't live through the day on that bleak mud bar and they had no way of knowing when searchers would find them.

Ray crawled into the boat, and Bob and Cal inched it off the bar, broke a path through the ice to open water and rowed slowly out of the lee into the lake. But their hands were too numb to grip the oars and the skiff went out of control almost as soon as the full force of wind and waves hit it.

Spray froze to the skiff as it struck now, coating the boat with ice. Ray's clothes were stiff as armor, and the feeling was gone from his legs to the extent that he no longer felt the cold blasts of wind. As the boat grew heavier and heavier from its load of ice, it was swept across the Winona pool to the Wisconsin side.

Normally they would have reached safety in that area, but there was more torment ahead. The marsh had frozen in the night, and they grounded on the new ice 100 yards offshore. It was thick enough to gouge a big hole in the bow of the skiff, but the ice wouldn't bear a man's weight. Luckily the wind drove them up until the hole was above water, and there they sat, shelterless and wretched, with no way to get to shore.

It was there a plane found them about an hour later. The plane, a Cub trainer piloted by Max Conrad of Winona, had been in the air since shortly after daylight, shuttling back and forth across the bottoms, spotting lost hunters, empty boats, deserted gear and stranded dogs, dropping sandwiches, whiskey, matches and cigarettes, even dipping low enough to shout down words of encouragement to the men as they were found. Nobody in the rescue teams that day did a better job.

Conrad flew low over the boys, wagging his wings, and shouted a message they could not undrestand. Then he was gone, but it wasn't long before they heard the steady throb of a powerboat and then saw the Army Engineers' launch *Chippewa* approaching.

She couldn't reach them, for they were out of the river channel in shallow water, and it took the crew close to an hour to break through the marsh ice and get to them with a skiff. Before they were through Ray's dad and a friend, who had been out all night looking for the lost trio, showed up in a boat with a powerful outboard. They carried Ray back to the launch, peeled off his shoes and frozen clothing and, even though he was only 14, gave him a man-sized slug of whiskey. He took it like a man, too.

Bob spent a week in a Winona hospital for treatment of his frozen hands, but he came through all right. Cal went home that same afternoon. Ray had a long bout with gangrene and lost part of a foot. He also lost an astonishing amount of weight, dropping from 143 pounds to 85 during his recovery. Christmas was less than a week away when he got out of the hospital, and he decided it would be the best Christmas he would ever have.

Ray became a teacher in La Crosse, Wisconsin, and has hunted ducks on the Mississippi bottoms many times since that fateful night, but there are certain precautions he takes on every trip. He wears special boots, even on the warmest days, and carries an emergency kit containing extra wool socks, warm gloves, a down-filled hat, compass, knife, matches in a water-tight container, even a small flare gun.

"I never go without that kit," he said. "There are too many mistakes in the world to make the same one twice. And besides, I still remember how the wind sounded that night back in 1940."

A Very Tough Bear

CARL JOHNSON, who lived in Cadillac, Michigan, had for several years devoted all his spare time to bear hunting. He owned the best pack of bear dogs in the Midwest, with which he had racked up a record of 25 kills (it has subsequently climbed to 125). At the time he was president of the Michigan Bear Hunters Association.

Carl had no idea when he answered the phone that evening in May 1950 that he was about to embark on his toughest bear hunt. The call came from Alex Van Luven in Brimley, a small town in the Upper Peninsula of the state. Van Luven, an experienced woodsman, had hunted coyotes, wolves and bears all his life.

"We've got a bad bear problem up here again," Alex Van Luven announced, coming straight to the point. "Bears have been raiding sheep pens and orchards and knocking over beehives ever since last summer. The last few weeks one big bruiser has been getting too fresh. He walks out around cabins in broad daylight; kids going home from school have seen him three or four times. He's got everybody's hair standing on end. I don't like the way he's behaving."

Carl Johnson would ordinarily have laughed off such an alarm. Wasn't it absurd for a community to consider a black bear as a menace to human life? Ordinarily, yes. Two years before, however, a black had killed a three-year-old girl, carrying her off from a cabin a few miles west of Brimley. He knew that the people around there hadn't forgotten that tragedy, and that Alex hadn't forgotten it either. He didn't blame them for their present concern. If Alex was upset, Carl thought, there must be good cause. Alex has had so much experience with bears; surely he would recognize a bad actor when one was on the prowl.

"We've tried traps but he's too smart," Alex went on. "Suppose your dogs could rout him out and handle him?"

"We'd like nothing better than to try," Carl replied.

Man-eating bears are a rarity, such a rarity that if you mention the subject to the average outdoorsman, he will almost certainly laugh outright in ridicule. But the scoffers are wrong.

True, it's close to unheard of for a bear to turn into a genuine man-eater, that is, a bear that attacks and kills a human without provocation and then carries off the victim to feed on afterward. But it does happen. There have been at least three substantiated cases of that happening in the United States and Canada. Strangest of all, each time the man-eater was a black bear, not a polar, grizzly or big brown.

The first incident occurred at a lumber camp on the Red Deer River in southern Alberta in May of 1906. Two men, named Heffern and McIntosh, were chopping wood near the cook shanty when they saw a bear come out of the brush on the far bank of the river. The only other man around the place at the time was Wilson, the cook. They called to him to come out and watch the bear. He did, never suspecting that he was walking to his death.

The bear marched into the river, swam across and shook itself as a dog on leaving water. Then it charged the three men headlong and without warning. McIntosh and Heffern made it into the cook shanty, only 30 feet away. Wilson un-luckily overran the door. He went racing on around the build-ing with the bear gaining on him at every bound. He was al-most back to the safety of the door when the bear felled him with a blow across the neck, probably killing him instantly.

From the shanty the two men bombarded the bear with everything they had at hand. They landed a cant hook and a can of lard solidly at short range, but the bear wasn't distracted. It picked up Wilson's body, dragged it off a few yards and stood over it, guarding its kill. Heffern and McIntosh made a run for the bunkhouse where they had a revolver. They came back as close as they dared and fired several shots without scoring a hit. The barrage caused the bear to back off, but it took its time about it. Then the bear picked up the dead man once more. It carried him a hundred yards out into the brush, determined to feed. When one of the lumberjacks showed up with a rifle a few minutes later, however, the bear cleared out without its prey.

Ernest Thompson Seton, the great wildlife writer who could always find an excuse for bad behavior in any animal, thought that the bear probably had rabies. There was, however, no more evidence of rabies in that bear than there is in a lion or tiger that attacks a man. Instead, it seems simply to have been a rare instance when hunger made a bear unusually bold, bold enough to attack and kill a man for food.

In the fall of 1924, a black bear killed a Finnish trapper named Waino, in the Port Arthur district of Ontario. The face and neck of that bear were bristling with procupine quills, a condition that has provoked some of the worst instances of man-eating tigers in India. Newspaper accounts of the tragedy reported that Waino's rifle had been fired once and had jammed when he attempted to lever in another shell. Whether his shot provoked the bear's attack, however, or whether he shot in self-defense as the bear was coming at him was never made clear, probably because it couldn't be determined. In any case the bear, which was an unusually big black, had come back to its kill. There was proof of that; the bear was shot while actually feeding on the body of the trapper. On the basis of that alone, the bear has to be listed as a true man-eater.

The man-eating black that attracted more attention than any other, frightening a dozen counties in northern Michigan into a state of near panic, was the one that chose a little girl as its victim. The attack occurred at the lonely fire-tower cabin on Mission Hill, in the Marquette National Forest, a few miles inland from Lake Superior and 15 miles from Brimley. The date was July 7, 1948.

Arthur Pomerankey, the ranger who lived in the cabin, was on duty at the forest headquarters at Raco, 15 miles away. It was a hot summer afternoon. Pomerankey's wife was busy in the kitchen of the cabin when she heard a scream. Looking out the window, she saw her three-year-old daughter Carol Ann scrambling up the steps of the back porch to get away from a small black bear. The killer, which weighed only about 150 pounds, was snarling at the girl's heels. The frightened child was reaching for the screen door when the bear grabbed her by the neck.

Horrified, the mother ran screaming from the house, caught up the first weapon at hand, a broom, and gave chase. But the bear refused to be scared off. It lumbered across the brush-bordered clearing and disappeared into the woods, still carrying Carol Ann.

The mother made a frantic phone call to her husband. After the alarm went out by radio, a posse of more than a hundred men armed with rifles and shotguns quickly gathered and began to search for the little girl. Alex Van Luven headed the search. He had his best dog with him, leading it on a leash.

Less than a quarter of a mile from the cabin, one of the searchers found a small blood-stained shoe. The dog picked up the trail from that and followed it into a dense thicket. They found the child's mangled body there. The bear had killed Carol Ann with a single bite through the back of her neck. It had carried her only a short distance before stopping to feed. The searchers had interrupted the bear and driven it off. Alex used his head. He sent one of the two men with him back with the tragic news. The other, a commercial fisherman from Lake Superior named Wayne Weston, was left to guard the body. Turning his dog loose on the track, Alex took out after the bear himself.

But it was to fall to Weston to take revenge on the bear for its atrocity. He had a very short wait. Within five minutes after the dog's bawling had faded in the woods, and while Alex was still within hearing of a rifle shot, the bear showed up. It was brazenly returning to finish its interrupted meal. Weston did not see it approach and had no warning until it stood up on its hind feet and stared him in the face, over the top of the bush, only 20 feet away.

"I was so scared for a second I hardly knew whether to shoot or not," he told Alex later.

But he wasn't long in making up his mind. He smashed a shot into the bear's mouth; it knocked the man-eater down. As the bear, thrashing and growling, attempted to drag itself away, Weston finished it with four more shots.

Wildlife experts from the Michigan Conservation Department moved into that case and investigated the atrocity with modern crime-detection methods. The carcass of the bear was flown to a veterinary lab at Michigan State College, in downstate East Lansing, where it was painstakingly examined. The department was looking for the answers to a number of questions. Had some kind of injury driven the bear to attack the child? Was it diseased? Had it once been a pet and so lost its normal fear of man? Human flesh in the stomach proved beyond all question that Weston had killed the bear that had attacked Carol Ann. Other than that proof, however, the experts couldn't determine much. There was no collar mark, no sign of injury, no trace of disease, no clue at all except the bear's physical appearance: the killer was lean and hungry. The blueberry season, when all bears feast, was still a couple of weeks away. The experts concluded hunger had possessed the beast.

Public reaction was pretty violent. For the next two or three years people in northern Michigan became jittery even over a black bear track—one found around a farm was enough to throw a scare into a whole neighborhood. Any bear seen near dwellings or at garbage pits at the edge of a town—and plenty were seen, of course—touched off something close to hysteria. There was an open season on bear the year round, and widespread clamor for a bounty. Any suggestion that, as game, bears ought to have some protection met with angry opposition. Blackie just wasn't to be trusted in that country. The tragedy resulting from the misbehavior of one perverted black bear had condemned the entire species to the status of outlaw, so far as the average resident was concerned. One can hardly blame the people for being vigilant, either, even though another man-eater might not show up in Michigan for the next 50 years.

Two years after the tragedy of Carol Ann, when Alex

phoned Carl, popular feeling about blacks was still the same. The two men made their plans quickly during the call. Carl picked seven dogs to do the job: Banjo and John, Bum and Barker and Hack, all hounds, and two airedales, Rocky and Duke. Banjo and John were the best of his pack, old and case-hardened, dead certain on a track and rough on any bear they closed with. The airedales could be even rougher. Barker and Bum were youngsters, with plenty of staying power. Hack, a new addition to the pack, was an airedale and Plott hound cross, bred in Tennessee. The dog had established a good tracking reputation in the southern mountains. Carl figured that if those seven dogs couldn't handle a mean bear, no dogs could.

Carl reached Alex's home around supper time the following Thursday. He had two companions with him: Howard McDaniel of Manton, and Danny Porter, a farmer from Boon who kenneled and helped train his dogs. Alex and an Indian named Joe would join them for the hunt. When the first red was beginning to show in the east the next morning, they drove out of Brimley on the old Mission Hill logging grade in the direction of the now deserted cabin from which the bear had carried off Carol Ann Pomerankey.

They parked a few miles out of town and turned north from the grade, toward Lake Superior, leading the dogs. Alex felt sure the bear they were looking for was somewhere in that area.

"I've studied his tracks a dozen times; I'll know 'em if we find 'em," he said to Carl.

Three or four times during the morning they came across bear sign where a black had either overturned rocks, looking for mice, or cuffed a crumbling log apart to get at a colony of ants. Twice the scent was fresh enough to make the impatient dogs tug at their chains and whine, but Alex looked things over carefully and then shook his head.

"Not the right bear," he said each time.

They had been walking four hours when they found sign that was fresher than any they had seen. It was at the border of a small clearing where an old logging camp had stood years before. A bear had really worked the place over. Banjo and John put their noses down to a mauled stump and begged to go, bawling, lunging into their collars.

"Pretty hot," Carl told Alex.

Alex nodded, not saying anything. He was going over the ground foot by foot. At last, in a patch of bare sand beside a log, he found what he was looking for: the clear imprint of a bear's front and hind feet. He studied the tracks for a minute.

"That's the one," he said crisply then. "Let 'em go."

Johnson slipped Banjo's collar. The hound made a preliminary circle along the edge of the clearing, testing logs and brush and ground for bear smell and announcing each new find in a gruff bellow. Fifty yards ahead Banjo lined out, singing cold trail. John was turned loose next and went tearing off after him.

The rest of the dogs were kept on leash. To be worth his salt in that part of the country a bear dog must be deer-proof. Deer are not hunted with hounds in the north; a dog that will take a deer track is worse than useless. Johnson's pack had been well-trained on the score, but to let a young dog go on a cold bear track is asking for trouble. Banjo and John could be trusted no matter what the provocation, but the others would have to stay on their chains until the bear was up.

The bear had traveled on dry ground, and the two hounds were having trouble. They felt their way so slowly that for a couple of miles the men kept them in hearing without any effort. Then the track turned toward the big Salt Point Swamp on the shore of Lake Superior. As the dogs hit wet ground, their pace quickened. Banjo and John were a long way ahead when they jumped the bear.

Turned loose at the border of the swamp, the rest of the pack went pell-mell to join the chase. Five minutes later all seven dogs were making music on a smoking hot bear track, but the clamor faded away fast. Blackie had never been dogged before, but he knew what all the noise meant, and he was going places.

Carl and Danny Porter followed the pack into the cedar and alder tangles, while Howard McDaniel and Alex and Indian Joe scattered in the hope of getting ahead of the bear. On a hunt such as this one it's essential for at least one of the hunters to follow the hounds and, if possible, to keep within hearing distance of them. Otherwise there's likely to be no one around to finish the job after the hounds have brought the bear to bay.

Carl and Danny did their best, but they had lost track of the dogs before pushing half a mile into the swamp. It was two hours before the men heard the familiar baying again, and then it was only a broken pulse beat of sound far off to the north.

The day had turned hot now, with the blazing heat of late spring. Carl and Danny pushed through the swamp, panting and streaming sweat. Taking a needed breathing spell, they stood and listened as the hound music began to grow louder. The bear was coming back.

They separated then, picked stands and waited. Carl found a place on an old brush-grown logging road from which he could see in three directions. For many minutes it sounded as though the dogs were going to drive the bear straight to him. When the chase was less than a hundred yards away, however, it swung suddenly to the west. The bear crossed the logging road and plunged into an alder thicket, disappearing out of sight.

Carl assumed the track-down was close to a finish then, but he was wrong. The bear was a running fool. Even though it was old, it was lean and tough. In ten minutes, it had again taken the pack out of range of Carl's hearing. Carl learned afterwards that the bear had led the hounds miles inland, through some of the roughest country in his home range, before it had turned back to the Salt Point Swamp.

It was not until three hours later that Carl and Porter heard the dogs once more. They came down into the swamp a long way off; the men knew from the sound of the chase that the dogs had at last overtaken the bear. It would be making a running fight, cuffing off the plucky dogs as it went. Carl could vouch that every dog in the pack was an expert in the business, and by now he figured the bear would be very tired. No bear could keep up that pace much longer. Carl tried to hurry, knowing they would be needed when the bear finally came to bay. But hurrying was something no man could do in that swamp.

The bear made a stand in the worst hellhole Johnson had ever seen. At some time in the past a gale, roaring in off Lake Superior, had mowed a wide swath of destruction through the swamp, tipping big spruce and cedar trees at crazy angles and piling them every which way. Young cedars and alders had grown up through the mess. It was now a green jungle that was over ten feet high and so thick it shut out the sun. The shin-tangle and leatherleaf underfoot completed the labyrinth—a totally wretched place in which to corner a bear.

The two men couldn't run in the maze, they couldn't even walk in it. Clawing at the heavy growth, they climbed over windfalls and crept through the young stuff on hands and knees. All the while, the sounds of the most blood-chilling bear-and-dog fight they had ever heard raged from the heart of the thicket ahead of them. When Carl and Danny were only 50 yards away and worming in for the kill, the dogs were no longer baying. They were screaming. Carl said afterward that it made his hair stand up to hear them.

The men lost sight of each other. Carl got so close to the bear he could hear it pop its jaw and even caught the heavy grunt of its breathing above the snarling and growling. He could even smell the bear's odor, which was mixed with the stink of churned mud and stagnant swamp water. But he still couldn't see either the bear or the dogs. The bear had backed in under a big windfall and was behind a solid green wall of young cedars.

Over all the other racket, the growling and worrying of the two airedales could be heard; the pair was doing its special job at close quarters. Carl was less than five yards away when Rocky, the bitch, suddenly ripped out a savage bawl of defiance and rage, followed by the sound of close-quarter flailing and scuffling. She had grabbed and was hanging on; that meant that the dogs knew Carl was there, even though the bear probably didn't know it yet. Then Rocky came sailing out of the cedars, flying through the air end over end. The blow she had received must have injured her, perhaps badly; however, before Carl could get his hands on her, she whirled and went back into the middle of the fight.

Carl inched deeper into the thicket, crawling on all fours. Suddenly the bear lunged out of its corner, roaring at the dogs, letting Carl see it at close range for the first time. He got a good look and didn't like what he saw. The muddy, bedraggled bear, now only three or four steps away, must have weighed close to 400 pounds. It was raging and frothing. The boar-like eyes were blazing red, its ears laid back, teeth bared, the hair on its neck all pointing the wrong way. It was the meanest looking thing Carl had ever seen.

Carl tried to jerk up his rifle, (an old converted British Army .303 with which he had made all of his bear kills) but the barrel caught in the brush. Just then Duke, the other airedale, flashed between Carl and the bear, so that he couldn't have shot anyway. Carl admitted afterward he wasn't sorry the dog had interfered.

Then once more the bear ducked back out of sight under the windfall. As Carl started to crawl closer toward the cedar wall, the fight suddenly stopped. The uproar died out all in an instant, making the swamp as still as a cemetery—and just about as cheerful.

Carl knew the bear had broken bay. He waited where he was for the dogs to pick up the track and drive it out of the thicket. The silence, however, hung on. The unnatural stillness made the skin prickle on the back of Carl's neck.

Then the silence was broken by the whimpering of a dog. Carl pushed into the windfall, where he discovered the answer to the riddle. His dogs, that he had bragged were a match for any bear, had quit cold. Five of them lay where they had fought, sprawled on their bellies in the water and the trampled muck, panting, whining, and licking their cuts. Banjo and Rocky were missing.

78

Porter came crashing through the brush.

"What happened?" he asked.

"We got licked out," Carl said glumly, "and we've lost Rocky and Banjo."

As the two men stood in that eerie, cramped hole, which smelled of swamp and bear, neither of them could blame the dogs for quitting. "My stomach turned over, and I decided I'd had all I wanted of that bear myself," Carl related later to Alex.

Porter suggested searching for the missing dogs, but Carl didn't have much heart even for that. He had seen Rocky knocked sprawling, and he was sure that Banjo had been hurt as badly. Probably both dogs had crawled away to die.

Suddenly Carl's spirits were raised as, off to the west, Banjo's rolling bawl rang out. It was clear and loud and defiant. The old hound hadn't quit after all. Banjo was still in action, driving the bear, and venting his hate. Shouting for backing, the dog bawled again—a triumphant, throaty war cry. On its heels, Carl and Danny heard the flat, thudding smash of a rifle shot. Although they didn't know it, McDaniel's .300 had had its say, and the hunt was over.

It took them half an hour to get to the area. They soon found Alex, McDaniel and Indian Joe. They were standing, looking at the bear, which was lying dead on the ground. Even dead, the bear was a tough-looking character. Banjo was sprawled on the ground near by, battered and exhausted, and Rocky lay on a hunting coat, whining from the pain of a broken jaw. McDaniel told Carl that the bear had run headlong into him as it was crossing an old logging road with both dogs snapping at its heels. After rounding up all his dogs, he went home.

Carl heard no more reports from Brimley about a trouble-making bear. It wasn't seen at the roadsides or around homes anymore, and there were no more incidents of a bear committing malicious acts of mischief as before. Carl knew that Alex had been correct in his identification of the track that hot spring morning. They had killed the right bear.

Had they done away with a potential man-eater? Probably not. There is no reason to believe that two of them would turn up in the same community in a space of two years. Left to itself, the bear they killed would have gone on stealing sheep, raiding orchards and scaring people. The chances are slim, however, that he would ever have mustered enough courage for a deliberate attack on a human. Maybe he would have liked to. Carl was convinced it had been vicious enough for it. But like most bears, it probably lacked the final touch of nerve.

At any rate, the hunt had eliminated a nuisance that had alarmed an entire neighborhood. It had also proved to Carl's satisfaction that his pack of seven dogs was a match for any bear, no matter how mean or tough.

Hell in Cold Water

THERE WAS no hint in the sky of weather trouble as the 30-foot trolling boat *Roamer* cast off her lines, backed away from the dock and moved out across Munising Bay. Her skipper, Captain Fred Lukowski, was at the wheel and Donald Martin, the 14-year-old helper and cabin boy, was busy coiling lines and making things shipshape. Jim Oxley and his six guests, aboard for a fishing trip, started to ready their deep-trolling gear.

A brisk wind had blown earlier in the morning, holding the *Roamer* temporarily at the dock, but it had died now to a light breeze. Crossing the blue, wind-ruffled bay, no one on board had reason to think that this would be anything but a pleasant, everyday fishing trip for big lake trout a few miles offshore on the reefs of Lake Superior. The skipper had no warning that it was his last day on earth, nor did any of the rest suspect that they were heading into an experience through which none of them would have believed he could live.

Jim had done considerable deep trolling for lakers. It was a sport he preferred to any other, and Munising, in the Upper Peninsula of Michigan, on the south shore of the lake, 150 miles west of Sault Sainte Marie, was his favorite trolling port. He had brought six novices along this time. Five of them, Fred Fendt, Walt Gottleber, Westal Riddick, Charlie Lea and Eddie Williams, worked at the tool manufacturing plant Jim operated in the village of Holly, 50 miles northwest of Detroit. The sixth man was Maurice Johnson, a friend from Flint, Michigan.

The trip had been planned weeks ahead as a Fourth of July outing; however, they had reached Munising a day early. Now, shortly before noon on July 3, 1949, the carefree and hopeful fishermen were on their way out to the trolling ground.

Outside Grand Island, seven or eight miles offshore, they came in over reefs where Jim had landed some top-notch lake trout on previous trips; Captain Lukowski gave the nod to put the spoons down. He cut the speed of the *Roamer* and the men paid out the metal lines from the heavy trolling rods and settled down to the uneventful and patience-trying job of waiting for a strike from a trout on the bottom of the lake, 50 to 75 feet under the keel.

It was soon apparent that the group had picked a poor day for trolling. The weather looked favorable, the wind was right, the water not too rough—but the lakers weren't having any. The men kept their spoons down deep, where they tapped the rocky reefs every now and then, while the skipper angled back and forth over the trout grounds. The *Roamer* rolled lazily in the light swell that was coming in from the open lake, and the rod tips dipped and rose. Nobody got a strike.

Two other boats were trolling not far away and, as far as Jim's party could see, their luck was no better. It was the poorest fishing Jim had ever encountered on those grounds. By the end of three hours he was fed up. As host, he was about ready to suggest that they give up for that day and go in, but before he could speak things were taken abruptly out of his hands.

The men heard a sudden far-off roll of thunder in the southeast, over the land. When they looked in that direction they saw that an odd black cloud was rolling up over the hills behind Munising. It was growing and climbing fast. They watched it for a minute or two. Then turning to Lukowski, Jim said, "That looks dirty."

The captain nodded. "Squall," he grunted. "Better get your lines in."

He swung the wheel over, and the *Roamer* came around and put her nose toward the wide channel between Grand Island and Wood Island. She had two or three miles to cover before she would have any kind of lee. Meanwhile, the men had grandstand seats to watch the oncoming storm. Off to the west, the two other boats had turned and were running for the shelter of Wood Island. As things turned out, their occupants were luckier than those of the *Roamer*. They didn't make harbor before trouble hit, but the wind veered around the island in such a way as to break the force of the storm for them.

The *Roamer's* skipper poured gas to his engine, and the boat hammered down into the channel. The squall was moving off to the northwest, passing around, traveling with such frightening speed that the men concluded they were going to outrun it safely. The storm slashed by them a mile or so to the north, a pitch-black cloud mass veined with lightning flashes. Then the wind freshened sharply and rain started to pelt down.

Nobody aboard realized it at the time, but what they were witnessing was the tortuous maneuvering and wandering of a genuine tornado. It had swept through Munising, wrecking docks and ripping the roofs off buildings. On Grand Island the tornado picked up a summer cottage, rolled and twisted it across the beach and slammed it down squarely on top of another.

While the fishing party was still eying it apprehensively, the ominous black cloud wheeled around into the southwest, then turned suddenly and bore down on them like a live thing, driven by a screaming wind out of the west.

"It's coming," somebody yelled. "We better get life jackets on!"

The life jackets were stored in a locker down in the cabin, where they weren't easy to get at, but the men clawed them out and tied them on. One of the party helped the skipper into his while he stood braced at the wheel.

The core of the storm struck the boat with a sledge-hammer blow. The solid wall of wind and rain brought big seas with it, roaring and foaming, their black-green crests smoking with spray. The mountains of dark water picked the *Roamer* up and slammed her down.

During that first wild rush of wind and sea and rain, Jim knew the *Roamer* was in serious trouble. The storm had caught the little 30-footer broadside, and she was wallowing in the trough of those heaving hills of water. It was too late now to bring her around and put her head into the wind. If she survived five minutes in the trough, it would be a miracle. Either she would be swamped or be smashed like an eggshell by tons of solid water pouring down on her.

After the second huge sea hit, there was a shout from the stern deck. Maurice Johnson was overboard. Swept clear of the deck by a gray-green wall of water, he was clawing and fighting to stay afloat. He was the one man in the party unable to swim a stroke; two or three of the others lunged toward the rail in the hope of aiding him, just as the waves relented. The reprieve was short; the next sea slewed the stern of the boat around within the reach of the man floundering in the water. He grabbed a post and, with a little help, hauled himself back on board. But a minute later he was thrown headlong off the slanting deck of the careening *Roamer*, along with the rest of the party.

As the boat lurched far over on her beam ends, a giant sea broke against her hull and rolled her down out of sight.

"I flung myself as far from her as I could, felt stinging cold water close over my head, and fought to get back to the top

where I could breathe," Jim said later, describing that terrible minute.

He came up, gulped in a lungful of air and saw heads popping out of the water all around him. As the boat rolled up, all but submerged now, swamped and sluggish, Jim noticed the skipper floating free of her. During that minute of initial panic, he saw that there was something wrong with him. He didn't seem able to do much for himself.

Jim, an experienced swimmer, battled to keep upright in the mountainous waves. Supported by his life jacket, he was able to take a quick count. He could find only eight bobbing heads. In the roaring confusion of the storm he managed to get a glimpse of each face. Charlie Lea was missing.

"Where's Lea?" he bawled. A voice shouted back that he must still be in the boat. Starting for the *Roamer* just as it was heaved up on the crest of a frothing sea, Jim saw Lea's head wash past one of the cabin windows.

He flung himself ahead, grabbed a railing near the bow and fought his way aft to the cabin. There were two or three others hanging on to the rail by that time. The cabin roof was made of plywood, and he was told afterward that he had ripped most of it away with his bare hands. Somehow he and the others smashed their way in and dragged Lea out to the momentary safety of open water. Then they finished tearing the cabin top away, and Jim started to help some of them find a handhold on it. It made a poor, makeshift life raft, but it was better than none.

They were in a bad spot. Lake Superior is the biggest body of fresh water in the world. Maybe it isn't the coldest; it couldn't be much colder and still be water. So clear and pure that big freighters pump their drinking tanks full in midlake, Superior maintains a year-round temperature close to that of spring water, never varying far from 45 degrees. They'll tell you, in the little fishing villages around the shore, that it never freezes over in winter, and that is true. Ice fields extend out for ten to twenty miles, but there is always open, restless water in midlake. They'll also tell you that the ice never thaws out completely in summer, and that comes close to being true, too.

It is reputed never to give up the bodies of those who drown in it. Jim knew when he felt the icy chill of the water bite through his heavy clothes in those first few minutes that numbing cold was one of the worst dangers they faced.

On top of that he was the only really capable swimmer in the party of seven. Johnson could not swim at all; the others were only fair swimmers. In his younger days Jim had swum as far as six miles at a stretch, and he had no fear for himself on that score. But he seriously doubted that the others could keep afloat in this rough water, even with the help of their life jackets.

During the first few minutes they were in the water, everything was confusion and panic. Jim had few clear memories of that part of the experience, but he remembered having helped two or three men to the improvised life raft and seeing to it that they had a handhold.

Jim was scared himself those first few minutes, too scared to think very clearly, and the rest were in about the same shape. But after he had swum around the swamped boat a couple of times to make sure that the whole party was accounted for and that everybody had some hold on the floating wreckage, he realized that he was not as cold as he had expected to be. In fact, he wasn't cold at all; so far the disaster was less dreadful than one might have anticipated. He began to think that maybe they would all get out of it alive after all.

During the first quarter hour in the water, Jim concluded that a man dressed in warm woolen clothing, as he was, has little to dread from the cold water of Superior if he keeps moving. Supported by a life jacket, a fairly strong swimmer can survive hours in the lake without any real ill effects, Jim declared later. He knew because he had done it. But on the other hand, a man unable to swim or one who stops swimming and just floats in one place will be finished off by the cold in a fairly short time, he said.

But even if the cold water wasn't so bad, looking back later on the ordeal as a whole, it seemed to Jim like a nightmare in slow motion. There was nothing they could do but hang on and wait. The seas were running 20 to 30 feet high. One minute the men were perched on a crest from which they could see an inferno of foaming, tortured water stretching away on all sides. The next they were thrown down into a deep hollow, walled in by the heaving flanks of great seas and the arc of the stormy sky overhead.

Everyone kept a grip on something. Most of the party were clustered around the wreckage of the cabin. The *Roamer* was still afloat, with three or four feet of her prow showing above water but her stern was submerged. Clinging to her and not daring to let go, Eddie Williams was taking a merciless pounding against her planking as the seas heaved and rolled the sodden wreck back and forth.

Nobody tried to talk. For one thing the noise of the wind and the water would have made talking difficult. For another, they were all trying to save their breath and strength. There was some praying, but most of it was silent.

Every few minutes, just as soon as Jim began to feel the chill of the water, he let go of the raft and swam around it, or over to the wreck and back, to keep his blood circulating.

The wind continued to blow a howling gale for nearly an hour after they had been swamped. Then it started to fall away and, although it was still blowing hard, the seas came at them a little less savagely.

They had been in the water about two hours when Captain Lukowski simply let go of the raft and floated away. No one realized at the time that he was dead. They were probably too numbed and too preoccupied with their own troubles by then to realize that Lukowski had slipped away. The skipper had seemed dazed and had not spoken all the time he clung to the wreckage. The men decided afterward, when they learned that Lukowski had died of a heart attack, that he must have been stricken at the wheel of the *Roamer* when the squall first struck. Probably he had hardly known what was happening after that.

All the time they were floating in the water, the timbered shore of Grand Island, two miles away across the wind-lashed channel, seemed to beckon mockingly toward them. Time after time as the raft was lifted by the heavy waves, they glimpsed the high sandstone cliffs of the island, sometimes half blotted out by rain, sometimes sharp and clear and seeming to be much closer than they really were. Jim kept turning over in his mind the possibility of swimming there to get help. He wondered whether he could make it; the more he thought about it, the more he was sure that he could.

But it wasn't a very sound idea. The island's outer end, which was closest to them, jutted out of the lake in sheer cliffs. There was no beach at their foot. The seas were thundering and smoking in foam-laced fury at the base of that long rampart. No swimmer could have survived the breakers there to make a landing. Even if Jim was lucky enough to blunder into a tiny, sheltered cove, Grand Island was close to twenty miles around. There were few houses; he would have a long hike before he could find help.

He wasn't, however, thinking about the disadvantages of

the scheme. All he could think of was that there was land off there to the east, within swimming distance. The afternoon was slipping away. If they weren't rescued before dark there would be no hope for any of them. Nobody could find them in that storm-tossed lake during the night; by morning rescue would be too late. Jim realized the outlook for himself and the others was bad. Then a few minutes after the skipper had drifted off, he kicked himself resolutely away from the raft and started to swim toward the distant island. He didn't know at the time that young Donald Martin had struck bravely out after him, either unwilling to let him make the try alone, or believing as Jim did that the best chance for the whole party lay in one of them getting ashore.

After half a mile, Jim noted that the power was going out of his strokes. Then he saw a boat coming up the channel to the south. It was a speed boat, and it was streaking along, knifing through the tops of the seas and throwing out a high V of white foam. He stopped swimming and rested in the water, watching it and listening to the distant, full-throated roar of the engine. It was the sweetest sight, the sweetest sound he could remember in his whole life.

If only the speed boat could see the wreck, if only it didn't pass them by. There wasn't much of the wreck for the boat to see, no more than two or three feet of the bow of the swamped *Roamer* and the half-submerged dot of the makeshift raft. Both were still being completely hidden each time the heavy seas rolled.

But they were seen. Jim saw the oncoming boat swerve and lose speed. The roar of her engine died away, the white V around her prow disappeared, her nose fell and she lay wallowing in the sea.

It was then that he discovered that the Martin boy had been following him to Grand Island. The lad's nerve broke at the prospect that the rescue boat might not find him out there in the empty lake by himself, halfway between Jim and the wreck, and for the first time that afternoon he yelled loudly and lustily for help.

After taking aboard the exhausted men who clung to the *Roamer,* the speedboat headed for the two swimmers. It stopped to pick up Donald, then streaked for Jim. It came alongside and stopped. The rail was within his reach. He lifted an arm, but it fell back into the water, numb and impotent. His last ounce of strength was gone, and they hauled him aboard as limp and helpless as a bundle of wet rags. During those dragging, tortured three hours, Superior had hit him harder than he had realized.

The rescue craft circled to look for Lukowski, but when it became apparent that he couldn't be found without a long search, the speedboat wheeled and roared back toward Munising. Everyone knew by that time that the skipper of the *Roamer* was beyond help, and the rest of the party needed immediate attention if the storm's toll was to be kept from mounting still higher.

The rescuer was Captain Everett Morrison; his boat was the fast cruiser in which he carried tourists along the foot of Pictured Rocks, east of Munising. He and Captain Lukowski were neighbors. They had a standing arrangement that if either was caught out on the lake or did not get in on schedule, the other would give a hand.

A Coast Guard boat from Munising also was out looking for the *Roamer* at the time Captain Morrison picked up the survivors, but it was searching on the east side of Grand Island.

It would have made the find in another half hour or so, but that would almost certainly have been too late, at least for Charlie Lea and Fred Fendt. They were both unconscious when they were taken aboard Morrison's boat, and Fendt was so blue and lifeless when he reached the hospital at Munising that the others thought he was dead. But hospital attention quickly brought both men around. They were released the next morning, in astonishingly good condition.

Eddie Williams had suffered the worst hurts of any of the party, from being pounded against the hull of the *Roamer*. Lea had lost a fair share of the skin on the side of one leg, but nobody had been injured critically.

Captain Morrison went back out on the lake as soon as all the survivors were safely ashore. He came in again shortly before dark with the body of the skipper.

Jim went back to Munising three weeks later with a companion on another trolling trip. He took certain precautions that time. Before they left home they purchased a seven-man war-surplus, rubber life raft. When they left the dock in Munising for the trolling grounds that raft, fully inflated, was lashed snugly in place on top of the cabin of their boat.

They had good luck that day, catching eight trout in three hours.

Jim did two things on that trip that were important to him, in addition to getting in a couple of days of deep trolling. First, he presented Captain Morrison with the finest waterproof watch he could buy, along with the grateful thanks of the six other men and himself. None of the others was present. They had had all the deep trolling they wanted for that summer.

Second, when Jim came in from fishing the first afternoon

he changed into his swim trunks and took a dip in Munising harbor just to find out how cold the water of Lake Superior really is under normal circumstances. When he dived in, it was like plunging into liquid ice. The numbing, stinging chill tore the breath out of his throat, and when he came up he gasped to himself, "Oxley, you're a damned liar! It can't be this cold!"

Handgun versus a Brownie

CECIL RHODE has always believed that if he hadn't seen that red squirrel and stopped to fool around with it, the incident would never have happened.

Maybe that hadn't been the case. Maybe the bear had been hunting and had mistaken him for a small moose. Or perhaps she had known he was a human, but just hadn't wanted him in the neighborhood. Cecil, however, blamed the closest shave of his life on a casual encounter with a squirrel.

At the time he was on a pack trip in a remote section of Alaska's Kenai peninsula, along the Chickaloon river. He was traveling alone and on foot, carrying his grub, sleeping bag and other equipment in a packsack. The main purpose of the trip was to get some pictures of the big Kenai moose. It was October, their rutting season, and a good time to stalk them with either gun or camera. Cecil had told his wife, when he left their cabin on Kenai Lake, that he would be gone 30 days, but the moose hunting was exceptionally good and time had slipped away fast. He had been out 35 days that morning in 1947 when the bear jumped him.

By that time he had walked better than 250 miles, carrying a pack that averaged about 60 pounds. Hunting big game with a camera is no soft job. But he had made some good moose pictures, including close-ups of big bulls and a movie record of a brisk scrap between a rival pair. During the 35 days, he had not seen another human.

It was getting late in the fall, and the weather had turned bad, with a lot of cold rain. Then the rain had changed to snow. A foot had come down in one night, a powdery fall that started to soften and settle as soon as the sun came out the next morning. Rhode decided to make one more trip out from his base camp, and then start for home.

A few miles from camp, down along a small creek that ran into the Chickaloon, he had located, on the side of a mountain, a big bench grown up with willow, aspen and cottonwood. There was plenty of moose food there, and an unusual concentration of moose. In the gray afternoon light of the day before, shortly before the snow began to fall, he had seen a big bull there with seven cows in his harem. If they were still together, Cecil wanted pictures of them. He left camp right after breakfast and headed that way.

He was carrying a Colt .38 double-action handgun. Up to then, on all his trips when he was after pictures and not meat or trophies, he had never packed anything heavier than a .22 automatic for picking off ptarmigan, grouse and rabbits for the pot. But his wife had worried about bears, and she had finally talked him into switching over to the .38. It was a good thing, too. Had he stuck to the .22, it's doubtful he would have come back from the Chickaloon.

If he had been going intentionally to hunt brown bears, he would have carried a rifle, but he needed to save weight on this trip and wanted both hands free for his cameras. He knew there were stray brownies scattered all over the Kenai, but since the place where he was headed was primarily moose range, and since he would be hunting nothing but moose, he had decided to risk it without a rifle.

"I've learned my lesson," he said later.

Handgun versus a Brownie

Cecil was taking good care of the handgun. He had it in a shoulder holster, where it wouldn't be in the way or catch in the brush, and also where the action would stay clean and dry. It never entered his mind, however, that he would have to turn the .38 on an enraged brownie.

He followed the small creek back toward the bench. When he was almost directly below the place where the moose had been yarded, he left the creek and started up the side of the mountain, picking his way through open stands of spruce and birch. He was moving as soundlessly as possible. When stalking game with a camera, he made it a rule to behave like an animal as much as possible, watching the wind and moving slowly and quietly.

He was within 300 feet of the bench, climbing carefully in the soft snow, when he saw the red squirrel. It was feeding on cones in a thin patch of alder. Curious as to what it would do, Cecil broke his rule about keeping quiet. He walked over, talked to the squirrel in an undertone and shook the alders a little, until it set up an excited chattering. Cecil realized afterward that between them they could have made noise enough to reach the ears of a bear up on the bench. When she heard the brush rattle, she might easily have mistaken the sound for that made by a moose; even if she heard only the scolding of the squirrel, she would have known instantly that something out of the ordinary was going on.

When the adventure was over, Cecil learned from the tracks that she had come around the mountain from his right, on a moose trail that followed the bench. As far as he could tell she still had been up there, unaware of his presence, when he stopped to tease the squirrel. But about that time, she had turned off the trail and started down to investigate.

He left the squirrel and went on, looking for the best going up the mountainside. Seventy yards ahead was a thick stand of young spruce, roughly circular and about 100 feet across. He would have to go around it. He picked out a route along the lower edge and plodded up.

He was 20 feet from the thicket when he heard a sudden commotion on the far side. It sounded like a bull moose breaking brush, which meant a chance for pictures. He decided to set his camera up and be ready for the moose at close range if it came through the thicket.

He was leaning forward and sidewise to ease an arm out of his pack straps when, through the spruce, he caught sight of a patch of brown 30 yards away. For a second he took it for the bull. But something about it wasn't right. He crouched for a better look under the branches—and found himself staring at a bear head that looked as big as a washtub.

In one quick glimpse, he took it all in—ears, muzzle, color. The head vanished in the snow-hung growth, and then Cecil heard the noise of a heavy animal crashing through the brush, running straight at him.

He got out of the packsack as easily as an eel sliding through a greased chute, jerked off his gloves and whipped the .38 from its holster. While he was doing those things, the bear came all the way through the thicket. As he swung the gun up, her big brown head broke out of the brush just four steps from him. Then, seeming to float to a stop, the bear halted.

Cecil never knew why, after that lightning-fast rush through the spruce tangle, she didn't finish her charge, unless she had thought she was stalking a moose and her surprise at finding herself facing a man caused her to stop short. Anyway, the break in the charge gave him the chance he needed.

She stood at the edge of the brush, so close he could have flipped a marble into her face, acting as if she had lost track of him. She lifted her head and cocked it to one side, and her nose wrinkled as she tested the wind. Cecil was reluctant to risk a shot from the handgun if he didn't have to. It was no weapon for the job, and he didn't want to shoot unless he was sure she meant business.

Was he scared? Put yourself in his shoes. The bear must have weighed at least nine hundred pounds, and she had trouble written all over her. When he paced the distance later, it was exactly 11 feet between her tracks and his.

"You can bet your last dollar I was scared, and I'm not ashamed to admit it," he recounted later. "But lucky for me, I wasn't rattled. I knew my only chance was to stand still and count on the .38 to do the job if it had to. And somehow I believed it would. Nevertheless, I recall the phrase 'This is it!' ticking through my brain over and over again."

It all happened faster than it can be set down here. After a second or two, the bear lowered her head and Cecil decided not to wait any longer. He was sure she had made up her mind to come for him and, with her head down, he had a chance to smash the 158-grain bullet into her skull, where it wouldn't be likely to glance off, and through her brain to make a quick kill.

At that range he couldn't miss. He brought the gun down on her head as deliberately as if shooting at a target, aimed about an inch to one side of center and fired. He saw the slug smack into her and blood flew. She didn't go down, but slumped like a boxer knocked half off his feet. For a second or two, Cecil felt pretty good; however, that feeling didn't last long.

The bear straightened up again and stood staring at him;

Cecil leveled the gun, ready to pour in another. Then, while he waited for her head to drop again, she did the last thing in the world he expected. She turned, slowly and calmly, as if nothing at all had happened, and then disappeared in the thicket.

She moved as if she were a pretty sick bear, but Cecil couldn't count too much on that. For maybe a minute he heard nothing more from her. He waited, tense and ready, expecting her to come at him again from any one of a dozen places. Then, at the far side of the spruce clump, all hell broke loose.

She let go a series of roaring bawls that were terrifying enough to turn a man's hair white. There was a scuffling racket that sounded like a bear fight, and suddenly he heard a cub squall. That was his first inkling that cubs were in the act, and it wasn't a pleasant thought. It explained a lot of things, and it meant, almost certainly, that the show wasn't over. He could count now on the protective mother to be really vindictive.

In the first few seconds after she disappeared in the thicket he had looked around desperately for a tree. The nearest one he could climb was a dead spruce, standing by itself in the open about twenty feet to his left. But it had a tangle of bleached branches extending all the way to the ground through which he would have to claw before he could reach the trunk. It wasn't a tree he could climb in a hurry. All the same, he started to edge toward it, moving very carefully. If the bear had forgotten where he was, he didn't want to do anything to remind her.

Her fight with the cubs didn't last long, but it was a nasty brawl while it lasted. Cecil could hear more than one cub squalling; the old lady seemed to be cuffing the daylights out of the whole family. When the racket stopped and the horrible noise of her bawling died away, he felt sure she was coming back after him. He stopped sidling toward the tree and braced himself, with the Colt cocked and ready, trying to watch the entire edge of the thicket at one time.

She did exactly what she had done before, except that this time she came through the brush without making a sound. She appeared without warning, 20 feet to his right.

Her head was lowered, giving him a good target; he didn't hesitate. He leveled down, fired and heard his second bullet thud into her skull. It was a good solid hit, and again she flinched and humped from the impact, sagging down without going off her feet. She didn't bawl or slap at herself; the flinch was the only sign she gave that she was hurt. An instant later she pulled herself together, stepped out of the brush and came along the edge of the thicket at a rolling walk.

Cecil Rhode had never known another minute like the one during which he stood and watched the wounded brownie lumber toward him. He held the cocked Colt on her head, expecting her to come those last few feet in a sudden roaring rush. But instead, keeping to the edge of the brush, she skirted Cecil by four or five paces.

When she was directly in front of him, she gave him the best target he had had. Her head was broadside then, and he knew he could put a shot into her skull just below the ear. Such a shot offered a chance of reaching the brain and putting a quick end to the bear. It was a tempting gamble, but the risk was also pretty terrible. If he failed to kill her outright, she could be on him in a single lunge.

If she had swung her head to look at him, if she had stopped or even hesitated, he would have shot. But she didn't. She walked on as if she no longer knew he was there. It seems logical to believe that, even without penetrating the brain, his two shots driven deep into her skull had dazed her, and that, after being hit, she did not know where he was. Except for his gun arm, Cecil didn't move a muscle while she was in sight.

When the bear was just beyond the place where he had shot her the first time, she again turned into the thicket and circled slowly toward the cubs. When she reached them there was another brief argument, with bawling and slapping and squalling. And now, still not daring to try to get into the tree, Cecil crouched almost on his belly in the snow and for the first time got a look at the entire family. There were three cubs, youngsters born the previous winter, which appeared to weigh between 60 and 100 pounds.

A minute or so after the argument ended the four bears started to move off up the mountain. They went very slowly. The old girl was having a hard time, and the cubs were running around her in circles, puzzled and alarmed. As soon as they were far enough away that he could move without attracting attention, Cecil inched cautiously over to the spruce, wormed his way in among the branches, and climbed like a squirrel.

Beyond the thicket the old bear was laboring a step at a time up the steep snow slope with the three cubs in frantic attendance. He could see blood on the trail behind her.

She didn't look around or pay any attention to the racket he made in the tree. He was in a position now to pay her back for all the trouble she had made him. When she was about 25 yards off, her broad back was an easy target. He squirmed into a comfortable position in a fork, laid the Colt across a branch and let her have it between the shoulders. The result surprised him. She spun half around, fell over backward and rolled all the way to the foot of the slope.

That was a jubilant half minute. He had broken her back,

he told himself, killed a brownie with a handgun. But he hadn't. After a moment, she picked herself up and started to climb again, working painfully up the mountain toward the bench.

Cecil had the gun cocked and the sights lined on her once more, still bent on revenge, when it suddenly occurred to him that he was throwing away a lot of his limited supply of ammunition. A quick mental inventory told him he had only nine shells left.

He was 40 miles from home and wanted to get in another day or two of picture taking. He realized now that this was indeed bear as well as moose country, and that he might need those nine shells urgently before he got back to the cabin on Kenai Lake. Certain that the bear would die of its wounds he decided he couldn't afford another shot.

He stayed in the tree for half an hour after the four bears had disappeared up on the bench. Then he climbed down, looked over the tracks and blood sign and started after them. Maybe it wasn't wise to trail the wounded brownie, with only a handgun as a defense, but Cecil still felt certain she was going to die. The more he thought about it, the more he wanted her pelt, which was a beauty, to remember her by.

He took plenty of time. He went up on knolls to look at the trail ahead and even climbed trees, scouting out the country to make sure he wasn't walking into an ambush. It took most of the afternoon to follow the bears for a mile and a half. Then realizing that he could just about get back to his base camp before dark, he gave up.

He was confident that the bear would die in the night. The next morning the snow was going fast, but there was enough left for tracking. He left camp at daylight and went back to pick up her trail. It showed less and less blood; the sign eventually dwindled to a small clot here and there on the snow or the brush.

Cecil stayed on the track until noon, following it another mile. By that time the snow was gone and, when the trail led down into an alder patch, he quit. He still believed she was dead, and still wanted her pelt, but not bad enough to follow her into the alders with the Colt.

Looking back on the adventure, he was not so sure she had died after all. The clotted skeins of blood had been few and far between where he left the track at the edge of the alder patch. He hadn't damaged her brain or she couldn't have traveled that far. The shot that had hit her in the back probably amounted to no more than a deep flesh wound after all. The best guess, he concluded, was that she had had nothing worse than a bad headache for a week or two.

There were a lot of unanswered questions about the encounter with the brownie that bothered him for a long time afterward. Had she originally noticed him because of the commotion he and the squirrel were making? Had she left the bench and come after him because she was hunting, because she resented his presence near her cubs, or because she was simply looking for trouble? And having found him, when she broke out of the brush the first time 11 feet from him and the second time about twice that far away, why hadn't she kept coming and finished what she had started? Finally, when he had hammered those two ineffective shots into her head, what had kept her from reacting the way a wounded brownie is supposed to do, the way they have on countless other occasions, all the way from Admiralty Island off the Canadian coast to Unimak Island in the Aleutians?

Cecil Rhode would never know the answers, of course.

And nobody among the Alaskan guides and hunters of his acquaintance claimed to know them. But a neighbor of his on Kenai Lake summed things up very well.

"You just weren't born to be killed by a brown bear," he said after Cecil told him about the experience. "Or if you were, the day ain't arrived yet!"

Night without Fire

WHEN AXEL ANDERSON pulled his only book of matches out of his hunting coat pocket and found it wet from melted snow, he had a hunch he was in trouble. He was sure of it after he tried to light the first match and most of the striking strip tore out of the book—a crumpled scrap of sodden paper—and came away in his hand. He didn't think he was going to die, not then. But a few hours later that thought would be gnawing at him. Axel knew enough about the woods to realize that his predicament meant he was in for a very tough time.

The date was Sunday, November 18, 1951. Axel had left his deer camp, in the roadless Rainy Lake country of northern Minnesota, on the Canadian border a hundred miles above Duluth, shortly after dawn. The 64-year-old Minneapolis factory foreman had been hunting deer off and on for about ten years. There was nothing to warn him that the next forty-eight hours would subject him to an ordeal almost beyond human endurance or that he would escape death by the narrowest of margins. He had no inkling that it would be six months before he would see his neat, white house in the outskirts of Minneapolis again, or that he would spend six dreary months filled with illness and pain such as he had never known. Nor did he suspect that he was starting out that morning on two good sound feet for the last time in his life.

He was camped with a neighbor, Louis Shomshak, and

two acquaintances, Cliff and Sonny Sonnenberg, a father-and-son team, in Shomshak's cabin on the northeast side of Crane Lake. Anderson had hunted in these woods once or twice before, but it was still relatively new territory to him. He hadn't carried a pocket map of the area, nor had he even bothered to look at a map before leaving camp.

He struck out that morning, with the other three men, into an unfamiliar section northeast of camp, where one of them had seen deer beds and sign the day before. A wet snow had fallen in the night and now lay heavy on brush and trees, bending the small stuff to the ground, and the going was hard. Axel and Sonny Sonnenberg found fresh deer beds and Axel picked himself a stand on a rocky ridge, intending to wait while his partner made a short drive. But, sweaty from walking, he quickly chilled in the cold wind and moved on to get warm.

Wandering through the timber on that overcast morning, he found the track of a big deer and followed it. It was probably during the next hour that he unknowingly became confused in his directions. Apparently the deer had been leading him north while he believed he was going south. After failing to jump the deer, he tried a stand once more, planning to wait there for the other members of the party. But finally he became so cold that he decided to give up and go back to camp by himself. Completely confident of his whereabouts, and believing himself to be a mile or so due east of the cabin, he took a compass reading and then headed west.

Again fresh deer tracks lured him off his course. Shortly before noon he came out on the shore of Crane Lake and met another hunter there who had just come across the frozen lake from the west. The stranger was Wilbert Ward, a 38-year-old chemist at the Federal Cartridge plant in Anoka, a suburb of

Minneapolis. Neither man guessed it at the time, but this stranger would later save Axel's life.

The two stood for a few minutes exchanging the small talk that passes between hunters when they meet in the woods. They spoke of the snow, hunting conditions and the deer sign they had seen. Axel mentioned that he was with the Shomshak party. Ward said that he and two other hunters were staying at a cabin east of Trout Lake. Then Axel and Ward parted, each believing he was headed for his own camp. One of them was wrong.

Although completely unaware of it, Axel was by this time thoroughly lost. He was traveling northwest along the shore of Crane Lake, directly away from the Shomshak cabin. At the north end of the lake, lacking both a map and detailed knowledge of the country, he had struck westward into a wild and rugged tract where there was no trail, no hunting camp, nothing to help a lost man find his way out. Ahead of him lay only the trackless, lake-dotted and stream-laced wilderness of Superior National Forest.

He soon found more fresh deer tracks, and since they led in the direction he thought he wanted to go, he followed them. The tracks angled south, then north, then back south again. It was only after he had given up trailing the deer, shortly before three in the afternoon, that Axel became really concerned about being lost.

Although he had only a hazy notion of the distance he had covered, he still believed that camp lay ahead of him, somewhere to the west. But he decided against going on now. The sun was getting low and it was turning very cold. Better light a fire, gather a supply of fuel while there's daylight, and spend the night in the woods.

He collected an armful of dry pine, stripped off birchbark for kindling, and reached for his matchbook. It was then, when the matches failed him, that he fully realized for the first time what he was up against.

He had left camp that morning with the equipment a deer hunter usually carries—rifle, shells, compass, sheath knife, whistle for signaling, length of rope, pocket hand warmer and several chocolate bars. One necessity, a waterproof, metal matchcase, was lacking. Axel had overlooked it in a bureau drawer while packing for the trip, and it was this oversight that was to bring about the most terrible experience of his life.

Once he became certain that he couldn't make a fire, he reconsidered his situation carefully. He decided that camp had to be near by and concluded that his best bet, instead of stopping for the night, was to keep traveling west. So he tucked the damp matchbook into the neckband of his shirt, hoping his body heat would dry the remaining matches, stuffed his supply of birchbark under his coat, and started working westward.

He was very tired and the going was bad. In many places he had to crawl on his hands and knees to get past windfalls and snow-bent evergreens. He came to a frozen stream and took thankfully to the ice where the walking was easier. As he walked he carefully probed for thin places with a stout stick. Two or three times he left the stream to climb high ridges, looking for landmarks, but he found none. Feeling the first licks of panic, he began to hurry, still hoping to reach camp before nightfall.

Then, with darkness at hand, real disaster struck. He heard the noise of a waterfall a short distance upstream and turned toward shore to detour around it. When he was only a couple strides from the bank, the ice let go under him and he was plunged belt-deep into black, bitterly cold water.

He fell forward and his arms were thrust under the water. The front of his clothing, from the shoulders down, was drenched. The bottom of the stream was strewn with big boulders and he slipped and fell twice more getting ashore. As he climbed out, wet from head to foot except for his shoulders and back, his Marlin, which had been dunked when he went through the ice, froze so solidly that he found it hard to work the action. When he saw how quickly the water on the rifle turned to ice, Axel had to accept the cruel fact that he had little chance of surviving. The temperature, now close to zero, was dropping steadily.

Axel faced an intensely cold night under almost the worst possible conditions. He had lost his birchbark kindling and without it there was little chance of a fire, even if his matches dried. He was tired and hungry and wet. The pockets of his coat were full of water, his hand warmer would no longer work, his mittens were drenched and freezing, and his feet were sloshing in his boots. Only one thing was in his favor. He was warmly dressed in wool underwear, heavy wool pants, shirt and hunting coat, a thick outer pair of wool socks over a thin inner pair of rayon, and rubber-bottomed pacs on his feet.

He stumbled to a log, groping his way in the gathering gloom, sat down and pulled off the pacs. He wrung out his socks and his felt inner soles as dry as he could and also squeezed as much water as he could out of his pants. He relaced the boots loosely, hoping the circulation of air around his legs would dry his clothing. The frozen mittens seemed worse than useless, so he hung them in a tree and left them.

Standing there in the darkness in that wild and lonely spot, shivering in the still cold, sheltering his numb hands in wet pockets, stamping his feet to restore some degree of warmth to them, Axel weighed his desperate situation with calm reason and came to the conclusion that his only chance for survival lay in backtracking to where he had left Sonny that morning. He would try it, he decided, as soon as the moon rose.

He leaned against a tree and stomped his cold feet steadily for two or three hours. At last the eastern sky brightened and a full moon, looking like a cold, silver disk, floated up over the timber. But even before the moon appeared, Axel realized he was too tired to follow his own tracks back to camp that night.

Nevertheless, he knew that he must keep moving as long as he could. To give in even for a minute to the consuming urge for rest was to invite freezing and certain death. If he should let himself sink down to the ground he knew he would doze off into a sleep from which he could not hope to awake.

He used his knife to cut dry twigs in the desperate hope of starting a fire. In fumbling to replace the knife in its sheath, he slashed through his belt. Under ordinary conditions that would have been no more than a humorous mishap. But for Axel it meant he would have to hold his pants up with one hand while he walked.

He licked that problem by using the length of rope in his coat pocket as a belt, but in getting it out he dropped both his knife and sheath. He pawed for them in snow that stung his hands like live coals, found them only to drop them again, and finally gave up trying to pick up the sheath. He did, however, manage to pocket his knife.

He went back onto the ice and laid out a circular path for himself about 300 yards long. While he was covering it for the second time, he found places where water had seeped up into his tracks, darkening them. These spots he avoided, knowing they spelled thin ice.

The details of that long and dreadful night blurred as Axel continued to walk without letup, pacing his beat on the frozen river. Fighting off numbing weariness and agonizing cold, not daring to stop, he became aware, ironically, that it was a beautiful night, windless and clear, with the moon and stars bright overhead, the snow sparkling and creaking underfoot. Sometime toward morning he ate the last small piece of the chocolate he had brought away from camp nearly 24 hours earlier.

During the night he kept seeing what he thought were birch trees on shore, but each time he investigated he found only the gray-white trunks of aspens. Then at last he found a birch, and near it a dead aspen with dry branches that would burn readily.

Peeling off a handful of the birchbark, he stamped a clear spot in the snow and built up a little pyramid of dry twigs. Now if only he had one match that would strike. He drew what was left of the book out of the neckband of his shirt, guarding it with cold-stiffened fingers. The first match caught and its tiny feeble flame glowed in his hands. As he held it against the birchbark, the curling tendrils ignited and flared and yellow flames danced up through the little tepee of sticks. A fire at last! Fate, however, played an incredible and fiendishly cruel prank on the lost, half-frozen man.

Axel crouched over the fire for a minute, gloating, exulting, holding his hands to the wonderful, unbelievable warmth. Then, straightening and stepping back for more fuel, he bumped into an overhanging balsam from which a great clod of snow came away in a miniature avalanche. It fell squarely on his tiny blaze, and the fire hissed and died. Once again the night was cold and still.

He tried desperately to get a second fire going but it was no use. After the remaining match failed to strike, Axel tasted utter black despair. He went out on the ice and began walking

his beat again. He kept it up, breaking through into shallow water a couple of times, until daylight.

Then, still clinging to the misbelief that his camp lay to the west, he started trudging off in that direction. His feet were without feeling now and he realized they had frozen during the night. His boots and pants were stiff, crackling as he walked, and his nose was frosted despite the fact that he had kept his face covered with a handkerchief. Unless he stumbled onto his camp, which no longer seemed likely, or a rescue party found him, Axel realized that his time was growing short. He figured he might be able to live until nightfall, but he knew there was no chance of surviving through another night without fire.

Back at camp his three companions were pushing a widening search for him, spreading the alarm as they went. In midmorning Shomshak and the senior Sonnenberg, searching together, blundered onto Wilbert Ward, the hunter Axel had met the day before on the shore of Crane Lake. The encounter was one of those thin cords of coincidence on which human life sometimes hangs.

Ward had had no occasion to think further of his casual meeting with Axel. But he recognized the missing man from his description and, reconstructing their meeting, sensed instantly that Axel had been lost and traveling in the wrong direction.

The members of the search party had been concentrating their efforts in an area to the north and east of their camp where Axel had last been seen. But Ward set them straight. "You won't find him around here," he told Sonnenberg and Shomshak. "He's off to the west of Crane Lake somewhere. When he left me he was traveling like a man who thought he knew where he was going. He could be miles away by this time—if he's still alive." There had been no fresh snow, and no wind in the night. "There's one sure way to find him," Ward pointed out. "We can pick up his track where I saw him last and follow him from there."

The two other members of Ward's hunting party had come along by that time. It was decided they should return to their camp, eat lunch and then bring food back for Ward. As things turned out, however, they never caught up with him. He traveled too fast.

He led Shomshak and Sonnenberg to the place where he had met Axel. There it was decided Shomshak should go back to his cabin, on the slim chance that Axel might have found his own way in by that time, in which case he would need help and attention. Ward and Sonnenberg took Axel's trail. One of the first things Ward did was to find a good clear imprint of the missing man's boot, measure it carefully and note identifying marks. He wanted to make no mistake in the event they came across the tracks of other hunters, but this wise precaution proved needless. Where Axel had gone there were no footprints but his own.

The two men took the track about an hour before noon. It led in a westerly direction, as Ward expected. The going was bad, through thick brush and a great deal of down stuff. About two-thirty in the afternoon they came to the place where Axel had tried to light his first fire. By that time Sonnenberg, who had been tramping steadily since daylight, was pretty well worn out. Ward decided he could travel faster by himself and he knew time was running out, so he urged Sonnenberg to follow their track back to Crane Lake, go on to camp and arrange to have food, blankets and a toboggan sent out. It was late enough now that Ward knew he and the lost man, if he was still alive, would have to spend the night in the woods.

For the next 20 hours Wilbert Ward was to do exactly the right things, the cool-headed, sensible things that had to be done, which was all the more remarkable in view of the fact that he had had no experience and little training to fit him for the job he was taking on.

Born in Georgia and reared in Oklahoma, with no opportunity for deer hunting, he was comparatively a novice in the deer woods, having hunted in Minnesota only three years prior to that fall. As a youngster, however, he had belonged to a Boy Scout troop, and later had served as a Scout leader, and he called now on what woodcraft he knew.

Alone, he was able to make better time. He stuck doggedly to the track, finding two more places where Axel had tried, unsuccessfully, to start a fire. With not much more than an hour of daylight left, he came to the black hole where the lost man had gone through the ice. Ward's first thought was that this was the end of the trail. But a few yards away, on shore, he found the log on which Axel had sat to empty the water from his boots. Near by were the man's frozen mittens, his knife sheath, and a telltale pile of unlighted twigs. Ward's hopes for rescuing Axel sank pretty low as he studied those pathetic bits of evidence. The man he was trailing was undoubtedly in worse shape than he had anticipated. Indeed, it seemed unlikely that he could still be alive.

Ward wasted little time in speculation. Whatever slender chance remained hinged now on his overtaking Axel before darkness halted his search. He left the knife sheath and mittens as markers to guide any rescuers who might follow him, stopped briefly on the ice to study the hard-beaten path where the lost man had paced all night, and then hurried on.

Axel's day was discouraging. Two planes flew over during the forenoon, high up. Although he realized from their altitude that they were not searching for him, he tried desperately to attract their attention, running back and forth on the ice and waving his arms. But as each plane droned on and disappeared, he sank deeper into despair.

In the afternoon he began to see what looked like men

walking the ridges on either side of him, but when he got close they turned out to be the snowbent tops of small trees, swaying in the wind. A few times he thought he heard voices. He was eating snow to allay his burning thirst. Shuffling along on feet that felt like wooden stumps, he kept thinking he saw the ridge from which he had started hunting the morning before. The day, like the one before, was harsh and cold.

Late in the afternoon a third plane snarled over, flying low. It vanished behind the next ridge to the west, and Axel was convinced it had landed there. He told himself it must have come down at a camp, and for the first time that day hope burned up in him. If he could reach the place before dark he would get out alive, after all. He was trying to hurry to the foot of the ridge when he heard someone behind him call his name. Hardly daring to believe his ears he turned around and saw the stranger he had met on Crane Lake the previous noon, running to overtake him.

Darkness was close at hand now. The two men still faced a night in the woods with almost no food—Ward's total supply consisted of a bar and a half of candy—and the long, grueling walk out. Ward moved swiftly and efficiently to make the best of a bad situation. He gave Axel a candy bar to eat, led him to high ground, found a sheltered spot in the lee of an over-hanging rock ledge and cleared away a place for the older man to rest.

By a curious coincidence, Ward himself was dangerously short of matches. Usually he made a point to carry a liberal supply on his deer hunts. This time, through an oversight, he had exactly four. But they were dry, and one was all he needed.

He gathered birchbark and grass for kindling, heaping up a tepee of dry sticks, and for the second time in 36 hours

Axel witnessed the miracle of fire born from a single match. But now it was no tiny blaze, to be smothered by a cascade of dislodged snow. The flames leaped up through the stack of dry wood, roaring and crackling and, for the first time since he had fallen through the ice, Axel began to get warm.

Ward rolled a log up to the fire for him to sit on and went at the job of drying his outer clothing and thawing and removing the boots from his frozen feet. It took time. When the first boot and heavy sock came away the thin inner sock remained, frozen solidly to the foot. When Ward had worked that free the two men could see ice between Axel's toes. In fact, his entire lower foot was encased in a thin sheath of ice.

After Ward had gotten the other boot off, he went to work on the frozen feet, alternately rubbing them gently with snow and massaging them with his bare hands, while Axel rubbed his frostbitten nose. It took an hour and a half to thaw his feet enough so that he could move his toes once more. Big, black and blue patches under each arch hinted at the real extent of the damage. Ward put his own socks on Axel while his wet boots and socks dried.

Once Axel, propped on the log before the fire, was dry and thoroughly warm, Ward let him drift into much-needed sleep. The rescuer, however, could not permit himself the luxury of even a brief nap. He collected wood and fed the fire throughout the night, awakening Anderson at intervals, rubbing his feet and moving him around to try to take the worst of the stiffness out of his exhausted body.

At daybreak he gave Axel the remaining half bar of candy and they moved out. The first mile was pretty bad. Axel's feet were so badly swollen that they had had to leave off his heavy outer socks, and he was stiff and sore to a point that made movement extremely difficult. Ward carried the two rifles and Axel shuffled along, clutching the back of his rescuer's hunting coat to help keep his balance. Twice when going ahead to test thin ice, Ward broke through; however, each time he took off his boots, emptied the water, and wrung his socks dry. The two men plodded slowly, painfully on toward Crane Lake.

At the place where Axel had gone through the ice, they collected his knife sheath and mittens, the latter still frozen hard. An hour before noon the two men, coming out on the lake, found snow writing saying that food and blankets were on the way. They had walked only a short distance on the open lake when a small rescue plane circled in and landed near them. Their long ordeal was ended.

Bad luck had even dogged the air search for Axel. His hunting friends had called on the sheriff of Rainy County, Henry Saarinen, for help. He in turn had enlisted the services of a local plane. In landing at the Shomshak camp, the rescue plane had gone through the ice and cracked up.

It was a second plane that picked up Axel. He was first flown to a nearby resort, given hot food and treated initially by a doctor who happened to have been hunting in the area. Then Sheriff Saarinen drove Axel to the Veterans Hospital at Fort Snelling.

As the rescue plane flew off that bleak afternoon, Ward started walking back toward his own camp. He went by way of the Shomshak cabin and told the anxious hunters there that he had found Axel alive and that he had been flown out. In describing how he had overtaken the lost man, Ward said, "I saw his red coat ahead of me when I rounded a bend and fired a couple of shots, but he didn't hear them. So I ran him down."

When he was released from the hospital months later, Axel

had only crippled stubs for feet. The medics had found it necessary to slice away the flesh of both heels and part of the bone of one, and amputate all ten toes to about an inch back of the joint where toe and foot are coupled.

Even while he was still in the hospital, Axel was telling friends that once his feet were completely healed and he was fitted with special shoes, he intended to make one more trip to Crane Lake and hike into the place Ward had found him. He wanted to prove that he had seen and heard that plane roaring low over him about an hour before Ward had overtaken him near that wooded ridge in the wilderness. He was going to find the camp where he was certain the plane had landed. Although his blue eyes twinkled mischievously, his friends could tell he was dead serious about disproving Ward's claim that his imagination had played tricks on him.

Ward had found Axel seven miles from the Shomshak camp, which was six miles from the place where they had met on the ice of Crane Lake. Axel had covered the six miles in something like 28 hours, Ward in about five and a half. He had been in an area where no search would ever have been made, since no one but Ward had suspected that Axel had headed off in that direction. Axel's frozen, lifeless body might have lain undiscovered in the woods for years, perhaps forever, the exact place and manner of his death an unsolved riddle.

Ward's role as hero did not end with rescue. The following summer the Minneapolis chemist was awarded the Minnesota Safety Council's Honor Deed Citation for having saved Axel Anderson's life—the first person ever cited in that state for having rescued a hunter in distress.

The Cruel Cold

THE BEAR was walking across rough ice when Tommy Richards, at the controls of the Cessna, spotted him. Richards, John Osborne and Dick Wilson were hunting the arctic pack off Point Hope, on the northwest coast of Alaska, between Kotzebue and Barrow. From an altitude of just under 1,000 feet, the bear was only an indistinct shadow moving on the ice fields, a white speck in a vast white world, but Tommy made him out the instant he came in sight behind a pressure ridge. A Kotzebue Eskimo and as able a bush pilot as one could find in Alaska, Richards had eyes like a hawk.

He banked the plane and pointed down for the benefit of John and Dick. Then he lost altitude in a wide turn until they were low enough so that the bear, noticing the giant bird swooping toward him, broke into a lumbering run. At 100 feet above the ice the three men had a good look at him as he galloped off, swinging his long snaky head from side to side and watching over his shoulder.

He was a big polar bear. They estimated his pelt would square out close to eight feet. He would certainly make a fine trophy, just what they had come for, and Wilson could feel his heart thumping with the excitement of his first close contact with the great white king of the arctic.

"We'll have to maneuver him out onto smoother ice," Tommy shouted above the roar of the Cessna's single engine. "Can't land on that stuff down there."

This bear hunt was something Dick Wilson had dreamed about for a long time. In the retail clothing business for 30 years and long interested in hunting, he had managed to sandwich in quite a few good trips for moose, elk, bear, goat and sheep. Now he wanted a polar bear to top his list.

He had left his home in Inglewood, California, on the morning of March 20, 1955, and flown to Nome, where his friend, John Osborne, met him at the field. John was an Alaskan working for the Alaska Native Service. Dick had known him since 1948, when he had been a guide, and they made their first hunt together, a successful trip by cruiser after brown bears. They considered each other excellent companions on any hunt.

From Nome they flew north to Kotzebue, where they engaged the Cessna with Tommy Richards as pilot from Wien Airlines. At that season the most practical way of hunting on the far-reaching pack ice that lies offshore is from the air. In fact that's the only way, unless the hunter is willing to travel on foot and use dog teams, as the Eskimos do. Aerial hunting may seem like an easy way to collect a bear-skin rug, but if the hunter is sportsman enough to land and then stalk and kill on foot, after spotting his trophy from the plane, it isn't as easy as it sounds. And the element of unforeseen danger is always present, as Dick and John were to discover.

The skis of the Cessna rose off the snow-covered field at Kotzebue about nine Thursday morning, March 24, and Tommy headed the plane northwest for the vicinity of Point Hope, 150 miles up the coast. John and Dick had walked out on the shore ice the afternoon before to sight in their rifles—a .30-06 Springfield Sporter and a Winchester Model 70 in .300 Magnum caliber, respectively. They had loaded the plane with cameras, caribou-skin sleeping robes, emergency gear, sandwiches and other supplies. As eager and excited as a couple of kids on the morning of a picnic, they were ready for the adventure of their lives.

Tommy flew a zigzag course, scouting a belt of ice about 50 miles wide. They saw bear tracks beneath them several times, and once he pointed out a red stain on the ice where he had guided another hunter to an unusually large bear only a couple of days earlier.

At the end of three hours he nosed the sleek red plane down for refueling at Point Hope. While it was being serviced, John and Dick visited the village and introduced themselves to Ed Sipes and his wife, teachers at the native school, and to Mark Kinneeveauk, an Eskimo, who, unknown to the hunters, would play a crucial role in their lives 24 hours later.

When they returned to the plane Tommy was ready for the take off. They thundered away to the south, back toward Kotzebue; it was only ten minutes later when Tommy pointed out the bear on the ice below.

The problem now was to herd him into an area on which they could land within striking distance. They stayed low, only a couple of hundred feet above the ice, and circled over him. The bear didn't like the buzzing plane, but he didn't show much alarm. He alternately ran and walked, breaking into a lumbering lope whenever Tommy buzzed him uncomfortably close. A few times he plunged into leads and swam across, and once he came to a big area of open water and tried to shake the plane for keeps by swimming and diving. At the end of about five miles he decided he had had enough. He turned to face the aircraft, reared up on his hind legs and stood swinging his massive white forepaws at it like a boxer sparring for an opening, daring the giant bird to come down and fight. That was a sight Dick and John never forgot.

The ice beyond the bear looked good to Tommy.

"We'll land and take him on," he shouted.

The plane slanted downward, no more than 100 feet over the bear, without budging him. Half a mile away the skis made a silk-smooth contact with the frost-covered ice. The Cessna coasted across the white surface as slick as a big toboggan, lost speed and stopped.

There was no warning before the sudden, terrifying crunch of three inches of hard new ice breaking beneath the skis. The plane slipped into black, bitterly cold water, which swirled up over the floor of the cabin with frightening speed around the legs of the men, and covered the seats. For one awful minute Dick thought they were going down like a stone. But then the wings settled on unbroken ice farther out, which held the weight of the plane and stopped the crazy, jolting dive.

John was in the back seat, next to the door. He thrust a shoulder against it and tried to force it open, but it was blocked by broken ice. John weighed 200 pounds, all bone and muscle. Belt-deep in the rising water, he twisted around and smashed into the door like a bull going for a red cape. It inched open far enough for him to squeeze through and he was gone. The ice-weighted door banged shut behind him.

Dick was next in line. To reach the door he had to crawl over the front seat. Halfway over, straddling the back, his left foot became wedged under something up front and he was stuck, unable to go either way. While he was fighting to free himself, he felt the relentless icy water creeping up.

All his life he had heard people talk about drowning like a rat in a trap; now he knew exactly how it felt. He hung there, unable to free his foot and barring Tommy's only means of escape, until the water filled the cabin to within three inches of the roof. Turning his face up against the ceiling, he gulped in the remaining precious air. Beside him, Tommy was doing the same thing. Later Dick remembered crying out, while they choked and strangled on sea water, "I guess this is the end of the line!" But if Tommy had bothered to answer, Dick could not recall what he had said. In fact, he couldn't remember Tommy's speaking at all during those horrible moments while they were fighting for their lives.

Looking back, Dick was surprised that the Eskimo hadn't cursed him to get out of the way. But he had said nothing.

"He had guts, that boy had!" Dick remarked later.

While their air supply dwindled, the two were fighting like madmen at the wedged door. Dick never knew how he freed his foot, but suddenly he was no longer held fast. Clearing the front seat, he threw every ounce of strength he had against the door. With Dick out of his way at last, Tommy was able to add his weight to the push. The door wrenched open, and Dick pitched through feet first. He went down a dozen feet before he could level off and swim for the surface, free at last of that devilish, awful trap.

When his lungs were close to bursting, he broke up into the air; the sunlight and the ice and the water had never looked half so good to him. John was perched precariously on the left wing of the plane, with water streaming out of his clothes. He reached down and hauled Dick up beside him, as Tommy popped to the surface a few feet away. He swam to them and together they helped him out of the water. Then all three crawled along the wing to solid ice and climbed down.

It would be hard to imagine men in a sorrier predicament.

They were drenched from head to toe, and afoot on the open ice, with food, sleeping robes and all their gear, even the dry socks they had carried for such an emergency, lost in the submerged cabin of the Cessna. The temperature stood at 15 below zero, and a knife-keen wind was sweeping the ice, blowing at about 12 miles an hour. The worst of it was that they had no way to kindle even the tiniest spark of fire.

They huddled there, wet and wretched, teeth chattering, knowing well how slim their chances of survival were.

"What time is it?" one of them asked.

John had lost his watch, but Dick still had his, which had stopped at 13 minutes past two. They knew then that they had about five hours until dark. Tommy estimated that they were about eight miles from the nearest land, across rough and broken pack ice seamed with leads and patches of open water. But he and John were old hands at dealing with emergencies. They knew they had no time to waste on feeling sorry for themselves; the three of them had a job of walking to do.

"We'll go south," Tommy decided. "Better ice that way." Their clothes were freezing now, the bitter wind turning them into crackling suits of armor. These seemed to give some protection from the cold. Once they started walking things weren't too bad.

They trudged across the ice for about a mile and a half, climbing pressure ridges and detouring around leads, before they realized there was no hope of reaching land by following that route. Too much open water was in the way. Reluctantly, they reversed their course, slogged back to the plane and struck out once more: this time toward Point Hope, which Tommy estimated lay between 12 and 20 miles to the north.

They hadn't walked 300 yards when John had another

close call. The patch of new ice he was walking over gave way under him, plunging the heavy man into the freezing water once more. Dick saw that John couldn't get out by himself; the strong current running beneath the ice was threatening to tear loose his handhold and pull him under. Dick edged down as near as he dared and got John by the wrists, but couldn't drag him out. So he yelled for help to Tommy, who was 100 yards ahead and unaware of John's mishap. The pilot came back at a dead run, and together they managed to get John once again on solid footing.

Ten minutes later he broke through again. But this time by twisting his body across the ice as he went in only his legs became submerged, and he managed to wiggle out without help.

About two miles north of the plane the men found their way blocked once more by a maze of open leads. With sinking hearts they once again turned back, faced by the prospect of having to spend the night on the open ice. Tommy, however, wouldn't give up. He struck off across the ice a third time, walking to the east, hoping to find a direct path ashore in the hour or so of daylight remaining. By that time Dick was too exhausted to walk any farther, and John decided to stay with him.

"If I make it I'll fly back for you in the morning," Tommy said with a cheerful grin as he trudged off.

The two men watched the pilot until he was out of sight. They could only wait and hope and worry. Would he reach the beach, or go through the ice and drown? Speculating about it did no good, but Dick and John couldn't get him out of their minds.

Shortly after they had lost sight of Tommy, darkness settled over the pack, the starlit darkness of a moonless night. The hours lagged terribly. The temperature dropped, and the wind continued to blow with cruel steadiness. Dick's legs were throbbing with pain, but his feet were comfortable—a sensation he realized meant they were beginning to freeze. John was in a little better shape, since he was wearing native caribou-skin footgear. Dick had on thick wool socks and sheep-lined house slippers inside fleece-lined flight boots. That sounds like a warm outfit, but the socks and the lining were soaking wet, so that they offered little or no protection against the bitter cold of the arctic night.

Although there was gas to start a fire with in the Cessna's tanks, they had no way to get at it, and no material to keep a fire going even if they had succeeded in starting one. They searched for shelter and finally found a block of pressure ice that was turned up on one side and big enough to afford some protection. But crouching behind it, they discovered that the temperature was so low that they couldn't stay in one place long enough to get any benefit out of the shelter. There was no choice: either keep moving or freeze to death.

John tried to build a bigger shelter of snow but had to give up when his hands started to freeze. He was wearing only light cotton gloves. Dick had none at all; his were down in the submerged cabin of the plane, along with his spare socks and those precious caribou-skin robes. He knew that his hands were freezing, too, the fingers slowly turning numb and stiff. He told John about it and together they cut Dick's wool scarf into two pieces and wrapped one around each of his hands. That was to save all of his hands but the tips of his fingers.

Apart from their concern for Tommy, two worries hounded John and Dick all through that terrible, long night.

Would the morning dawn clear, and would their partly submerged plane stay up long enough for searchers to spot it from the air? Only the wing and part of the tail, which were resting on the ice, remained above water now. Sooner or later the plane would take the final plunge. As long as any part of it was in sight the rescue planes that were sure to take off at daylight would have a good marker to spot; however, once it was gone the planes would only have a pair of tiny specks on the vast ice fields to look for.

Every now and then, all night long, they heard the sharp crunch of breaking ice as the water-logged Cessna settled a little lower. Each time that happened they knew their chances were slimmer. If fog should lay over the ice and sea the next morning, they knew they would have no chance at all of being found in time. They said nothing about it, but both men knew there was a limit to the number of hours they could survive on the open ice in frozen clothing. Their feet and hands were already freezing.

They walked up and down, keeping their backs to the wind. Dick's feet, which felt like wooden stumps, caused him to stumble and fall repeatedly, but each time John prodded him up and Dick made himself walk again. John had directed rescue work in the arctic often enough to know what to do to keep them going, and if he was discouraged he didn't show it. Twice toward morning Dick dropped down behind a sheltering hummock, falling asleep the instant he hit the ice, but each time John had him back on his feet in a hurry. John fell a few times, too, and when that happened Dick turned the tables and urged him up. They were so tired and cold that neither cared much whether he himself lived or died, but a spark of mutual concern for the other kept them both going. Alone, it's doubtful either would have lived through the night. Together, they wouldn't allow themselves to quit.

Hour after hour they walked and fell, got up and walked again. Dick prayed to himself as he plodded back and forth across the ice. They didn't talk much, except to hope for fair weather in the morning and to wonder how Tommy had fared. They counted their steps, trying to make the hours pass more quickly, and as the night wore on, they made a game of estimating time by trying to clock off 15-minute intervals and checking against each other's blind reckoning.

Daybreak came about six. To their enormous relief the dawn was frosty and clear, with a beautiful red sunrise over the low coast in the southeast.

"We won't have long to wait now," John predicted cheerfully. "Whether Tommy got ashore or not, the alarm is out. There'll be planes over the ice in an hour."

He was right about it, too. The planes didn't come close enough for the two to see them, not at first, but they heard the far-off drone of the first motor shortly after sunrise.

They had eaten nothing since breakfast the morning before, and their bellies were beginning to gnaw and cramp. Lack of food and sleep, and the long cold night, had sapped their strength, and it was more difficult than before to stay on their feet and keep awake. Now close to the end of their endurance, they reeled and staggered, falling more and more often and getting up with greater difficulty each time.

It was midmorning before they heard a plane near enough so that they could dare to hope rescue was at hand. It droned along beyond their sight, flying toward Point Hope, and a few minutes later they heard it come back, still hidden in the frost haze along the horizon.

"He's getting warm," John declared. "He'll spot us on the next pass."

They learned later that the hunters' disappearance had triggered a search of major proportions. Every Wien Airlines plane was up that morning searching, as well as other flyers from Kotzebue, and before they were found the 74th Air Rescue Squadron at Ladd Air Force Base was in the act, too.

It was an hour before noon when the throb of a plane off to the south began to grow louder.

"There he comes!" John shouted. "Flag him down!"

A second later Dick made out an oncoming aircraft, headed straight for them. He whipped out a soggy red handkerchief and waved it as he had never waved before in his life. John joined in, and the two went on waving and dancing around on the ice while the plane bore down on them. They found out later, however, that their frantic efforts at signaling had been futile. Although the wings of their Cessna had slipped under the water, luckily the tail still rested on the ice; it was that blob of red, not the signalling of the men, that attracted the attention of the search pilot. The doomed plane would plunge to the bottom later that day, almost as though aware it had served its final usefulness.

Half a mile away the approaching pilot dipped his wings in sudden salute; the men knew they were spotted. The plane was the most beautiful sight they had ever seen. It rocketed over, and the pilot banked it in a sharp turn and swung back to pick a spot for a landing. John and Dick watched, hardly breathing, as the plane's skis touched down on old ice 50 yards beyond the Cessna. When the ice held they yelled and whooped like two Comanches.

The pilot was John Cross, a Wien Airlines man. The first

thing he said to the exhausted men was, "Where is Richards?" Their hearts sank all the way down to their boots. So Tommy hadn't made it ashore, after all. John and Dick couldn't have felt much worse if rescue had passed them by. But Cross wasn't discouraged.

"He's on the ice somewhere. We'll find him," he predicted.

He hustled the two men into the plane, and ten minutes later they were at Point Hope crawling out and onto Mark Kinneeveauk's dog sled for the short ride to the village school where they could receive emergency treatment. Cross immediately whipped his plane around and gunned it off the ice without a second look at them, on his way to search for Tommy in the area where the two men indicated he must have disappeared the night before. He found him, too, but another rescue plane was already down beside him. Cross went down and picked Tommy up and flew him directly to his home in Kotzebue for first-aid treatment.

What had happened was that Tommy had crossed a strip of newly frozen, thin ice, onto a big floe, and found his way ahead blocked by open leads. Then he discovered he couldn't get back across the thin ice. He had been able to see the tail of the Cessna as long as daylight lasted, but had been too far away to see John or Dick, and so had no idea of how they were faring. He had spent a miserable night on the floe. Feeling as much concern for John and Dick as they were expending on him, he had even worried over the possibility that a bear might come along and attack them.

At the village school everything possible was being done for John and Dick by Ed Sipes, his wife and the natives of Point Hope. An Eskimo named Daniel Lisbourne massaged

Dick's frozen feet for four hours with hardly a letup until they thawed and the blood was going in them once more.

"And maybe you think they didn't give me hell about that time!" Dick said later. "It isn't freezing that hurts, it's thawing out!"

Both men had frozen fingers and toes, although John's feet and Tommy's had come through in better shape than Dick's, thanks to the native footgear they were wearing.

When everything possible had been done in the way of first aid, Cross loaded Dick and John into his plane again for the flight down the coast to Kotzebue. At the native hospital there, they slept that night under warm wool blankets. Although their hands and feet were wrapped in dressings, the two men were able to rest comfortably.

Three days later John was flown to a hospital near his home in Nome and Dick to one at Fairbanks. The morning after Dick arrived Dr. Paul Haggland, a top-notch surgeon with an interest in hunting about as keen as his own, came in to look him over. It was not until three weeks later that the doctor broke the news to his patient: Dick would have to lose the little toe on his right foot.

"It isn't much good for anything except to grow corns on, anyway," Dr. Haggland kidded.

The loss of his toe was the most serious result of Dick's exposure to the cruel cold. He had lost 25 pounds during the ordeal, and he also lost most of the nails on his frostbitten toes and fingers, but they soon grew back. It was nine weeks before he was able to put his feet to the floor; however, within five months he had discarded his crutches. He was able to get around fairly well then in a loose, comfortable pair of bird-shooter boots, although his toes were still stiff and touchy. The doctor told him he would probably always have some discomfort in his feet.

As for the other two members of the trio, Tommy was flying again in a short time; John, who also lost some of his fingernails and toenails from frostbite, was soon back at his job. Everything considered, the three of them came through the ordeal in remarkably good shape. In Dick's case, the Eskimos at Point Hope called it an outright miracle that he had lived, considering his age and the fact that he came from the warm climate of southern California.

Despite his experience, Dick was not discouraged about hunting in Alaska. He made a date to hunt Dall sheep with Doc Haggland as soon as his feet were in shape, and said that he would like nothing better than to go back to Kotzebue and have another try for a polar bear. Even though Mark Kinneeveauk gave him a fine pelt from a bear he had killed three weeks before the accident, Dick still wanted one of his own. He figured the one he tried to collect that unlucky March day was still up there . . . waiting for him.

Arrow for a Grizzly

THE HUNTING party stopped for lunch beside a small glacial stream in a pretty little valley in the Yukon Territory. Cold rain was falling, but Alex Van Bibber, the outfitter and chief guide, produced a stub of candle, flattened and discolored from long carrying in his pocket, lighted it and held it under a pyramid of wet twigs. They dried slowly and crackled into a brisk, small fire that licked cheerfully up the sides of the smoke-blackened tea pail.

The men ate cold goat ribs and Yukon doughnuts—a variety fried over an open fire in bear fat. Huddling around the fire, the riders welcomed the rest and were warm and comfortable, in spite of the weather. The horses wandered off a short distance, picking at whatever forage they could find.

When the last drop of tea was gone and Alex Van Bibber was stamping out the embers, he happened to look toward a mountain a half mile up the valley and spotted a bear working down the steep slope.

He lifted his glasses for a quick look.

"Black," he announced.

Everyone looked and agreed. It was a black; nothing to get excited about. However sportsmen may feel about them in the rest of the United States, in Alaska and also in the Yukon, the black bear is regarded by guides and hunters alike with about the same contempt a trout fisherman feels for a sucker. Up there grizzlies and browns are the bears that count.

The party, however, stood around for 20 minutes, just watching this fellow amble down off the mountain. He was taking his time, stopping every now and then to dig for a ground squirrel or marmot. He gradually worked his way into a patch of willows and finally disappeared; then the five men climbed back into their saddles.

This was a bow hunt for moose, goats, Dall sheep and grizzlies. There were seven men in the party, plus Tiger, the young Husky that Alex had brought along to keep grizzlies out of the cook tent, and a string of 21 horses. The hunters were Fred Bear, a manufacturer of archery equipment in Grayling, Michigan, and Dr. Judd Grindell, from Siren, Wisconsin. Both were bow hunters of vast experience; in fact, Bear had one African bow hunt behind him. Don Redinger, a Pittsburgh photographer, had come along in the hope of taking good action pictures of a bow hunt for trophy game, something Bear had also wanted to try. Redinger was using a movie camera with a six-inch telephoto lens; he was too busy with his camera to try any hunting on his own. Redinger was the cameraman who later went to Africa with the Texas sportsman, Bill Negley, to film the first elephant bow shoot.

In addition to Alex there was a second guide, an Indian named George John, and a wrangler and a cook. Ed Merriam, the cook, came originally from Virginia, but he liked the Yukon better. Joe House, the wrangler, had quit a two-dollar-an-hour job in town to shag horses for the same reason. He liked it. The only time he had ever regretted it, he said, was when he went out after the horse string one frosty dawn and blundered into an old sow grizzly with two cubs. She had gone for him and he had had to run for it. Coming to a steep bank, Joe had seen one of the horses at the bottom of it, directly below him, and he had made a flying leap astride, only to find the horse was one he had hobbled the night before. Luckily for both of them, the bear had given up at the top of the bank.

The party had left its take-off point on the Haines Highway 93 miles above Haines on the morning of August 26, 1956. Base camp was established now on Devils Lake, in rough and roadless country near the southwest corner of the Yukon, three or four days' ride above the British Columbia border and east of Alaska.

For Fred Bear the trip had a two-fold purpose over and above the fun that goes with every big-game hunt. Most of all he hoped to kill a grizzly with an arrow. If he succeeded he would be the first man, so far as he knew, to take a full-grown silvertip that way since Art Young and Saxton Pope had hunted down, under permit, and liquidated a big trouble-making grizzly in Yellowstone National Park, in the early 1920's.

Besides wanting to take a grizzly that way, something he had dreamed of for years, Fred wanted to test a new type of hunting point that he had recently developed—a razorhead. This arrowhead was a single-blade broadhead that mounted a removable two-edged razor blade, very thin and hard, to do its cutting. He had experimented with it for three years at his archery plant. Having used it on antelope and other thin-skinned game in Africa, he was eager to try it on something bigger and tougher. His bow quiver now held three hollow glass shafts mounted with these new heads; he also had a reserve supply along. Given the right chance, he would find out just what the razorhead was capable of.

His bow was also one of his own make, a Kodiak model with a draw weight of close to 70 pounds. Made with a maple core, faced and backed with fiberglass, it would shrug off heat, cold or moisture, and cast an arrow with great power and speed. So far as equipment was concerned, he was ready for business. Fred's success on this hunt depended now on the grizzlies and his markmanship.

Alex didn't relish the idea of guiding a bowman, and he cared even less for the combination of a bowman and a photographer. He had made that clear in advance, and Fred admitted his reasons were sound: the average guide in the Yukon and Alaska figures to put his hunter within 200 yards of a grizzly or brown bear; the rest is up to the hunter. If the client is using a modern rifle at that range and can't connect, he doesn't deserve a trophy. If brush, poor visibility or other conditions make it necessary the guide will move him in, say to 100 yards, but that's about the limit.

Alex had understood before they left his headquarters at Champagne that he would have to do a lot better than that for the bowman. Fred had killed his last game with a rifle 25 years before. The bow had been his sole hunting weapon ever since. Whatever he took on this trip, grizzly included, would be put down with an arrow. He had no intention of risking a bad shot at a range in excess of 50 yards, and 25 or 30 would be more to his liking. However good it is on other accounts, the bow is not a long-range weapon. And at 25 yards a wounded grizzly can spell bad trouble if not killed in its tracks, something no arrow, however well placed, can be counted on to do. Alex knew the outcome of such a situation might well be up to him, and he didn't like the idea. Not that he was short on physical courage. He had plenty of that. He had Indian blood from his mother, and his father, a mountain man from Virginia, had gone to the Yukon many years before and cut such a swath that his name was still legendary there. Alex had been brought up to be afraid of nothing.

What was worrying him was that his reputation as a guide might suffer should things go wrong. For one thing, when you have to stalk as close as you do in bowhunting, there is always a chance of spooking game and the possibility of losing an outstanding trophy, for which one may have waited and worked for weeks. For another, Alex didn't like the idea of possibly being responsible for losing a hunter—even a crazy bowman— to a wounded bear, or for having one get badly clobbered. All in all, he said frankly that he wished Fred and Grindell would use rifles, but he knew there was no chance of that. Before the hunt started, he had rather reluctantly promised he would see it through and do the best he could for them.

The base camp at Devils Lake now turned into little more than a place to pick up supplies. Days of unbroken rain and snow turned the mountain tundra into a soggy sponge. Alders and scrub willows dripped as the men rode through them. Autumn was near in that high country; the weather was getting steadily worse. In the five weeks the hunt lasted, the party would see only five days of sunshine. Fortunately everyone had good rain gear (Fred was wearing a two-piece outfit of coated nylon, which was so waterproof he could sit in a pool for hours without getting damp) and dry bedrolls. The well-equipped hunters roamed the mountains in the saddle day after day, hunting in rain, snow and fog and making side camps where they stayed for a day or two at a time.

They kept seeing moose and sheep in the distance, and enough grizzly tracks to keep them in a hopeful frame of mind. Goats, always hard to stalk, were plentiful in the region. Except for the lower lakes and valleys, the country was all above timberline. Alder crept up the draws and canyons, and thickets of buckbrush cloaked the lower hills, which were all decked out in autumn colors. Above those brushy hills, the cliffs and ridges and peaks shouldered up, seamed with slides and canyons and ledges, and draped much of the time in fog or cloud. None of the country was flat, so the advantage was all with the nimble goats.

They finally got a day of blue sky and sunshine, and from a side camp on Upper Hendon Lake, Fred and Alex spotted three goats, including one very good billy, high on a mountain above the Hendon River.

It took the two men three hours to get up to them. They made a careful and patient stalk, and they were only 20 yards away when gravel crunched under their boots, causing the three goats to bound to their feet. For a second or two they stood broadside, caught flat-footed and staring in amazement. They looked like animals carved from mountain snow; it was one of the most beautiful sights Fred had ever seen on a hunt.

He drove an arrow through the biggest billy, missed with his second shot as the wounded animal was racing away but finished it with his third. They found it lying at the edge of a ledge in a side canyon. There was no way to get down to the spot without ropes, and it was too late in the afternoon to spend any more time on the mountain. They got back to camp after dark, returned with ropes the next morning and retrieved the goat, a fine 200-pound billy with nine-and-a-half-inch horns.

Two days later Dr. Grindell killed a good-size blonde grizzly, but not with the bow. Grindell and George John stalked the bear to within 150 yards; the guide flatly refused to go closer. He had an overwhelming fear of grizzlies and carried bad scars on his neck, arm and shoulder as proof that his aversion was not an idle whim. On a hunt a few years earlier he had tackled a grizzly at close range with a .30/30 and muffed the job. The bear grabbed him by a shoulder and came near killing him before his hunting partner got a shot into its head. Since then George John simply wouldn't go near a grizzly if he could help it. He regarded Bear's and Grindell's determination to take one with a bow as downright foolhardy.

Nothing Grindell said could change the Indian's mind. Realizing his hunting time was running out and fearful he would not get another chance at a grizzly, Grindell reluctantly borrowed the guide's rifle, a 6.5 mm. Mannlicher. He killed the bear with a single shot through the heart.

It was a couple of days after this kill that the hunting party, stopping for lunch in the high valley, watched the black bear feed down the slope of a near by mountain. As the bear went out of sight in a big willow thicket and the men rode away from the ashes of their little fire, Fred was doing some serious thinking about a black-bear hunt.

Their course up the valley was leading them along the foot of the mountain, only a quarter mile from where they had seen the black. The more Fred turned the situation over in his mind, the more unwilling he was to pass up the bear just be-cause it wasn't a grizzly. This black was the first bear he had been close to on the hunt, and it was big enough to rate as a good trophy. More important, here was an opportunity to try his razorheads on a tough, thick-skinned animal. There was the bear in the willows up ahead. Fred knew the guides wouldn't bother with it unless he insisted, for Alex hadn't agreed to hunt blacks. Fred decided to insist.

Just then they topped a low rise and saw the bear again. It

was on the side of a ridge across the creek and, while they watched, it walked down into a draw, out of sight.

"What do you say?" Fred asked Grindell.

"A bear is a bear," Grindell replied. "Let's go get him."

They climbed down from their horses, stripped off their rain gear and chaps, and started for the ridge. Redinger unlimbered his camera and trailed them. Alex and George John stayed in the saddle, watching with tolerant grins. This was a bear hunt they intended to sit out. That was all right with Fred. He and Judd could handle it by themselves.

Their position as they approached the ridge put Grindell on the right. He signaled he would climb that side. Fred circled around to the far slope, where they had last seen the bear. He rounded a low knoll and saw it less than 100 yards away, digging for a marmot. The bear had its front legs down to the shoulders in the hole it had excavated, and it was intent on what it was doing, trying to watch all sides at once to make sure the marmot didn't pop out of another entrance and get away.

The bear's rump was toward Fred; it was easy for the hunter to back off, crouch down and creep up to a small boulder 25 yards behind the bear. There he rose in a half crouch on one knee, with an arrow ready on the string. But before he could draw, the bear whipped its head around his way, looking for the marmot—and time stood still.

Fred was looking into the bulldog face of a grizzly bear just 75 feet off. Now, for the first time, he noticed the telltale sprinkle of gray hairs in the rain-wet pelt. He would have seen the silvertip hairs if the bear's fur hadn't been wet. Although Fred had come to the Yukon to kill a grizzly, he had never intended to tackle one with the bow all by himself, unbacked by a rifleman. He had made that clear to Alex. Although Fred had complete confidence in the killing power of a well-placed arrow, he also knew that an arrow-shot bear is not likely to die on the spot. A wounded grizzly is a terrible thing to face, especially alone. It had been agreed that Alex would be behind him with a .30/06 any time Fred got close to a grizzly. But at the moment Alex was sitting in his saddle on the other side of the creek, chuckling with George John about bow hunters who wasted time stalking a black bear.

Fred had also never intended to face a grizzly without a sidearm. When planning the grizzly hunt, he had bought a .44 Magnum Smith and Wesson and had put in a whole summer of practice with it. The Canadian Government and the Mounties at Whitehorse had been very co-operative about giving him a permit to carry it, and the Yukon Game Commissioner had also authorized Alex to carry a rifle while guiding the bowman. The authorities didn't want any accidents on this bear hunt, any more than the hunters or Alex did.

Fred's Smith and Wesson, however, was heavy and awkward; the shoulder holster interfered with the use of his bow, so he had gotten into the habit of carrying it in a regular holster hung on his saddle. And that was where it was now, back on the far side of the ridge with Alex, George John and the horses. Fred was on his own. If he killed the grizzly, it would have to be with his bow, without rifle backing or any other help.

It was a tough spot. It was also the challenge of a lifetime, and one that seemed too tempting not to accept. Fred weighed the situation for only three or four seconds, just long enough to determine that if the bear came at him he would have time to dodge and get a second arrow on the string. Later he realized he had probably been wrong about that.

Still crouched down behind the boulder that was barely

big enough to break his outline, Fred brought the bowstring back and let drive. He didn't know it at the time, but Redinger had come up behind him to within 150 yards and was covering the entire incident with his camera. Hearing the snap of the bowstring, the grizzly jerked its burly head around in a lightning-quick move as the arrow sliced into its rib section. The bear let go a short, gruff growl and whipped sidewise, snapping at its side, not where the arrow had hit but where it had come out. The arrow had knifed all the way through the grizzly's body, shearing off, Fred found out later, a rib and cutting through lungs, diaphragm, liver and intestines; it still had had power enough to bury itself, above the razorhead, in the hillside.

The grizzly bit at its side for as long as it would have taken to count to three. Then it swung around and came for him, growling and bawling. Fred braced himself to dodge; he was no longer sure he would have time to use a second arrow.

Next the bear did something for which there was no apparent logical explanation. It turned, perhaps because it changed its mind in mid-charge. More likely, however, it turned because it had failed to locate the cause of its troubles; all bears, Fred knew, are notoriously near-sighted. There seemed to be no other reason why, once it started in to get revenge, it shouldn't have kept coming.

But it didn't. Halfway to Fred, it turned up over the ridge. He didn't think it wise to call attention to himself with another arrow, so he let the grizzly go. Grindell saw it come down the other side of the ridge, about 75 yards off. The bear ran 80 paces, spun around two or three times in tight circles and then went down to stay.

This was Fred's fiftieth big-game kill with a bow, a total

representing hunts in the United States, Canada, Alaska, and Africa. He had itched to take a grizzly for years, and now he was about as happy as a hunter can be. As things turned out, he was fated to share the honor soon with Bill Mastrangel of Phoenix, Arizona. That same September Mastrangel reported killing a grizzly with a bow in British Columbia.

The bear was no giant, but it was big enough to make a fine trophy. Although it was gaunt and thin, it had the silver-tip's typical massive head, shoulders, powerful legs and long claws. Mountain grizzlies don't grow as big as their fish-eating, seaside cousins. Location and food supply considered, this seemed to be a fairly good one, and when they took the pelt off, they uncovered a streamlined carcass that was all muscle and sinew.

Most of the time it's the medium-sized bear built for speed and power and endurance, not the real big bruiser, that makes trouble for a hunter. The big ones know better. Grizzlies of the size Fred killed are the cocky young toughs that have not yet learned their lesson. It was one in this same class that had mauled George John, and another that had killed a hunter in that same part of the Yukon only a year or two before.

When they opened up the bear to see what the arrow had done, they found a hole in the diaphragm so big that the stomach had jostled through into the lung cavity as the animal ran. It had bled white inside from the cuts made as the razorhead slashed through its vitals.

Fred was asked many times after the hunt whether he would tackle a grizzly again single-handed, with nothing but a bow. He admitted it was a tough question to answer. In the first place he had not done it intentionally, and he emphasized that he would not recommend that any hunter try it deliberately.

But if he had a similar opportunity, and especially if he was above the bear with a rock or cover of some kind to duck down behind after releasing his arrow, he said that he would respond again to the challenge.

"I guess that's the way it is when you're after trophy game," he explained.

Squall of Content

LES TASSELL awoke from deep sleep chilled by the sense that something was wrong. He lay quietly in his berth, listening. The ship's clock chimed eight bells. Midnight. Then there was no further sound in the still Florida night, not even the lapping of water against the Don-Jo's planking. There was no reason to feel uneasy, but Les did, so he slipped out of the berth and padded up on deck.

Everything was shipshape, exactly as it had been when Les had turned in two hours before. The night was calm and fine, the velvet sky was sprinkled with stars that seemed almost close enough to touch and the sea was smooth as glass. The 33-foot cruiser lay motionless on the black water, not even tugging at the bow and stern anchors that had been put down.

One thousand feet to port, Content Key was silhouetted against the starlit sky, a low black shape broken by the outlines of mangrove trees and a few scattered scrub palms. There was not even a surf on the ragged coral beach. It would have been hard to imagine a more peaceful scene, and yet Les could not shake off the haunting feeling that something was wrong.

Most people believe that close calls aren't telegraphed ahead, that a man never knows beforehand that trouble is coming. Trouble just happens.

Les Tassell disagrees. Half a dozen times in his life, he has experienced in advance a strong sense of impending danger. Call it a hunch, premonition, or the presence of a guardian angel. Whatever it is, Les felt he was being warned on that calm February night in Florida Bay. If he had paid closer attention, he and Ruth, his wife, might have been able to avoid the most horrible experience of their lives and been able to save a good boat. But he didn't listen to the small voice of warning. Instead, since everything seemed snug and safe, he went below and turned in again.

This cruise was actually a venture in skin diving, a sport that was new to Les. Two years before he and Ruth had sailed the Don-Jo from her home port of Holland, Michigan, across Lake Michigan to Chicago, down the Illinois ship canal into the Mississippi River, which they followed down as far as Cairo, then up the Ohio and through the TVA lakes to Guntersville. At that point their wandering by water was temporarily ended. The cruiser was hauled out and shipped overland by truck to Jacksonville, Florida. Next they cruised down the inland waterway of Florida's east coast to Fort Lauderdale, which became their port of operations for the next two years. Les and Ruth fitted the Don-Jo with outriggers and fighting chairs for deep-sea work. After that they went down to Florida from their home in Grand Rapids, Michigan, two or three times each year. They arranged to spend at least a couple of months during the winter cruising and fishing.

The Don-Jo was a Chris-Craft, with twin screws and powered by two 95-horse engines. She had cabin space for four people and was well-equipped for cozy living.

In January of 1952, Les hired a mate, Ed Boshead, before setting out from Fort Lauderdale, in order to free himself from the full time job of running the boat and thus have a chance to do more fishing. The Don-Jo lazed south from Lauderdale into the Keys, then west as far as Marathon, where the Tassells spent two weeks of varied fishing in ideal waters. At sea they filled the box with kings, dolphin and hard-fighting jack crevalle, and every now and then they hung and released a good lusty sail. Between trips, however, it was almost as much sport just to loaf on the dock and catch the rainbow-colored parrot fish and the other "reefers" that abounded in the shallow crystal clear water.

Two weeks of fishing and loafing slipped away quickly. The skin-diving bug, however, was biting Les harder and harder. His interest in the sport had been kindled by the new mate. Ed was an experienced and enthusiastic diver. The more Les listened to his descriptions of the underwater world and the action spear fishing provided, the longer he watched the parrot fish and mangrove snappers swim around in the clear depths, thumbing their noses at onlookers and fishermen alike, the more Les itched to go down and take them on in their own element. Before the two weeks were up, Les had bought fins, a snorkel mask and a spear, and was practicing diving in a pool near the beach at Marathon. The day finally arrived when Ed decided Les was ready for the real thing.

The next morning broke fine and clear, so they backed away from the dock and headed northwest, out through the Spanish Channel, for the little dot of coral and mangrove known as Content Key. Tipsters at Marathon who knew the waters well had told them there wasn't a more productive fishing ground or a better place for skin diving anywhere in the keys.

The run from Marathon through the Spanish Channel was as pleasant as any Les and Ruth could recall. There was not a cloud in the sky, and the waters of Florida Bay, lying between the keys and the tip of the mainland, were as unruffled as a millpond. Frolicking porpoises rolled on the shimmering surface of the sea, while overhead clumsy-looking brown pelicans planed and wheeled. Now and then they drew in their wings and landing gear and plunged abruptly into the blue water, reappearing an instant later, gulping down a fish. The Don-Jo's engines purred like contented cats, Ruth soaked up the sun on the after deck, Ed busied himself with minor chores and Les lolled at the wheel. It was one of those perfect days, in the middle of the Florida winter, when a fisherman itches to shove off from the dock.

The charts showed that deep channels flanked by coral reefs ran all the way to Content, a fact born out by the surface colors of the water. Although it was certainly tempting fishing water, they passed it up, hurrying to get to their destination.

They ran out into Florida Bay and made a wide turn, approaching the key from the north. Content, they saw, was a low blob of gray coral, only a few feet above the sea at high tide, which sloped down into a mangrove swamp on the south side. They slowed the Don-Jo's motors as they approached and cruised back and forth over a series of coral reefs, looking things over. The water over the reefs was about ten feet in depth; the channels between were deeper. Since the cruiser drew only three and a half feet, the Don-Jo was able to work in to within 300 yards of the beach without being in any danger of going aground. There they dropped the bow anchor, backed off 50 yards, and put down the stern anchor. Now the boat was secure and wouldn't swing in the light offshore breeze.

The two men liked what they had seen of the sea bottom. There were plenty of deep holes and shadowy caverns along the coral ledges, the sort of places skin divers look for, so Ed and Les got into swim trunks, lowered the eight-foot dinghy and rowed away for a closer look.

It didn't take the skin divers long to realize that they had come to exactly the right spot. The shoal waters over the reefs were teeming with permit, jack crevalle, yellowtails and other fish. In the shallows to the south of the island, offshore from the mangrove swamp, they rowed over manta rays as wide as the dinghy was long—dark, ugly batwinged things that sprawled flat on the sea bottom. Two or three times they saw the high dorsal fins of cruising sharks cut the water around them.

There was plenty of exciting material here; however, they agreed to leave the big stuff alone, at least until Les had a day or two of spear fishing under his belt.

By the time they finished their leisurely row around Content, it was too late in the day for diving. As they headed back to the Don-Jo for dinner, the two men made big plans for the next morning. In a place where such a variety of fish life abounded and the coral reefs provided such ideal conditions, Les felt confident, and Ed agreed, that even a novice spearman could be sure of plenty of action.

The evening was as fine as the day had been. The light breeze died and the sea turned glassy calm, with the stars shedding almost as much light as a young moon. When darkness had fallen, the night-roving denizens of the coral reefs staged as entertaining a show as the Tassells had ever watched.

It began when thousands of tiny phosphorescent shrimp— glowworms of the sea—started to swim to the surface in pairs to mate. After spawning, the shrimp drifted down again, lighting the water with an eerie radiance. Suddenly a school of foraging minnows slashed through the shrimp, which scattered like drops of liquid fire. On the heels of the minnows, a pack of yellowtails raced in to kill and feed. After the yellowtails had passed, the sea grew quiet. The cycle of begetting life and taking life had begun again.

The three of them sat watching and talking for a couple of hours. After Les took a last look at the anchor lines, made a mental note of the location and outline of the key in case a wind came up during the night, they turned in.

It seemed to him that he had no more than dropped off to sleep when he was aroused by that strange, disturbing sense of misgiving, which had sent him topside for a look.

When he got back to his berth he lay awake for an hour, restless and worried, yet not knowing what was troubling him and telling himself he was behaving like a nervous old woman. Eventually, he dozed off again.

Suddenly he was awake and aware that wind-driven rain was pounding against the windows, while the rolling and pitching Don-Jo bucked hard at her anchor lines. He slid his feet into slippers and raced for the deck. As he stepped out of the shelter of the cabin, the wind tore at him with clawing fingers and hissing rain almost blinded him. Sudden squalls are common off the tip of Florida; they pass quickly. Les knew the Don-Jo could ride out any ordinary storm without danger. Then as he rubbed his eyes clear of water, he looked off toward the key. His hair stood on end as he made out its black, surf-fringed outline through the storm. The Don-Jo was much closer to Content than it had been earlier. Les realized in a flash that the boat was dragging its anchors and that the raging wind was driving it toward the treacherous reefs offshore. Les ducked back into the cabin.

"Roll out," he bawled to Ruth and Ed. "We're going aground!"

All three of them were on deck in a matter of seconds. There was only one way to save the boat: head for the open sea. Les kicked the engines alive, and Ed started to heave in the stern line. At his hail of "Anchor up!" Les threw in the clutch with the engines roaring full astern. The boat shouldered back into the seas and staggered under their impact. A shudder ran the length of the Don-Jo just as it was beginning to gather steerageway. Then the starboard engine sputtered and quit. Les sensed what had happened even before Ed shouted the word. In the darkness on the heaving afterdeck, a loop of anchor line had slid into the sea unseen, been sucked in and fouled the starboard screw. For the duration of the squall, they would be on one engine. Before he tried, Les knew that one engine could not drive them through the seas that were smashing down on the Don-Jo.

He kept her on full astern, but the one engine wasn't powerful enough; inevitably they drifted down on the bow anchor. Ed scrambled to get it up, while Les, fighting the wheel, tried to bring the reeling Don-Jo around and head her offshore. But the squall was too severe. Then the Don-Jo struck a reef with such a jolting crash that all three of them were sent sprawling on the deck.

The next sea lifted the Don-Jo and smashed her down again. The Tassells and Ed heard the boat's ribs and planking splinter as the storm pounded her cruelly on that coral anvil. No boat could live long under such conditions.

"It's time to get ashore," Les shouted to Ruth and Ed.

He knew they were wondering, the same as he was, whether they could make it to the beach, but none of them voiced any doubts. They got into life jackets. Then Ed and Les unlashed the dinghy and slid it down to the deck from its cradle on top of the cabin. Hurriedly they grabbed up blankets, food and a few articles of clothing and tossed them in. Ruth remembered a big glass jug of fresh water. They got it and stowed it securely in the dinghy. By this time the Don-Jo was low in the water. Each succeeding sea was lifting her and tilting her at crazy angles, breaking her back across the reef and hammering her bottom.

The deck was awash, and the wind was blowing black sheets of water over the top of the cabin by the time they had the dinghy ready. They saw then that there was no possibility of rowing in. The little eight-foot boat wouldn't have stayed afloat a minute with three people aboard it in that roaring surf. They considered just putting Ruth in, since she was a poor swimmer; however, they quickly decided that the risk of the dinghy's capsizing or swamping was too great. If they were to reach the beach at all, they would have to do it by hanging on to the dinghy.

They shoved the little boat off the tilting deck of the Don-Jo and slid into the water beside it. None of them had really gauged the savage fury of the sea until that minute. But there was one factor in their favor. The wind, which had driven the cruiser aground, was carrying the dinghy toward shore. If they could keep their grip on it and avoid being mauled on the ragged, flinty floor of the sea, they would get out of this disaster all right. The storm was going to put them on the beach in a few minutes.

But just then a great lace-crested roller lifted them, almost tearing the boat out of their hands. It passed and Les felt what seemed like the slash of a stone knife on his knees as they struck and were dragged across a sharp ridge of coral. Floating now in the storm-tormented water, the three of them were lifted again and then dropped. For a second or two Les was on his feet, standing on smooth rock. He stole a glance back in the direction of the Don-Jo. It was many yards behind, rolling soddenly. Les could see then that they had made good headway toward shore.

But he never knew how they made it all the way in, except that the instinctive, grim determination to live shared by all humans seemed to carry them through the welter of foaming water and across the snag-toothed reefs. They swam and crawled through the shallower water; the last 50 yards they walked and dragged the dinghy along through the shoals, as the breakers tried to suck them back into the sea. As soon as they could, they lifted and carried the craft, knowing it had to be beached without being damaged. It was their only means of getting off the key when the storm abated. The burden and the footing, which was as treacherous as broken concrete, caused them to stumble, slip and fall. But after what seemed an eternity, they realized there was no longer any surf around their feet. They were ashore. They were bruised and cut and battered; their lungs were nearly bursting for lack of breath; and they had swallowed a great deal of water. But they were ashore.

They lugged the dinghy well up the beach to a clump of mangroves. The dinghy was still seaworthy. Then they looked around for some shelter for themselves, but there was none in sight. There was no dry wood to start a fire. Now that they were out of the water, the cold rain and the relentless wind quickly chilled them to the bone. They wrapped themselves in the blankets they had brought ashore, turned the boat on its side, and, cold and wet and wretched, huddled together in its lee, thankful to be on land.

The next four hours, until the gray of daylight began to stain the eastern sky, were the longest any of them could remember. At daybreak the storm was slowly subsiding; however, it was still raining and blowing hard. The crabs in the mangroves around them were a constant worry to Ruth. They were a small variety, with one huge claw out of all proportion to the rest of them that they snapped shut with a loud cracking noise. The crabs were all around them and kept up their racket during the remainder of the stormy night. Ruth's jitters lessened as it grew lighter; now at least the crabs wouldn't be able to crawl over her in the dark. Les realized he hadn't been as much comfort to his wife as he should have been, but his attention had been diverted by the sound of the Don-Jo breaking up out on the reef. Hour after hour he heard the rhythmic crunch and smash of the seas pounding her; the sounds were loud and clear even above the noise of the storm.

Although there was still a heavy surf running at daybreak, within an hour the sea had calmed enough for Les and Ed to row out in the dinghy to have a close look at the wreck. The cruiser lay low in the water, and the upper hull and cabin didn't look badly damaged. Les knew better, however, than to hope for much. When they got aboard they found that the Don-Jo was actually a total loss: bottom torn out, engines smashed and screws and shafts twisted into scrap. During the predawn hours, the seas had swept the inside of the cruiser clean of equipment and belongings.

The Don-Jo was a gutted boat that couldn't be salvaged. The two men rowed back to the beach. After a cold snack that passed for breakfast, plans were made for getting away from Content Key.

They couldn't all leave in the dinghy. It was decided that

the best plan was for one of them to go for help. It would be a long row. The nearest human habitation there in the unpeopled keys was along Highway US 1, the bridge-and-causeway road that leads out to Key West. That was about 20 miles away, down the Spanish Channel, in which the water was pretty choppy. The reefs would break the worst of the seas, however, and the wind would be with the rower all the way. Ed volunteered for the chore, confident he could make it.

"I'll be back with a rescue boat of some kind before dark," he promised.

It was agreed that Ed would try to make it to the highway. They carried the dinghy around to the lee side of the island, where there was very little surf, and he shoved off. Ruth and Les watched him until the boat, far offshore, looked no bigger than a squat, two-legged beetle crawling across the gray sea. Then they busied themselves with gathering wood for a fire and putting up a crude tent, made from two blankets, against the possibility Ed might not be able to keep the promise he had made.

The day dragged. When they finished their simple camp chores, they explored the key, but that didn't take long. There was no evidence that anyone had ever spent any time there, nor any reason why anyone would want to. They ate cold food again for lunch. Late in the afternoon there was still no sign of Ed, so they began to make ready for another night on the barren island, reminding themselves that they weren't too badly off. They had food, water and material for a fire. It was Ed they were worried about. Had he made it to the highway without mishap? Would he have the endurance to row across 20 miles of open sea?

Then as Les was piling up a small heap of dry wood for

a fire, they both heard, off in the southeast, the distant thrum of a big outboard. They ran to the beach on that side of the key, where a skiff was planing in, throwing a high V of spray as it roared across the water.

The rescue boat was skippered by Speck Smith, a cottager from a key along the highway. Ed was in the boat; he was exhausted from the long row, as beaten a man as Les had ever seen. He was still game, however, and his only concern was getting Les and Ruth safely off the key. They were all back at Smith's cottage in less than an hour.

After the ordeal off Content Key, Les resolved to take heed the next time a small voice in the back of his mind whispers "Danger!"

The Widow Maker

IN THE Chicago Museum of Natural History there is a wonderfully realistic habitat group that depicts the gathering of 23 African animals at a waterhole. The central characters are a cow rhino and her calf, wallowing in the muddy seepage that trickles from beneath the replica of the roots of a huge fig tree. Behind them stands a little band of zebras, patiently waiting their turn. Across the waterhole, five giraffes of the rare reticulated variety are edging in, goaded by thirst, yet knowing better than to challenge Old Lady Horns for water rights. Their leader is a magnificent bull 17 feet tall. In back of the giraffes, eight Grant gazelles and a lone oryx look on, resigned to the fact that they'll get no drink until the lords of the place have had their fill, one after another. To the left, under the fig tree, two big elands are loafing in the shade. Evidently the first to arrive, they had refreshed themselves before the rhinos took over.

The scene is compelling because of its naturalness. Every day during the dry season, similar dramas are enacted around the precious waterholes scattered over the vast plains of Africa.

This impressive habitat group was designed and built by John Albrecht, staff taxidermist at the museum in Chicago for 19 years. It took him three years to complete the job, which included modeling the fig tree in clay, mounting the animals and arranging their grouping. Before that, however, he spent a year in Africa, an experience he had dreamed about, helping to collect and prepare specimens the museum wanted, including those used in the huge habitat group.

The expedition brought back over 80 trophies: antelope of various kinds, buffalo, lion, wart hog, wildebeest, aardvark and a few other rare ones. During the 22 years of John Albrecht's career in the museum field, he had collected and photographed trophy game on 31 expeditions, which took him from central Africa to the arctic regions of Alaska. That year-long expedition in Africa, however, had been the most outstanding by far. The most dangerous, too. It had nearly cost the young taxidermist his life.

Even now, more than 30 years later, when John looks at that habitat group, the memories of the expedition still forcibly thrust themselves upon him: the heat and sweat and thirst, weariness and dust, tormenting insects, narrow game trails and stinking waterholes, primitive villages, mountains and jungles, snarling leopard and charging buffalo, hardship and danger and camaraderie around the many campfires that were lighted across 1,000 miles of the loneliest reaches of Africa.

There were four in the party. It was headed by Major John Coates, an English sportsman whose family had been thread manufacturers for generations. The other three were Captain Harold White of New York, George Carey of Baltimore, and John. White, who stood six feet seven, without shoes, was called Babe.

As the expedition's taxidermist, it was John's job to make plaster death masks of the animals that were killed, measure them, supervise the skinning and preparation of the pelts, and clean the skulls and other bones. He was also responsible for collecting specimens of representative plants and for photographing scenes that could be duplicated for the habitat backgrounds. In short, he was charged with gathering the complex materials that comprise modern museum habitat groups.

The expedition arrived in Ethiopia, then known as Abyssinia, in September of 1928. It would disband in Tanganyika, far to the south, exactly one year later. The four men spent a month in the Abyssinian capital of Addis Ababa, getting their outfit together and making the elaborate preparations that are necessary prior to spending a year in the bush. During the month in the capital, they were lavishly entertained at the foreign legations. The wining and dining Emperor Haile Selassie showered on them topped all the other hospitality. They became fond of him and he of them; they were even afforded the privilege of eating off the famous solid gold royal dinner service.

Eventually, however, their preparations were completed, and it was time to get under way. The last big caravan safari to cross Africa headed south from Addis Ababa in October. Its ranks consisted of 60 natives who were to serve as gun bearers, cooks, skinners, drivers and general helpers. They had no trucks or vehicles of any kind. Their supplies, which were sufficient for seven months, and all their equipment were packed on 35 camels and an equal number of horses and mules. Each camel was toting 400 pounds, the other animals 160 apiece. They had had trouble finding, among the runty stock in Addis Ababa, a saddle animal capable of carrying Babe White; however, the Emperor had solved that problem by presenting him with a big, powerful mule from the royal stables. They promptly named it the White Onion.

The men had no way of knowing that when they reached the Kenya border seven months later there would be little left of the caravan stock except the mules; that all the horses and all but seven of the camels would be dead.

Major Coates engaged no guides or white hunters. Except for the gunbearers and the trackers, the four men were on their own. One of the most important members of the party, however, was their native interpreter, who spoke eight European languages and all of the Abyssinian dialects. His talents later earned him the post of interpreter at the court of Haile Selassie.

John's introduction to the savagery and brutality of Africa was abrupt and bloody. In the late afternoon the first day out of Addis Ababa, they made camp on the dry brushy plains a short distance south of the city. Shortly after dark, White Onion managed to untie his picket rope and strayed. One of the natives discovered that the mule was missing and aroused the camp. Still doped with sleep, John began to crawl out of his bag in the midst of the turmoil. Above the shouts he suddenly heard the clatter of an animal running toward him. Then something soft and wet and sticky was dragged across his face. John focused his eyes. He saw a sheep running . . . bleeding and trailing its entrails. They discovered later that the animal had been ripped open and half-gutted by hyenas at the edge of camp. Luckily they found White Onion before the hyenas found the stray mule.

Of the big five of African trophy game, the safari was after specimens of four—leopard, lion, buffalo and rhino. The museum had no need for an elephant, so care was taken to avoid elephant herds and lone tuskers. John's closest call of the entire safari was served up by a buffalo, but not before a couple of hair-raising encounters with leopard and lion.

With no water in sight, they had to make a dry camp one afternoon early in the trip, setting the tents in the center of the area with the natives and the stock scattered around in a crude circle. John had shot a couple of oryx that morning; however, it was not until camp had been set up that he was able to spread the salted skins out in the fading sun to dry. Once the sun goes down, John had learned, darkness comes quickly in Africa. Complete darkness fell during the short interval of supper. After the meal, John walked over to have a last look at the skins for the night.

They were gone.

He prowled around in the tall grass near by, blaming a skulking hyena for the theft. Then he found one of the skins. It had been dragged to the edge of a thicket. He got a flashlight from his tent and went back to look for the other skin. From the very spot where he had been standing two minutes before, he was startled, when he flashed on his light, by a pair of eyes that glowed like green coals.

He yelled for one of the boys to bring his shotgun. A boy came running. Babe, however, arrived at the same time and grabbed the weapon. John held the light on the target as Babe blasted the two eyes out. The range was only about 30 feet. With a coughing snarl, a big leopard went straight up into the air like a tomcat stung with an airgun.

There is hardly a meaner customer in Africa to deal with than a wounded leopard. The fact that this one was blinded by the shot (in examining the unfired load in the other barrel later, they discovered the boy had brought birdshot loads, not buck-shot) probably saved Babe and John from instant reprisal. Instead, they heard the cat thrashing in the grass and brush, all the time moving off. They had no stomach for crowding in close enough to finish the business, especially in the dark. The snarling eventually died away completely. They went back to the tents. Before turning in, however, John paced the distance from the tent in which they had eaten supper to the spot where the skins had been drying. It was just seven paces. The leopard had slyly stalked up through camp to within 25 feet of them in order to make off with its own supper: the oryx skins. It had managed to eat an entire one, salt and all, except for the tail and a scrap or two of the hide, before John interrupted the larceny.

John and Babe never did track down that leopard. There wasn't time in the morning; camp was broken and they moved out before daylight. It had become imperative to find water soon. They made a permanent camp in reticulated giraffe country, where they dug wells to insure a constant supply of water. The safari made that camp its headquarters for a month and a half, while it collected the five giraffe specimens.

The camp was also in lion country; they were hoping to pick up a fine maned male, but had no luck on that score. From the beginning of their stay in the region, they frequently heard lions roaring in the distance on the veldt. The first time John heard what is supposed to be the incarnate voice of the African night, he mistook it for a disgruntled stray bull from some native cattle *boma*, or corral, that was venting its feelings. He soon learned, however, what the noise really was.

One native in the safari, who was a renowned lion hunter, attributed much of his success to a lion call he had perfected. It consisted of a big clay jug and a tube of dry bamboo. The blast that resulted was usually a perfect imitation of a lion's roar. As proof that his call worked, he carried with him an ancient gun. Its stock had been half chewed off by a lion that had responded to his call and then charged him at close range. On this hunt, however, the call wasn't successful. Lions off on the plains would answer at daybreak and dusk, but they seemed to be wary. The native call was never able to lure a lion within gun range.

The lions, however, were bolder at night. Their forays then near the camp terrorized the stock. On two or three occasions some of the horses and mules broke their picket ropes and staged a real stampede when the cats skulked too close. The bad luck with lions persisted. In the seven months they traveled from Addis Ababa to the Kenya-Abyssinia border, the men were neither able to photograph nor get a good shot at a single one. When John finally got his first good look at one, it was by accident.

Word reached the base camp that there was a waterhole three days to the south that was frequented by an unusual concentration of zebra, giraffe, buffalo and other game. Since it sounded like a good place for pictures, John left the main party and headed down the dry bed of the Sagon River, taking along ten boys and two camels.

They found plenty of game sign. John and the gun bearer Syce (whom the whites had nicknamed Buck because of two prominent and very white front teeth) marched ahead. Syce was carrying the canteen and cameras, and John was toting his converted .30/06 Springfield sporter. The two men were acting as a spearhead to rout any lion or buffalo along the dry river bed that might make trouble for the little caravan.

The first day went well, but by the second afternoon they were running low on water. The two big canteens that were slung on one of the camels had developed leaks. By the time John made camp that second night, the water supply was down to the small amount in his own canteen, plus half a cup apiece for the natives.

The lack of water was affecting morale; camp that night was cheerless. John went out and shot a lesser kudu, knowing how the boys loved meat and thinking that it would bolster their spirits. They refused, however, to eat it, saying that the meat was too salty and that it would aggravate their thirst. John had been holding back the little stock of water, intending to start the boys off with it the next day. Before dark, however, the natives gathered around and pleaded so desperately for a drink that he gave in to them. To avoid the burning heat of the day, he marched before dawn and without breakfast, leading a thirst-tormented, depressed little band. The experience was so terrible that to this day it bothers him to see water spilling wastefully out of a faucet.

As the morning dragged on, he began to realize that serious trouble was shaping up; then shortly before noon as they rounded a bend in the river bed, the natives let out yells of delight. John was puzzled. All he could see was a little cloud of butterflies ahead, fluttering over a spot in the sand. There was no trace of moisture, nothing to hint that there was water near by, but the boys were besides themselves with excitement. They fell to their knees and started to dig. At a depth of three feet, muddy water began to seep into the hole. A little deeper they struck clear water, all they needed. There was cause for celebrating. They lighted a fire and cooked the kudu. They ate and drank their fill, then replenished the canteens. It was midafternoon before they pushed on.

John and Syce, half an hour in the lead, were taking a short cut across a wide loop of the river, walking on a dry sandbar close to the bank, when they jumped the lion. He was lying in a patch of shade under one of the many trees that overhung the bank. He must have been napping, since they had walked to

168

within 20 feet of him. When the lion bounded up, it seemed to John that he would have fallen over the beast with one more step.

Although it was the biggest lion he had ever seen, it was apparently as scared as John and Syce were. The startled beast ran the other way, crossing the river bed in long bounds. John had his rifle slung over his shoulder. Quickly unshouldering it, he snapped a shot at the rear end of the huge tawny cat just as it leaped up over the eight-foot river bank. The shot had no visible effect on the lion.

What happened next was an amazing demonstration of courage on the part of the native gun bearer. Syce carried a very small rhino skin shield. Its size was symbolic. To an Abyssinian, the smaller the shield the braver the warrior. Syce also wore a ring of buffalo horn in one ear—a decoration commemorating the fact that he had once killed a buffalo single-handedly, with nothing more than an old blunderbuss.

If one knows the meaning of the decorations, it is easy to identify the degree of bravery of a native Abyssinian hunter by what he is wearing. A bracelet of elephant ivory signifies its wearer has killed a lion. A similar bracelet of double width, grooved around the center, indicates a hunter has two lions to his credit. A visor of rhino skin tied around the head and turned up in front means that its wearer has exhibited the greatest degree of hunting skill and bravery—the killing of an elephant. Decorations, however, do not only indicate the killing of animals. Those warriors who have killed men often wear gruesome proof—the sexual organs of their victims—in the belief that the victims will not enjoy the privileges of manhood in the hereafter.

Syce ran up to John, kicked off his sandals and then showed

in pantomine what he intended to do. He would creep up the bank and stand there. If the wounded lion was waiting just beyond the rise, Syce's presence was sure to draw its charge. When the lion charged, the native planned to tumble back down the bank, giving John a chance to shoot.

John realized that the gun bearer had seen him consistently kill antelope and other game; Syce obviously believed the shot at the lion couldn't have been a miss. John, however, was not as certain. He didn't particularly like what Syce was suggesting. He hated, however, to give up the lion without making a decent try. To give himself all the room he could get, he backed as far away as the river bank would permit.

Syce padded off. He climbed the opposite bank as silently as a shadow and poked his head over. When nothing happened, he clambered up and stood in plain view. By that time John sincerely hoped that the lion had moved on. Syce finally climbed a low tree to have a better look. There was no lion in sight. John was relieved and disappointed; the two of them pushed on.

It was not until the safari got into Tanganyika, toward the end of the long expedition, that John finally got the chance to kill the lion he wanted. Lions were plentiful there, and they were as easy to approach as they had been wary in Abyssinia. On one occasion one of the hunters shot an ostrich and tied it down for bait. John set up his camera beside a thorn bush only 30 feet away from the bait and waited. Babe, Carey and Coates were covering him from three different angles.

In a matter of minutes, six lionesses and a big male walked out of a nearby *donga* and strolled over to the ostrich to feed. The cats paid no more attention to the photographer than to the bush he was standing beside. For an hour, while seven full grown lions, only ten paces away, growled over their dinner, John didn't move a muscle except to crank the camera.

"That's unpleasantly like sitting down right in the middle of them," he said, recalling the experience.

There were no specimens in that pride that the hunters wanted to shoot, so when the lions had finished with the ostrich, they were allowed to walk peacefully back to the donga. At the next camp John shot a good maned male. It was lying out in the open, and he walked up within 50 yards and killed it with a 150-grain solid point bullet from the .30/06. Unknown to him, there were four or five other lions lying near by. At the report of the shot, they jumped up and ran, all except one gaunt female. She lay down again in the dry grass with just her eyes and ears showing. Lashing her tail, she growled threateningly. When the hunters tried to move closer, she charged.

Since she wasn't large enough to be included in the Museum's lion group, they jumped up and down, waving their hats and yelling, and bluffed her out without having to shoot. Although she stopped her charge, the cat was reluctant to leave the dead male. It took the hunters an hour to drive her off. Only then could the job of skinning get under way.

While in Tanganyika, the safari saw as many as 60 lions in a day; the hunters took the six they needed in one week, choosing the specimens as carefully as a woman shops for a new dress.

After getting the lions, they went after buffalo. Crossing back into Abyssinia, they found prime buffalo country near the Kenya border. The big, black brutes were all over the area; it was a wonderful change after the fruitless months they had spent hunting for them in Tanganyika. They stampeded one big herd, saw a number of sizeable bunches, and looked at some good heads, but did not get a shot.

Then one morning John and George spotted a lone bull coming across a grassy opening, headed for a thicket where he was going to lie up for the day. His sullen, truculent character was immediately apparent to both of them.

"There's a widow maker," John whispered.

They had drawn lots at breakfast, and George had won the shooting privileges for that day. They had waited a long time for this chance. The bull looked exactly like what they wanted. George was eager to get a shot in, but he restrained himself until the buffalo was 70 yards off. Then he slammed in a heavy bullet from his 9.3 Mauser. It hit in the shoulder, a bit too high to be fatal. The bull wheeled and ran. George fired again. The shot had no apparent effect on the buffalo. The shooter yelled for John to back him up.

John was carrying his .30/06, loaded with 220-grain solid bullets. Unlike most sportsmen, he considers the metal-jacketed service bullet the ideal load to use against most of the world's trophy game. With it he has killed almost 300 head of big game, including elk, bear, caribou, moose, mountain lion, sheep and goats, and kudu, eland and African lion, and has lost only one cripple. That was an oryx he wanted for camp meat; it got into a herd and he couldn't single it out. He admits readily that the solid bullet necessitates the careful placing of shots; however that's a prime requirement anyway in shooting museum trophies.

John shot at the running buffalo. The impact of the hit drove the beast to its knees, but it got up again. John fired three more shots as it plowed through a small thicket; each of them spanked up dust from the black hide. Now he had only the rear end of the brute for a target. When the buffalo kept going, he knew that his last three shots had not done any major damage.

John and George wanted that bull as much as they had wanted anything else they had encountered on this safari. The hunters had come a long way to find the perfect specimen—this buffalo was it. When they examined the track, the two men found that it was strewn with blood. With the wish fathering the thought, they told each other the brute was as good as dead. He had at least five bullets in him, maybe six, and the first one each had fired were in vital spots. They both agreed that the buffalo couldn't go far or give them any real trouble; the time to go after him was right now.

John, George and the gun bearers got down on hands and knees and crawled into the jungle into which the buffalo had disappeared. The blood spoor led them along a twisting game trail. They realized later that their decision to track the wounded buffalo through the brush was reckless folly, a suicidal action. At the moment, however, it had seemed reasonable.

George took the lead. His bearer and Syce came next and John brought up the rear. When tracking a wounded buffalo in the brush, one place is about as safe as another. They moved very slowly and very carefully; it took them half an hour to go less than 200 yards. The heat in the thicket was stifling; sweat streamed off them. The only sound that broke the stillness was the loud pounding of their hearts.

Then in the dense green wall ahead John saw a patch of black. He didn't wait to identify it further. He raised up on one knee and shot twice. The buffalo went crashing away. John was sure it was carrying two more bullets now, but if they had done damage there was no sign of it.

The certainty that the wounded bull was still on its feet

and able to run had a pretty chilling effect on the hunters. They talked it over in whispers and agreed that it was too late to back out. With extreme caution, they crept ahead once more. At the end of another half hour the blood sign faded out.

They had come to a fork in the narrow game path they were following. Now they stopped for another brief council George was sure the buffalo had gone to the left. He started that way; the two bearers inched along behind him. John never knew why, but he stayed at the fork. In the stillness, he was straining his eyes and ears for a clue when suddenly he heard a low moan from the trail to the right.

Whipping his head around, he was surprised to see the buffalo standing in the edge of some thick stuff not more than 50 feet away. Its murderous horns and muzzle were thrust belligerently out of the brush. Camouflaged by light and shadow, the animal had evidently been standing there while the two men held their whispered conference. The realization made John's scalp prickle. There could be only one explanation of its behavior. John reasoned that by this time the bull was very sick, probably too badly hurt to take the initiative and charge unless prodded into it. The fact that the brute was still on his feet, however, meant he would have plenty of punch left once he got cranked up.

John made the first move. The buffalo was standing with its head high. John sighted on the side of it, meaning to drive his bullet in under the eye and up beneath the massive boss of the horns to the brain. It would have been the best shot possible under the circumstances, but the thick cover and peculiar light caused him to misjudge the bull's position. Actually the buffalo was facing him head-on; John thought it was standing broadside. The shot hit exactly where he intended, but the heavy bullet, they later learned, only ranged back along the neck and came out behind an ear, inflicting little more than a deep and painful flesh wound.

The new pain, however, touched off the buffalo as a match ignites a powder keg. The enraged brute reared up on his hind legs, pivoted and went crashing through the brush. Its

target was George and the two bearers. It had had them located all along, and it realized that they were closer and easier to get at than John.

At the place where the buffalo was hiding, the two forks of the game path paralleled each other and were only a few yards apart. The animal was on the men in several jumps. Tangled in vines and wait-a-bit thorn, George never even had the chance to get his rifle to his shoulder. It was all over very quickly, but for two or three seconds George and the two natives were sure their time had come.

John had the bull in sight all the time, and he sent another shot at the heart as it rushed the three men. George said afterward the huge black body seemed to spin in mid-air as John's shot hit home. The tracks showed that the buffalo had been just eight feet from the three men when the shot had deflected its charge.

The buffalo wanted to get at John now. Nobody would have believed that this big animal had eight or nine heavy rifle bullets under its thick hide. John knew he had made all the mistakes he could afford. This shot had to kill, or else. He stood squarely in the path of the charging buffalo, waiting for the one sure chance.

Hemmed in by green jungle on either side, there was room at the fork where John was standing for him to jump aside. He took in the situation with a flick of his eyes, holding his rifle on the onrushing bulk of black bull. Four paces away from him, it lowered its head, ready to catch up and toss the man. As those terrible, curved, black horns went down, John poured his shot over them into the top of the buffalo's neck—the spot into which a matador drives in his sword. Then John jumped aside so fast he went out from under his pith helmet.

It clattered to the ground, and the buffalo's forefeet came crashing down on it. The brute could have easily turned and had John on his horns with one lunge, but it was too far gone now to hunt the man down. As a last attempt at revenge, the buffalo stood goring and pawing blindly at the ground. Then it collapsed slowly, settling to its knees and rolling heavily over on one side into the brush.

George called John's name in a voice strained with foreboding and dread. John shouted back. Then he stepped out into the trail beside the dead bull and sat down very heavily.

The head of buffalo is over John's fireplace now in his home in the suburbs of Chicago. To this day, he refers to the bull as "the widow maker."

Search for a Boy

ON THE opening morning of the 1956 deer season Earl Harmon, his wife Helen, his 14-year-old son Earl, Jr., and his 16-year-old kid brother Ralph, were camped in a tent just inside the west boundary of Seney National Wildlife Refuge in the Upper Peninsula of Michigan. The huge refuge, a waterfowl sanctuary open to deer hunting, lay south of Highway M28 between Seney and Shingleton; it consisted of 96,000 acres of marsh, pond, timber, bog and swamp, which were laced with ditches and creeks and dotted with small islands of dry land, most of it roadless. The Harmons had entered it on a rutted truck trail, driving their panel truck three and a half miles in from the main road.

The Harmons were from the downstate city of Lansing. Earl Senior was a fairly experienced woodsman who had hunted and trapped in northern Michigan, Minnesota and Canada on and off all his life. Helen Harmon had spent several seasons in the Michigan deer woods, but this was the first trip of that kind for Ralph and Earl, Jr.

They ate a hearty breakfast of bacon and eggs and pancakes early, so that when light began to break over the swamp they were ready to start hunting. Helen, Ralph and Junior, as the family called young Earl, chose stands not far from camp, where they had seen deer sign the day before. Earl left them, driving the truck a mile or so down the trail to a spot he thought might be even more promising.

179

There was an inch or two of wet snow on the ground, but the day was warm and sunny and the snow started to melt almost at once. About an hour after daylight Helen heard a noise behind her. Turning her head, she saw an 8-point buck staring at her, only a few yards off.

"He was right over my shoulder," she said later, relating the incident, "and I couldn't get twisted around."

The buck spooked and lit out, and her shot, fired from an awkward angle, went wide. Disappointed and disgusted, she settled back, hoping for a second chance. It was Junior, however, not his mother, on whom luck smiled next.

About an hour after Helen had missed the deer, the boy heard two shots rap out just over a ridge from his stand, and seconds later something big and black came barreling across the hill, running straight at him. Although he had never seen a bear in the woods before, Junior didn't hesitate to act. He was carrying a 20-gauge Stevens single-barrel, loaded with a rifled slug. He slapped the slug into the bear at very short range, and the animal changed ends and hightailed it for the thick swamp at the foot of the ridge.

Junior's first deer hunt was off to an exciting start. He found puddles of blood on the track and followed it. It turned out the bear had nothing worse than a flesh wound, for the boy's father crossed the track by accident on a patch of snow five and a half miles away the following day. Although the bear was still bleeding a little, it was traveling steadily. Evidently the wound was not giving him much trouble.

But Junior supposed he had inflicted a mortal injury. He trailed the bear into the swamp for close to two miles before becoming concerned about the possibility of getting lost, then gave up. He figured on getting his dad to help him; they would go back later in the day if the snow lasted. As he was following his own tracks back to his stand, he had no way of knowing that he wouldn't see his father again for the better part of a week.

A couple of hours after noon Helen and Junior, drenched to the skin from melting snow, decided to return to camp and dry out for an hour. They found the tent deserted, but it was not surprising that neither Earl or Ralph had come in, since they had all been carrying apples, cookies and candy bars that morning. It had been agreed that they wouldn't come back to camp for lunch.

Junior and his mother went out again about three. It was only a short time until dark, so they walked less than half a mile from the tent. Helen picked a stand in a clump of pines on a low ridge, and sent the boy on to another clump a few hundred yards ahead.

They sat on their stands for about an hour without seeing game. Junior suddenly realized that the afternoon light was starting to fade. It was at this point that things went wrong. All his life he had been afraid of the dark, obsessed with that inexplicable, haunting fear that is buried deep in many of us. In the Harmon boy's case it was acute. At home he wouldn't step out of the house at night without a flashlight. As the dusk deepened, he began to worry that his mother might go back to camp without him, leaving him alone in the darkened woods. Merely thinking of that possibility made him decide on the spot to leave his stand and rejoin her. Junior was a real beginner in the woods. When he started back he didn't hesitate for a second, striking out confidently . . . in the wrong direction.

Before he had gone far he came to the edge of a dense, wet swamp. He turned back. Inadvertently circling, he encountered the swamp again. Now, scared and rattled, he resigned himself

181

to the fact that in order to get back to camp, he would have to cross it. He plunged in, clawing through alder and willow thickets, wading into icy water above his knees, fighting desperately to beat the darkness he dreaded, which was closing in quickly around him.

At full dark he stumbled up out of the swamp onto a low sandy ridge, scattered with a few pine trees. He was really afraid now, his mind ablaze with every tale he had ever heard of bears, wolves and the nameless terrors of the woods at night. But he was also exhausted. Finding a big pine with a canopy of low branches growing almost to the ground, he crawled underneath, stretched out and fell asleep.

Earl Harmon, Jr., 14, was now hopelessly lost in the 150 square miles of tangled swamp and marsh and forest that comprise the Seney Refuge. There was not enough snow left for searchers to follow his tracks. Worse, his frantic parents had no idea of the direction their son had taken. The date was Thursday, November 15. Winter was close at hand by that time in the Lake Superior country. The weather and the other factors of the situation were all against the boy.

He was dressed warmly, but not warmly enough for the ordeal that lay ahead. He was wearing three pairs of cotton blue jeans, a cotton flannel shirt, a light waterproof jacket, a heavy insulated outer coat with a parka hood, heavy wool socks over a light inner pair, and insulated boots. He had only one glove. He had lost the other while tracking the bear and had forgotten to pick up another pair at camp.

As for equipment, he had little that could be helpful to him. He carried his shotgun and nine shells, but he had no knife. Since he had not learned to use a compass, he didn't carry one. But worst of all, he didn't have any matches. He had argued with his parents that he wouldn't need them, since he didn't smoke. Junior realized now that until found he would have to face the November weather without fire.

When the light began to fade that afternoon Helen got up from the stump where she had been sitting and shouted for Junior. When he failed to answer, she walked to the clump of timber where he had gone. Her anxious calling from Junior's stand brought no response. When she could find no trace of the boy, she had to conclude that he had wandered into the woods and was probably lost.

She had made her way out to the truck trail and turned back toward camp, shouting Junior's name at intervals as she walked. There was no answer. It was pitch dark by the time the lighted tent loomed up at the side of the trail. At the tent she found double trouble. Junior hadn't returned to the tent, and neither had Ralph. Earl and Helen concluded they had two lost boys to find.

Returning to camp about four o'clock, Earl had busied himself with chores. He was preparing supper when Helen showed up, and was beginning to worry about the other members of the party. Helen's story confirmed his fears. They were comforted somewhat by the fact that both boys were missing. They assumed the boys were together. Actually, three days would pass before they learned that was a wrong guess.

Earl didn't bother to eat supper. After hanging a gas lantern on a tree near the tent, he started to drive back and forth over the rutted trail, honking the horn of his truck as he went. Every now and then he stopped to fire a shot. Earl had no way of knowing that by that time both Junior and Ralph were too far into the depths of the swamp to hear his signals.

A party of hunters from Detroit, camped near by, soon

learned of the Harmons' troubles. To help they drove into
Seney and spread the alarm. In less than half an hour, some
Michigan State Police were at the camp, ready to do all they
could; however, the organized search couldn't be undertaken
until morning.

Lost hunters aren't a novelty in Michigan's deer woods.
Most of the time they are found. Now and then they aren't.
The dangers of being lost are well-known and understood by
the public; consequently, the whole state hangs anxiously on
every report of a person lost in the woods. The report about
the two youths who had become lost in the vast reaches of Seney
swamp stirred public concern deeply. The plight of Junior and
Ralph generated banner headlines in Michigan papers and in
others far beyond the state's borders that cold November Friday. But there was action, too. All the machinery of a region
that was used to conducting full-scale rescue operations was
thrown instantly into gear.

The search got under way shortly after daybreak. State
police, conservation officers and fire wardens (the latter two
groups including experienced woodsmen who knew every foot
of the Seney country) headed up a posse of 100 volunteers,
which began the slow tedious job of combing the big swamp.
A state police plane flew a grid pattern overhead; the planes of
the Schoolcraft County Squadron of the Civil Air Patrol joined
in, some of them piloted by men giving up their own deer
hunting to lend a hand. The seven CAP pilots would burn a
thousand gallons of gas before the search was finished.

At the outset, the ground searchers agreed on a set of signals: two shots if the boys were found and four to call off the
search. The signals were ostensibly workable; however, the
shooting by hunters in the area, who were not involved in the

search, proved distracting. Despite this, the big search party worked through the bogs and marshes and ridges all that day. At nightfall Friday there was still no trace of either boy.

It was a clear night with little wind, but the temperature dropped far below freezing. The leaders of the search and its participants, as well as all who were following its progress, wondered how long the two boys could hold out in such weather. How were they surviving the long, cold hours of darkness? Were they wandering farther into the morass during the day? How were they enduring this ordeal which many thought would make short work of an older man? A persistent, bitter doubt began to gnaw at the optimism of the searchers. Rain and snow had fallen. Wouldn't the exposure to the cold, plus hunger and fatigue have taken their toll by this time? Doubt, however, never touched Earl. They'll be found in time, he assured Helen over and over again. They had to be. He spent his days with the search party, and at night after the searchers had disbanded, he went back into the swamp by himself, shouting the boys' names, probing behind logs and stumps with his flashlight looking for tracks, only to tramp back to camp long after midnight to catch two or three hours of sleep. At daylight, he was up and ready to join the others again.

Signs were posted on the boundaries of the refuge reading "Lost Boy—No Hunting." Every effort was made from then on to keep hunters out of the area. A Coast Guard helicopter from Traverse City joined in the search, reinforcing the state police and CAP planes, and by Saturday the ranks of the ground party had grown to 175.

Ralph Harmon found his own way out of the woods on Sunday morning, and it was only then that the searchers learned that the two boys had not been together. Ralph was in better physical shape than one would have expected from the report he gave of his ordeal.

Ready to go back to the tent the first afternoon, he had lost all sense of direction. He was carrying a compass but became confused as to which way camp lay. Like many an inexperienced hunter, when the compass failed to tell the story he wanted to believe, he decided it was out of order. Later he discarded it outright.

He struck into the timber in the wrong direction, much as Junior had, and kept going until darkness halted him. He was without matches, but was carrying a lighter. When he tried to use it to get a fire going, however, it proved to be either out of fluid or out of flint. In any case it would not light, and that ended his hope of a fire.

He had slogged through the swamp by day, trying desperately to find his way back to camp. The first night he slept under a pine tree. The second he found a sheltered spot beside a log, and on Saturday night he had the good luck to stumble onto a hollow log that was big enough to crawl into. It kept him warm that night, in spite of the sharp cold and the light fall of snow.

By a strange bit of irony, all day Saturday while Ralph was traveling due east through the swamp, he was hardly more than half a mile ahead of a group of searchers who were walking in that same direction from eleven in the morning until dark. Late in the afternoon the helicopter flew over him, and he waved frantically with a red handkerchief tied to the barrel of his .35 Marlin; however, by that time the search party was so close on his heels that the pilot of the whirlybird mistook him for one of the searchers and droned on.

Sunday morning Ralph decided to turn back west. The

'copter had come from that way and gone back that way. It seemed logical to believe that the camp or at least a road lay in that direction. He had crossed a deep drainage ditch late the afternoon before. In recrossing it, he found boot tracks in the fresh snow on the west bank—the first human footprints, apart from his own, that he had seen in 60 hours. Those tracks were like a lifebelt thrown to a drowning man; Ralph followed them until they led him out to the truck trail where he met members of the search party who hustled him off to a Munising hospital.

Now that the searchers knew that the 14-year-old Junior was alone in the swamp, their concern mounted. The posse dwindled to around 50 men that Sunday, because garbled reports had circulated that both boys had been found. By Sunday night, however, the true story had gotten around; Monday morning the crew was back in full strength. State police and conservation officers had been called to join in the search from as far away as Detroit and Lansing. The feeling was growing that the search must succeed within the next day or two if Junior was to be found alive.

Now, as if they had not already had enough bad luck, the Harmons got another shock. Helen received word that her father had died in Lansing. Knowing that she was needed urgently at home and that she couldn't actually take part in the search for Junior, she left camp reluctantly on Sunday afternoon. The distraught woman was conducted downstate by a relay of state police cars, leaving her husband to carry on at the camp for both of them.

The state police persuaded Earl not to go into the woods with the searchers on Monday. The strain, the sleepless nights and the terrible worry were taking their toll, and the officers figured he had about had it. So they kept him in a car and made him take it easy. But when the day's search ended and darkness fell over the swamp, he went in with his flashlight to search, alone, as he had done each night since the two boys had become lost. That night the bulb of his flashlight burned out sometime after midnight, and he was forced to work his way back to camp by moonlight.

Earl was still confident that his boy would be found alive. His faith never wavered; neither did Helen's. Earl knew from personal experience what it was to be without food and without fire in sub-freezing weather, and therefore knew how long a human can survive under those circumstances. During the days and nights of searching for Junior, Earl kept remembering similar days in December, 1944. He had been one of eight men cut off from their unit in a Belgian forest during the Battle of the Bulge. The group had taken refuge in an unheated cellar. Surrounded by enemy forces, the survivors had managed to hang on for 17 days until they were able to rejoin another unit. Eight men had gone into that cellar, two had come out alive. The bitter cold and the effects of unrelieved hunger, mostly the latter, had killed six men. But that had been a siege of 17 days. The boy can last at least a week and possibly much longer than that, Harmon assured himself again and again during the search.

Not all the other searchers, however, shared Earl's confidence. Although they were still doggedly plodding through the swamp from daylight to dark, few had any hope that Junior Harmon would be found alive. By Monday the search was in its final stage; it was now actually a search for the body of a dead boy, a frozen body huddled behind a log or under a tree somewhere in the recesses of the great marsh. The odds were poor that even a find of that kind would ever be made. Nearly 200 men walked through the Seney by compass line that Monday, five paces apart and always within sight of each other. They peered and probed into every sheltered spot where a lost boy might have lain down to spend his last night on earth.

Shortly after Junior had stretched out under the sheltering branches of the pine to get some sleep that Thursday night, a cold rain had begun to fall. Wet and chilled and wretched, he awoke sometime before midnight and got to his feet and walked to warm up. He was too miserable to be much afraid of the dark. He stumbled along, keeping on the ridge and avoiding the swamp, until he had warmed up enough so that his teeth stopped chattering. Then he crawled under another tree to rest again for a short time.

He followed that routine until daylight: sleeping in short snatches until the cold and wet woke him up, walking the chill off, huddling under a tree once more. Toward the morning the temperature dropped, turning the icy rain to snow. There was half an inch on the ground when the gray and cheerless day broke. The tree branches glittered under a coat of ice an inch thick.

The boy hadn't really missed not having any supper the night before, partly because he was scared and upset, and partly because he had been able to munch on cookies and apples and candy bars during the afternoon. By Friday morning, however, he was hungry; his hunger grew worse as the day went on. He tried to fill his empty stomach by stopping often to drink water. After that first day, however, the lack of food didn't bother him much.

Junior walked through the swamp all that Friday, trudging and stumbling from one ridge to another. At dusk he found a small island of dry land that had a clump of three or four ever-

189

green trees on it. Growing close to the ground, the trees effec-
tively broke the cold wind. He crawled into the center of the
clump and sat down to face his second night alone in the woods.
The dark no longer frightened him. For a time he thought about
his father and mother and Ralph back in camp. He knew they
would be worried and looking for him, but he didn't see how
they would ever find him in this wilderness. When darkness fell
he curled up on the ground and went to sleep.

He slept soundly through most of Friday night, awaking
with the first light Saturday morning, refreshed and ready to
tackle once more the problem of finding his way out of the
swamp. During the night his clothing had dried; now he was
warmer and more comfortable. The lack of food, however, was
beginning to tell. He had to stop frequently to rest that day on
the dry islands that dotted the swamp. Patches of snow still
covered the ground in spots, and two or three times he crossed
tracks in it that looked like his own, but he couldn't be sure.
Late in the day he found and recognized the clump of trees
under which he had slept the night before. He realized then
that he was walking in circles; however, he wasn't sufficiently
experienced in handling himself in the woods to know how to
avoid this error, which so many lost men make.

For Junior Saturday night was much like the two that had
preceded it. He found a sheltered spot under a tree and was able
to sleep, in spite of the cold. It snowed toward morning—a
light fall, but heavy enough to cover the tracks he had made
the day before. By now Junior had given up all hope of being
found or getting out alive, but this realization never caused him
to panic. He never cried. He saw a plane overhead that day, the
first he had noticed, but it was too far away for him to signal.
It didn't occur to him that it might be a search plane.

When he awoke Sunday morning he felt too tired to walk; however, he made himself get up and move on. With his energy just about sapped, Junior moved slowly now, even on the open ridges, and he only covered a little ground that day. Late in the afternoon he came to a stream about 15 feet wide. By that time he was too tired to take precautions, such as keeping dry. He plunged into the waist-deep, icy water and waded across. He dragged himself out on the far bank and continued to walk a while, but his pants and flannel shirt felt so heavy that he stripped off the wet shirt and outer pair of jeans and tossed them into a hollow stump.

He spent Sunday night just about the same way as he had spent the others. At dusk he crawled out of the swamp onto a dry ridge, and lay down beside a log. Although the weather was cold and stormy, he slept and afterwards couldn't recall suffering during the night. In all likelihood, he had been too weak by that time to feel discomfort.

Junior's endurance was running out; his days of wandering through the swamp were over. All day Monday he stayed on the ridge, immobile. His only movements were the few short trips he made down to a small creek at the edge of the marsh to drink. That night, for the first time since he had become lost, Junior slept in the same place in which he had lain the night before, beside the sheltering log. When he awoke on Tuesday morning, he was too weak to get to his feet.

The youth had managed to get through four days and five nights in the open, without food, without dry clothes and boots and without adequate shelter. But he had taken about all he could of the bitter cold, the freezing rain and the snow, the endless tangles of swamp and marsh and the torture of wading through the maze of icy streams. Yet he still didn't break down and cry.

A couple of hours after he awoke Tuesday, he began to be tormented by thirst. Since he couldn't stand, he had to crawl on his belly down the slope to get a drink from the little stream there. As he was starting to crawl back up to the sheltered spot beside the log, a Civil Air Patrol plane spotted him. The pilot, Lieutenant Howard Tennyson, and his observer, state trooper Harold MacNamara, saw Junior's small figure, face down, pitiably shuffling crablike in the snow.

Junior had seen planes in the air two or three times each day since Saturday, and once he had even noticed a helicopter hovering over the swamp; however, none of the aircraft had come close so that he could hope to attract its attention. Now he heard the roar of a plane that seemed to be coming straight at him. Was he imagining the sound of that engine? Or was he going to be found, after all? Hope blazed up in him. He tried with all his strength to stand up, but he couldn't. In desperation, he rolled over on his back and waved both arms frantically as the low-flying plane thundered over the tree tops. It zoomed up, turned in a tight circle and came back; Junior realized he had been seen.

The first thing that MacNamara threw from the plane was a small bottle of matches. Junior watched it fall and land in the snow at the edge of the marsh. He started to crawl to get it. Next the trooper tossed a roll of toilet paper out of the plane, holding on to the loose end. As it fell, the paper spun off the roll, laying a white ribbon across the swamp. This marker insured that Junior's location would be easy to spot. Tennyson climbed a few hundred feet and droned in lazy circles over the ridge on which Junior had been spotted.

"We've found him, we've found him," he was saying into the mike of his radio. In response to the report, police cars on the roads in the area of the refuge roared into action.

Young Earl was able to retrieve the bottle of matches and then crawl back to dry land. Breaking off a handful of dead twigs, he struck a fire, relishing the first real warmth he had known since Thursday as it began to seep into his cold-stiffened hands. He couldn't find enough dry wood, however, to keep the fire going, and it guttered down and died. No matter now. Junior knew rescue was at hand. There would be warmth and food and a bed to sleep in, as well as a reunion with his father and mother. He had dreamed of all these things during these past five days, but never expected to experience them again.

There were 28 men in the rescue party. They piled out of cars from the end of the truck road and started the final dash on foot through the swamp to reach Junior. The boy's father was in the last rescue car. Running in heavy boots, splashing through waist-high water, he overtook and passed 25 of the others in his excitement. As he neared a ridge, he saw the streamer of toilet paper draped across the brush there. He knew he was close. He shouted Junior's name. The was a faint answer from somewhere up ahead. As he hit the dry ridge with two other men, he saw Junior sitting on a log, stoically waiting for them. The boy managed a grin as they raced to him. The long search was over. It was none too soon. Eighteen inches of snow blanketed the Seney that night; more fell every day during the rest of the week.

The searchers quickly built up a roaring fire, cut the boots from the boy's swollen feet, stripped off his wet, brush-torn clothing, wrapped him in dry coats, and gave him coffee, a little milk from a thermos, and an orange. Because he had been without nourishment for so long, the food reacted violently in his stomach; however, by the time a stretcher had been rigged from poles and coats, he felt well enough to be lifted onto it and to start the three-and-a-half-mile trip through the swamp to the road. He was carried in relays by the rescuers. In less than three hours after the plane first sighted him on the snowy ridge, Junior was resting between warm blankets in the same hospital where Ralph was being treated.

Junior Harmon had lost 12 pounds during his five days in the swamp. His feet and hands had been frostbitten, but the case was not severe. All of Junior's fingers and toes were saved. On December 2, when he was released from the hospital after a 13-day stay, the boy was almost as good as new, and eager to return home to Lansing with his father and mother and Ralph.

During the five days he was lost in the Seney Refuge, Junior had only wandered about four miles to the south, and three or four west. He was found three and a half airline miles from the Harmon camp. How many miles Junior had actually walked by circling through the swamp no one will ever know.

The Harmons' hunting season had certainly gotten off to an unhappy start, but it ended on a brighter note. Helen Harmon returned to the camp in the Seney to go hunting once more with her husband. One day before the season ended, she killed a good buck. Ralph, who was released from the hospital in time for the season's windup, knocked over a deer that same day. The last day of the season, Earl wound things up in a blaze of glory by flooring a black bear.

Only Junior Harmon missed out on the hunting altogether that year. When deer season opened the following November, however, he was ready to go back to the woods with his dad and make up for lost time. He was really ready, too. He had learned to read maps, to use a compass, and he carried matches at all times. If night should ever overtake him in the woods again, he knew what to do. Light a fire, sit tight and wait for the rest of his party to find him in the morning.

Foot Race with a Grizzly

IN SEPTEMBER of 1948, Howard Copenhaver and two of his brothers, Gene and Wendell, guided a party of six hunters from Cleveland, Ohio, into the mountains 30 miles from the Copenhavers' home ranch on the Big Blackfoot, in western Montana. They were out for elk in the Marshall Wilderness Area. They camped on Danaher Creek, at the head of the South Fork of the Flathead, in prime game country. Snow had come early. The ground was patched with three or four inches, enough for tracking, and the prospects looked rosy.

Late the second afternoon one of the hunters killed a nice bull on Hay Creek, about two and a half miles above camp. It was decided that Howard would have the job of bringing the carcass down to camp the next morning. At daylight he saddled his horse and started out in the direction of the kill, leading two pack horses—a full-grown elk is too much for one. He didn't want to leave meat lying in the woods any longer than he could help, on account of bears. An elk or deer left overnight is likely to be half eaten by morning.

The bears are more plentiful some years than others. That fall was a bad one for the beasts; they were hungrier than usual. The berry crop had failed, and every bear in the mountains was on the prowl day and night, hunting for anything that would fill an empty belly. So Howard wasn't surprised to see bear sign several times as he rode up along the creek.

Half an hour from camp he encountered a jackpine thicket

that was too much for the horses, so he tied them and went ahead on foot to find the elk and pick a trail for the horses up to it. He hadn't walked far when he crossed another fresh bear track, and the farther he went the more sign he saw. He began to think that if he found the elk in one piece he would be lucky; he started to hurry then, impatient to run off any bear and salvage what remained of the meat. But he was too late. When he got to the place where the bull had been dressed out, he found only a few leavings and a broad, telltale trail where a bear had dragged the carcass.

Howard was mad. What guide wouldn't be if he had outfitted a party of dudes, herded them a hard day's ride back into the mountains with all their supplies and gear on pack animals, set up camp and spotted his hunters in first-class game country, only to have a thieving bear lug off the first kill? He had blood in his eye and just one idea in mind. To get back what was left of the elk and do it right away. And at the same time, he would teach the bear a good lesson.

He had hunted all his life and outfitted and guided for close to 20 years. With that much hunting experience, he should have taken a second look at the bear tracks before doing anything else. But in his anger he overlooked that little detail. The sign he had seen farther down the creek had been made by a black bear, and he took for granted this was one of the same breed. He knew it was big, for the elk would have dressed close to 400 pounds, but it didn't cross his mind that the bear might be a grizzly.

The trail was easy to follow. The bear had taken the elk up and around the side of the mountain, and it had made easy work of the carcass considering its weight. After 300 yards the track dropped into a series of deep washes and then angled up a steep slope toward an isolated stand of thick spruce. Howard knew he was getting warm. No bear would take an elk through there. The bear had headed for that thicket on purpose, seeking a good spot to stop and cash in on its night's work. Howard would find the bear in there somewhere, with what was left of the loot—which probably wouldn't be enough to pack out. He was getting madder by the minute.

He stopped at the edge of the timber and went down on one knee for a look; it didn't take long to find what he was looking for. Howard saw a patch of dark fur move behind a log, 25 feet up the hill, and then he made out the outline of an ear and saw an eye staring in his direction. The bear had seen him first.

The rifle he was carrying was light for the job. One day many years before, as a boy, he had shot a box of 8 mm. shells at a coyote, which had been about 1,000 yards off. He hadn't killed the coyote. His shoulder had taken a pretty severe lacing, and as a result of that incident, he had developed the bad habit of flinching when firing any gun that slammed back at him. He had never been able to get over it; consequently, he stayed away from the wallop packers. Most of the time he toted a .25-35.

"I know it sounds screwy for a man in my business, but I prefer that little gun and do better with it," he once explained.

Howard knew a .25-35 really wasn't rifle enough for a big bear, even a black; however, he figured if he put the treatment in at the butt of an ear he wouldn't have any trouble. The ear was conveniently exposed over the log, and Howard was close enough that he couldn't miss. As he brought the rifle up, slow and easy, the bear came up, too, fast and hard. It reared on its hind legs and let go a deafening roar that was enough to knock Howard's hat off.

That roar told Howard, a little late, that he wasn't dealing with a black. He had walked into a grizzly as short-tempered as a stick of dynamite, and all of a sudden the little .25-35 seemed hardly more adequate than an airgun.

They looked each other over for maybe ten seconds, although to Howard it seemed like a quarter of an our. He noted that the bear was a handsome old sorehead, with a dark, silver-tipped coat that shone like frost, even in the dim light under the spruces. He held the gun on the bear and waited for it to make the next move, hoping it wouldn't be in his direction. When the grizzly didn't move, Howard took a cautious step back, and then another. He kept backing up until he had a reasonable amount of yardage between him and the timber. The bear stayed put. Howard dropped down into one of the washes and then got out of there fast. He didn't intend to lead the pack horses back to camp unloaded, but he knew he would have to kill the bear if he wanted to claim the elk.

He decided to come in from above and try for a shot in the open, at something more than 25 feet. He made a big circle and worked warily down the hillside to the upper edge of the spruce thicket. He thought he knew exactly where he would find the bear. It would be on the elk or beside it, waiting. But he had figured wrong.

He was down on one knee again, trying to see under the branches, when the silvertip cut loose another roar so close behind him that he thought it must be looking over his shoulder. He spun around and stared the bear in the face. It was just six yards off.

It wasn't a pleasant sight. The grizzly was up on its hind feet like a man, eyes blazing, lips curled back and emitting a rumbling growl, the hair on its neck and shoulders all standing the wrong way. It looked 20 feet tall, and it scared the hell out of Howard.

He had no chance of stopping the bear at that distance with the .25-35, and he knew it. No matter where he hit it, the bear would keep coming until it got to him. There was only one thing to do: find a tree and, if he could reach it in time, climb. A grizzly can't follow a man into a tree.

It was a slim chance. There was just one tree of the right size anywhere near, and it was between him and the bear. When the hunters paced it the next forenoon, they found Howard had been ten feet from the tree, the grizzly eight. Howard didn't have time to think. He said later that he must have acted from instinct, or from something he had learned in the Army—that a surprise offense is often the best defense. He yelled in the bear's face and jumped for the tree.

His yell must have startled the grizzly for a second or two as much as the bear's roar had startled him, and Howard's headlong rush kept it off balance just long enough. He was already in the tree when the grizzly started for him and out of reach when it arrived.

When he started his dash he had had his rifle with him, but when he reached a safe perch about 20 feet off the ground, he missed it. Looking down, he saw the rifle lying two or three yards from the base of the tree; the bear was smelling and cuffing at it. He realized later that no man could climb at the rate he had to and hang onto a rifle.

The grizzly blew its cork over his getaway. It danced around under him, bawling and raging and clawing bark, tearing up the ground like a baited bull. Howard was high enough in the tree to see the elk carcass in the spruce thicket, about 20 yards away, and he kept hoping the fresh meat would lure the bear off. Finally it did. The grizzly turned and lumbered down the hill, stopping every few steps to throw a warning growl back. When it reached the elk, it lay down beside the carcass. The bear, however, kept its head turned toward the man.

The first thing Howard wanted to do was to get his rifle.

He gave the bear a quarter hour to settle down and get interested again in the elk. Then, he started inching toward the ground, lowering himself from one branch to another.

He was careful to make no noise; the bear paid no attention until Howard was almost down. Then suddenly it seemed to sense what was going on. It lurched to its feet with a bawl of pure hate and came streaking up the hill. A bear can really cover ground for a short distance when it wants to. Howard went back up the tree a lot faster than he had slid down. The bear tramped around again under him for a while, grumbling and snarling, but finally made up its mind it couldn't reach him and went back to the elk.

Howard gave the grizzly time to lose interest once more, and then he tried another cat-footed descent. The same thing happened. The grizzly let him get down to the lowest branches, then it bounced up and came raging for him.

It's hard to believe, but the man and the bear kept that up for more than seven hours, from half past eight in the morning until almost four in the afternoon. Howard lost track of how many times he went up and down the tree, but by late afternoon he was worn to a frazzle and realized that he couldn't keep at it much longer. Unless he succeeded in getting the rifle on the next try, he would have to give it up. And that would mean sitting in the tree and waiting for help to come from camp, a prospect he didn't relish. Gene and Wendell wouldn't start to look for him until dark, and Howard kept thinking how his brothers would probably blunder into the grizzly then. He wanted to prevent that. But how?

Unexpectedly, however, the bear's attitude changed. It must have been getting just as tired of chasing him as he was getting tired of climbing. Or maybe it merely became resigned to the situation—it couldn't catch Howard in the tree, and Howard wasn't going to risk coming down on the ground. As Howard started down for his final try, the grizzly, lying on the elk, was growling and blustering and balefully watching the man. When Howard reached the lowest branches, the grizzly stood up and bawled its resentment. But it seemed unwilling to be tricked into making any more runs up the hill, unless there was a fair chance of getting at the man. That gave Howard the opportunity he had been waiting for all day. When he had reached a point about his own height from the ground, he braced himself, legs tense and ready for a fast ascent. Cautiously he broke off a forked branch, reached out with it and raked the rifle up. He felt almost secure as he started back up the tree with the weapon in one hand.

But even before he was back on his perch, he knew he wasn't going to risk using his pea shooter on the grizzly, after all. There was only the slimmest possibility that he could kill it with one shot and, once it was hit and went off into the thick spruce, he wouldn't have a second chance. There was still Wendell and Gene to think about. If they came up along the creek after dark, hunting for him, the bear, unwounded, would be formidable enough. Wounded, it would be almost certain to kill one or both of them. Somehow Howard had to get out of this fix by himself, while it was still daylight.

During the day, he had looked the hillside over countless times, but now he took another look and thought he saw a way of escape. As near as he could figure, it was about 60 feet down the hill to the elk carcass, where the bear was lying. Thirty feet the other way, up the hill, there was another tree he could climb. Beyond that one was a third and a fourth, each a little farther apart. If he could make it to the first and then on to the others, by a series of dashes and climbs, maybe he could finally put enough distance between him and the grizzly so that the bear would stay with the elk and forget about him.

The first lap would be risky, but it was the only way to keep Gene and Wendell out of trouble. He would have 30 feet to cover, while the bear was coming 90. If he could get a running start, he figured he could make it.

He let himself down to the lowest branches. The grizzly watched every move he made, growling ominously. It took all the nerve Howard had to let go and drop to the ground. But once he was sure the bear wasn't going to get up before he hit the ground, he did it. He lit running. He heard a gruff bawl as the grizzly lumbered to its feet, and could hear it pounding up the hill in pursuit, but Howard's 20-yard start was too much for the animal. He was safely up the second tree before the bear got there, and he had even managed to get his rifle up in the tree with him.

The bear was snorting and tearing around at the foot of the tree, then after a few minutes, it gave up and went back to the elk. The next tree was about 50 feet farther up the hill. As soon as things quieted down, Howard dropped and went for it. It was duck soup this time. The silvertip again came charging after him, but it had too far to run now to cause Howard any real concern. It took four trees, nevertheless, and a total gain of 75 yards before the bear called quits. It chased Howard up those four, one after the other. When he came down from the fourth tree, the bear paid no attention.

To make sure, Howard backed away a few yards, one step at a time. When he saw that the bear stayed put, he took off up the hill, watching it over his shoulder. He made a wide circle to get back to the horses. Then he started for camp.

It was dark when he rode in. He had expected his long absence to have caused some anxiety, but nobody showed any. Somewhat to his annoyance, his story provoked more amusement than sympathy. It took him a couple of hours to convince his brothers and the rest of the party that he wasn't just spinning a tall yarn. It was hard for them to believe that a bear would keep a man in a tree for a whole day. They finally were convinced that Howard wasn't kidding. Before turning in, the party had everything arranged for settling the grizzly's hash the first thing the next morning.

"If he's still there," somebody put in.

"He'll be there," Howard predicted grimly. "He won't move ten yards as long as there's a mouthful of that elk left. If we want him, we'll have to run him out."

The six hunters and three guides left camp at sunrise, following Hay Creek for a couple of miles and then riding straight up the mountain to get around the bear. Howard remembered an open ridge that gave a clear view of the creek bottom, the hillside and the spruce thicket. They planned to post the hunters along that ridge, then Howard, Gene and Wendell would move down on the grizzly and flush it out. By following this plan there was no way for the grizzly to catch them with their guard down, as it had caught Howard the morning before. It was a good plan and it would have worked, except for one thing they hadn't figured on. Nobody needed to go into the brush and flush that grizzly out. It was ready to come out without any prodding.

After tying the horses a safe distance back in the timber, they moved down to the ridge on foot. Most horses will bolt at even grizzly sign in a trail; they knew they would be asking for a big package of trouble if they tried to take them anywhere near the bear. The men were bunched on the ridge 300 yards from the thicket, getting ready to send the hunters to their places. The bear was nowhere in sight. Then all of a sudden they heard a commotion on the hill below.

"Here he comes!" Gene yelled.

The grizzly had boiled out of the thicket and was plowing up the hill at a dead run, apparently hellbent on tackling all nine men. They let it come 30 or 40 yards, waiting to see if the bear really intended to go through with it. Then, pulling up and standing on a fallen log, the grizzly reared high on its hind legs for a better look. The men didn't wait any longer to see what the bear would do next, but they all agreed afterward that it would have kept coming if they hadn't killed it. The grizzly acted every bit as reckless and vindictive in the face of nine-to-one odds as it had the day before when it had put a lone man, without a gun, up a tree and kept him there for nearly eight hours.

Gene got in the first shot. He belted the bear in the shoulder with a 180-grain core-lokt from his .30-06, and the grizzly dropped off the log with a bellow that shook the ground. But it didn't go down. It whipped around, bit at its shoulder, pulled itself together and came pelting up the hill again, straight at them.

Then the mountain fell in on the bear: the men were yelling and shooting and the horses were rearing and plunging. Three or four good solid hits were scored.

The bear kept its footing through the whole barrage, but seemed to be aware that it was licked. Still roaring defiance, it wheeled and started the other way as Wendell spiked it in the back of the head with a softnose. The grizzly was less than 100 yards from the party when it went down.

When they skinned the bear they found it had copped nine hits, of which any one, given a little time, would have been fatal. The grizzly, however, had stayed on its feet until that final shot which had blown its brains apart. A bear that's aroused enough to attack man can absorb an amazing amount of lead.

"I was glad I hadn't tried for him with the .25-35 the day before!" Howard confessed when it was all over.

The hunting party went back later to look over the sign and piece together how the bear had managed to surprise Howard the day before. It had come out of the thicket on the downhill side, picked up the man's tracks and trailed him as a hound trails a rabbit, following him while he circled to get above the thicket. It had stalked Howard with the stealth of a cat. The snow was frozen and crunchy, yet the grizzly had crept up to within 18 feet of him—they paced the distance between Howard's tracks and the bear's, and even measured it with a steel tape—without a whisper of sound. Then it had stood up and bawled, ready for the final rush. Some hunters say an unwounded bear won't stalk a man, but that one certainly did.

The pelt squared nine feet, as beautiful a silvertip skin as any of the men had ever seen. They estimated its weight at not less than 800 pounds. Some of the eastern hunters, who had hunted Alaskan browns, thought the grizzly would go better than that. Whatever the bear weighed, it's a safe bet that no meaner grizzly ever roamed the mountains of Montana.

Strike of Death

BERNARD RUMSEY, an experienced snake hunter, had started out that summer morning in 1947 on a somewhat unusual errand. A group of women at the shop where he worked in La Crosse, Wisconsin, wanted to go after wild blackberries but were afraid of snakes. The thing that bothered them most was that they wouldn't know a rattler if they saw one. Bernard had tried to describe them and explain how they differ in appearance and habits from bullsnakes, blacksnakes and the other harmless kinds, but he could see he wasn't getting it across very well. So finally, to drive home his nature lesson and help the gals along with their berrying project, he said he would bring in a live rattler so they could both see and hear the kind of snake they had to watch out for. It should have been an easy promise to keep, after all the snake hunting he had done, but what he failed to reckon with was a combination of bad luck and a second of carelessness.

It was not an ideal time to pick up a rattler on short notice, since the month was August. Rattlers are often hard to find after they have scattered away from their winter denning places. But Bernard Rumsey knew a couple of spots that could be counted on to produce a snake or two most any time between May and the fall frosts, so he loaded his equipment in his car and started for a hilly area with big limestone outcrops, where he had always found rattlers.

He had along two items of equipment that he didn't usually

carry. One was a live-minnow cage to bring the snake home in. The other was a pair of long-handled tongs that a friend had rigged up from old pliers, for picking up live snakes. He had never used the tongs, but this seemed like a good time to try them out.

He found a snake on the first hill, but couldn't get a grip on its neck with the homemade tongs. He finally lost patience, pinned it down with a stick and had it in the cage in short order, but he had been a little rough about it. Looking the snake over, he saw it was injured badly, and he didn't think it would survive.

He decided that if he wanted to be sure of a live snake when he got back to town he had better catch another, so he drove to Burns Valley and there on the farm of a family named Knifel he found a big timber rattler, close to four feet long. It was lying on a flat shelf of rock, with brush and vines behind and a crevice at one side it could slip into as easily as oil running down a trough.

The snake was full of fight. It whipped into an S-shaped coil the instant Bernard reached for it, rattling angrily. He made two or three passes and got the loop over its head, but he couldn't hold the loop in place. Finally he held the snake down with his hook-stick, careful not to injure it, slipped the loop around and drew it tight.

He had left the cage in the car, so he had to carry the rattler back by the loop around its neck. A snake can be strangled if not handled carefully; to avoid that Bernard stopped every little while to let the snake rest its weight on the ground and get its breath. Even so, he arrived at the car with a snake that appeared to be dead.

He took the cage out, nevertheless, and opened the cover, a small board that slid under two cleats. Next he lifted the rattler by the loop, dropped it in and slid the cover shut. Then he opened his old pocketknife to cut the twine. It was a simple thing to do, but for the first time in all his years of snake hunting he dropped his guard for an instant. He slashed at the twine. His knife was dull, and he failed to notice that the force of his strokes had pushed open the cage lid a couple of inches.

Bernard's right hand was directly over that narrow opening when the strike came. It was like forked lightning. The fangs were in and out of his hand, between the thumb and first finger, before his eyes could even register the flashing movement or the flat, triangular head.

Bernard had been hunting snakes for 35 years, and he shouldn't have been surprised. Under the law of averages, he was almost bound to be bitten sooner or later. But somehow that swift, wicked strike was the last thing he had expected, and the feel of the fangs in his hand astonished him more than it hurt, right then.

He had had an intense interest in snakes as far back as he could remember. When he was a boy of 13, his father was running a tavern in the little town of Chaseburg, in southwest Wisconsin a few miles from the Mississippi. The boy was doing chores around the place one morning when two strangers walked in. They looked ordinary enough, except for one thing. The younger man was wearing a wide-brimmed felt hat with a band of tanned rattlesnake skin. Sets of rattles were tucked under the band all the way around.

Bernard couldn't take his eyes off that hat. Here was something he hadn't encountered before, a professional snake hunter. To the gangling boy, who had been fascinated by snakes since he was old enough to prowl, the experience was like being presented to royalty.

It turned out the two were a father-and-son team by the name of Brown, from the Minnesota side of the Mississippi. Rattler hunting for bounty was their business. In the boy's mind they were the most important men he had ever laid eyes on. He stood around, gawking at the hat and listening to their tales; by the time they left, he knew what he wanted to be when he grew up.

He had one big hurdle to get over. His dad hated and feared snakes like nothing else on earth. He had brought Bernard up on tales of the dreadful things they were capable of, and wouldn't let the boy have anything to do with them. But Bernard managed to get around that and started hunting rattlesnakes the year after he met the Browns.

The Rumsey family moved to a farm that spring, and one morning in May, while Bernard and Hugh Allen, the hired man, were planting corn they stopped at the end of the row to rest.

"I'll bet the rattlers are all out of their dens by now. Let's you and me take tomorrow off and go snake hunting," Hugh said, looking off across the broken hills toward the river.

Bernard had never wanted to do anything so much in his life. He cornered his father at the supper table, and they made a deal. If Bernard would walk four miles to the other side of Dodson Hollow to pick up the ten dollars a neighboring farmer owed Mr. Rumsey for a colt, his father said that Allen and he could hunt snakes on the way home.

The hired man and the boy left right after breakfast, poorly equipped to go snake hunting. They lacked boots, hooks, killing sticks, lunches, water and all the other essentials. In fact they had nothing but their enthusiasm, and pocketknives with which they cut green walking sticks.

Bernard had no luck collecting the money, but maybe that was just as well. He would probably have lost it anyway, in the excitement that followed. He and Hugh headed home by way of a long timbered hogback, with exposed rocks and ledges on the south slope. They climbed a fence along a sheep pasture and then started into an area of vines, brush and tall grass.

"This is where we'll find 'em," Hugh said confidently.

They hadn't gone 50 yards when Bernard saw something just ahead, glistening in the sun on top of a pile of loose rocks. He took a couple more steps and made out the heavy, sinister coils of a big rattlesnake. It was the first he had ever seen, and he didn't hestitate a second. He yelled for Hugh.

But just then there was a thrashing in the grass and vines downhill, where Hugh was probing around a big outcrop.

"Darn near stepped on one!" he yelled.

He clobbered his snake with his stick, and then started up the slope to give Bernard a hand. The boy was inching in, a step at a time, when there was a sudden movement in the grass close by his feet, and he heard a harsh, shrill buzzing that he had no trouble identifying. A second snake, coiled beside a rock only three or four feet away, was rattling in sullen irritation. He smacked it a clout that took the fight out of it, and two or three more blows finished the job. He had killed his first rattler, and he couldn't have been more proud if he had just been elected President.

Hugh disposed of the third snake, and then they found and killed a fourth. Later they located the denning place, a small hole leading back into the rocks. For many years that den remained one of the most productive spots for Bernard. He liquidated 22 snakes there one spring day, all in an area no bigger than an average city lot.

Before that first hunt was over, he and Hugh found a second den, a woodchuck hole with flat slabs of rock scattered over the ground around it. When they trudged home in mid-afternoon, tired, thirsty and soaked with sweat, they had accounted for 11 rattlers, then worth two bits apiece in bounty money. It had been quite a day for a kid just starting out.

From that day on nothing interested Bernard as much as rattlesnakes, and hunting them held more thrills and excitement for him than any other sport. He hunted mostly timber rattlers. The marshland massasauga, a smaller rattler, also is found in a few areas in Wisconsin, especially on the old wing dams along the Mississippi and in the river bottom. He killed massasaugas when he came across them and cleaned out dens of them a time or two, but he never made a hobby of going after them.

He hunted timber rattlers in Iowa and along the Root, Whitewater and Zumbra Rivers in Minnesota, as well as in Wisconsin. He also went out for prairie rattlers a few times in the Dakotas, Montana and Nebraska, but hunting them was not like hunting the timber variety, and he took only a few. At one time, when he was with the U.S. Cavalry on the Rio Grande, he had a go at diamondbacks, but without any success. Most of his hunting was done in the limestone bluff country along the Mississippi and such other rivers as the Wisconsin, Coon, Kickapoo, La Crosse, Trempeleau, Black, Yellow and Chippewa in his home state, and that's where his best kills were made.

Several Wisconsin counties have for years paid a bounty on rattlers. It ranges now from as little as ten cents to a quarter of a dollar for young or unborn snakes up to a dollar for adult specimens. But Bernard didn't hunt for the bounty. He hunted for the kick he got out of it.

He kept no accurate record of the number of snakes he killed, but during his best year he and a hunting partner accounted for as many as 500, and another year two of them took about 300. He estimated that he averaged around 75 a year from the time he had begun hunting them, for a total of between 3,000 and 4,000 snakes—maybe two miles of 'em if they were laid nose to tail in a straight line. The biggest he ever took measured an inch over five feet and had 12 rattles. Full-grown timber rattlers average a foot or so shorter than that.

Bernard still considers rattlesnakes the most dangerous creatures in the United States, and about the most unpredictable. He has killed a dozen at a den within a quarter mile of a farmhouse where the farmer said he had not seen one around his place in ten years. Again he has known them to turn up on doorsteps, pump platforms, under loose boards and rose bushes, and even in outbuildings and hay barns a mile or more from the nearest winter den. Like all snakes in the northern states, rattlers gather at denning places in the fall, spend the winter in hibernation, come out as soon as the weather turns warm in spring, and scatter widely over the countryside for the summer. They are most often found in hay and grain fields, where they hunt mice and other small rodents. Berry patches also seem to have a strong attraction for them, probably because of the heavy cover and also because birds and their nests are plentiful in such places. The timber rattler feeds on birds whenever it gets the chance.

Bernard has had these snakes rattle and strike viciously in his direction when he was as far as two rods away. On two occasions he actually stepped on one, and once, while climbing a ledge, he put his hand on a snake without provoking a strike. Another time he came within kissing distance of a big one when he peered up over a little shelf of rock where he wanted to set a coon trap. The snake just lay and watched him until he ducked down out of reach.

All his experience tends to prove that nobody knows what an individual snake will do in a given set of circumstances. They vary as widely in their behavior as any other living creature. One will be sullen, mean, aggressive, with a chip on his shoulder, ready to fight at the drop of a hat. The next will be lazy, good natured, slow to anger, willing to let you alone if you'll do the same by him. Still another will be wary, retiring, almost cowardly, sliding for cover the instant he sees you move or hears the vibration of your footfalls in his neighborhood. Of course, in hunting them you have to watch out most for the bad ones; the best rules to follow are don't trust rattlers and don't take chances.

Bernard is convinced that the seemingly erratic behavior of some rattlesnakes is accounted for by the partial or complete blindness that comes on shortly before they shed their skin. The skin loosens around the lips and over the eyes (snake eyes are lidless and the thin transparent scale that covers them comes off with the rest of the skin), and the eyes cloud over and turn a milky color as a result. At such times the snake apparently can see little or nothing at all. Some turn hostile, treacherous and vicious; others seem to go out of their way to avoid trouble, as if aware of their handicap.

A temporarily blind rattler gave Bernard one of the closest calls he ever had. He wasn't snake hunting that day, but stumbled onto the snake by accident. It lay beside a big rock and, the instant it heard him coming, it rattled and crawled under the rock. He cut a stout green stick and tried to punch the snake out, but it wouldn't budge. When the snake finally quit its incessant, dry buzzing, Bernard decided he had killed or disabled it, so he lay flat on his stomach to look under the rock. The rattler struck like a whiplash, but missed the man's face by inches. Next it came slithering out and took off, looking for a safer place. Not until Bernard overtook and killed it did he discover the milky-white, opaque eyes that explained why Bernard hadn't been bitten.

He thinks one of the most dangerous situations a man can get into is to encounter a rattlesnake that has no rattles. It has happened to him twice. Both times there was clear evidence that the rattles had been cut off, either by a snake hunter with a peculiar sense of humor or for bounty purposes. In each instance, the snake did its best to warn him off, coiling and vibrating its tail vigorously, but of course making no sound. One was lying in a little pocket on the face of a ledge, about waist high. Bernard was approaching the spot when his intuition warned him to stop and look ahead. It was a timely warning, too; if he had taken another step, he would have been within easy reach of the sullen, soundless coils.

For several reasons, Bernard does his snake killing with a cane about three and a half feet long, cut from a green sapling, rather than with a gun. One is that, in addition to the cane, he has to carry a hook-stick for getting snakes out of tight places like crevices and from under rocks. That means both hands are full. Also the two sticks are a help in poking into crannies and in keeping his hands off the ground (a first rule in snake hunting) when climbing outcrops and ledges. Finally, the hunter knows that when he runs into a den, the less noise he makes the more rattlers he will collect. For this reason, a stick is a far more effective weapon than a gun.

The biggest kill Bernard and three partners ever made in

one day took place on a hot morning in midsummer when the best time of year for running into groups of snakes is supposed to be past. When the four hunters drove to the home of one of the town-board members at noon to collect their bounty, they dumped 90 rattlers, old and young, in his yard. The man's eyes almost popped out of his head.

Despite all his experience in snake hunting, Bernard knew little about snakebite until that day in August when the captive rattler struck him as the lid of its cage slid back. He had always imagined the bite of a venomous snake would be extremely painful, like the sting of a hornet greatly intensified, but in his case it was nothing of the kind. He felt a swift, pricking sensation, as if his hand had been pierced by briars or two very sharp needles (as in fact it had), but the hurt was nothing compared with that of a bee sting.

His first reaction was surprise. Being bitten was something he had been careful to avoid ever since he went snake hunting the first time, and he couldn't believe it had actually happened. Then he became scared, scared bad. He knew he had been injected with the full dose of venom from a four-foot timber rattler, injected deep in his hand. Men had died from that within an hour.

He knew, however, better than to give way to panic, which has probably killed almost as many snakebite victims as the venom itself. By the time he had jerked his hand away, the snake was halfway out of the box, and the first thing he did was get it back into the box and shut the lid. Then he started thinking about first aid.

He was in a bad fix on that score. His knife was too dull to make the sharp cuts over the bite that were needed and, even if he had made them, he didn't have a suction cup. Because of bad teeth, he was afraid to try sucking the venom out, figuring the poison might do more harm in his mouth than in his hand. Nor did he have a bandage or material for a tourniquet.

Strangely enough, he still felt no pain. His hand was turning numb and starting to swell around the fang punctures, and minute by minute he could feel the numbness spreading up the wrist and into the arm, but the bite didn't hurt as he had expected it to.

Before he had time to shout for help, Mrs. Knifel came out of the house to see what was going on. He instructed her to knot his handkerchief tightly around his wrist to form an improvised tourniquet. Then he jumped in behind the wheel of his car and headed for the nearest doctor's office, in the town of Bangor. But almost before he was out of the Knifel yard, he realized he might not make it, so he pulled up half a mile down the road and asked one of the Knifel boys, working in a field there, to take over.

The doctor in Bangor had never treated snakebite and had no serum, so Bernard phoned a friend and asked to be driven to a hospital in La Crosse in a hurry. When he reached the hospital, his hand, which was swelling fast, had a curious flabby feeling, as if the flesh were turning to jelly. It also felt far larger than it actually was.

He still had no pain, but waves of nausea were beginning to sweep over him, and he vomited time after time. His mind was getting hazy, and a burning thirst made him ask for water after each spasm of retching. Sitting on the edge of a small table in one of the emergency rooms, he heard the doctor who was working over him tell a nurse to take his pulse. The doctor's voice sounded pretty far away. The nurse felt for the pulse.

"He doesn't have any," she said in a startled tone.

As she picked up his hand to examine the fingernails, he blacked out. That was about three in the afternoon. Bernard had been bitten about two hours before; the venom was beginning to take full effect. He regained consciousness around eight that night. His two children, Mary and Junior, were sitting beside his bed, waiting to see whether he was going to wake up or die in a coma. He recognized them, but he was too sick to remember what had happened. His right arm felt like a wooden stump, and from then until he left the hospital three weeks later, he could move it only by picking it up with his left hand.

His great need now was for snakebite serum, but only one tube was available in that entire part of the country. A wholesale drug salesman told Bernard weeks later that he had stayed up until long after midnight that night, making phone calls and trying to locate more, but without success. Win or lose, Bernard Rumsey was fated to battle out his ordeal with a woefully inadequate supply of the one medicine that would have helped him most.

"If you're going to hunt venomous snakes, keep a stock of serum on hand at all times and never go out without a good first-aid kit," he told friends much later.

When Bernard awoke the next morning, he was very sleepy and foggy, but the nausea was gone. His hand and arm were swollen to twice their normal size, but there was no longer any sensation of flabbiness. In fact, all sensation was gone; his right arm and hand were just so much dead weight.

The doctors were giving him sulpha drugs and penicillin. After coasting along for a couple of days and beginning to feel a little better, he decided maybe he was going to make the grade after all. He still had, however, a long way to go. Huge, bloody blisters appeared on his hand and arm now, the biggest covering the entire right palm. Between the blisters, the skin turned black and green. The discoloration spread up the arm and across his upper body, all the way to the center of his back and chest.

"You'd have had to see me at that stage to realize just what a dreadful thing snakebite is," he said later.

At the end of a week, he imagined he was about well. Then, almost without warning, the most deadly effect of all showed up. The venom of rattlesnakes, copperheads and water moccasins—the three most common poisonous snakes in the United States—kills its victims by destroying their red blood cells, whereas the venom of cobras and vipers attacks chiefly the brain and spinal cord, stopping the heart. The rattler poison which Bernard had absorbed had been working in his blood stream all that time, and now it came close to finishing him. He went suddenly into a very severe chill, and the doctors called for emergency blood transfusion.

Two transfusions exhausted the hospital's supply of his type of blood. Junior and Mary were rushed to the hospital, but theirs didn't match. Then a friend asked for help over a local radio program. Within an hour, 13 men who worked with Bernard and who had the right type blood were at the hospital waiting to donate.

Bernard was given ten transfusions. Then, when he was on the road to recovery once more, gangrene threatened his right arm. When the doctors broke the news that they might have to amputate it, he had one short word to say about that —no! A week of hot applications and more penicillin turned back the gangrene, and he walked out of the hospital after three weeks with both arms and hands intact. His right arm, however, was still useless and its skin was sloughing off. It took weeks of effort and exercise before he could use the hand on that arm to feed himself.

That was in 1947. He has never recovered completely and never will. As long as he lives that arm will be tormented by arthritis, and the hand was left so crippled that he can no longer write letters, shoot a pistol, or grip tools. The doctors told him his hand was mostly scar tissue; it still has the feel of something half frozen.

While Bernard was in the hospital, he promised his family and friends that his snake-hunting days were over. When warm weather came the next spring, however, a friend asked him to go out after rattlers just once more, to make movies. He could no more refuse than he could quit breathing. For ten years after being bitten, he did not miss a season.

Snakebite is a terrible ordeal to live through. Bernard Rumsey knows that first-hand. But to him snake hunting is the most exciting sport on earth and always will be, and there just wasn't any use in his trying to swear off.

The Circuit Rider

ROY MURRAY had a phone call one cold, February evening at his ranch, a few miles south of Boulder, Montana. It was his brother, Clarence, phoning to report that hunters had found the track of a big tom mountain lion at the head of Johnny's Gulch, on the divide between Crow Creek and Boulder River, about 14 miles west of Roy's place. The big cat seemed to be traveling in the direction of Roy's ranch. Clarence, who had killed quite a few lions on his own, couldn't get away. Did Roy want to take a crack at it?

He certainly did. Roy hated mountain lions and that hatred was to goad him for a week during the toughest hunt of his life—a hundred and fifty-mile track over rough country in bitter, winter weather.

" I challenge any man who has trailed lions through game country, and seen what they kill and how they go about it, to say a good word for them," Roy had said. "No other predator in the West can match 'em for blood lust and cruelty. Lord knows a wolf is bad enough—sly and slinking and vicious, but he's honest on one score. He kills when he's hungry, eats what he kills and is through killing until he gets hungry again. A lion will kill day after day out of sheer devilishness, for the fun of killing, taking nothing but a little warm blood and the liver and moving on to look for another victim. He has to be hard-pressed if he comes back to eat cold meat and it's lean pickings when a full-grown one doesn't account for 300 kills a year.

They don't kill clean, either. They maul and torture and play cat and mouse."

Roy had been born in Minnesota and had grown up in Canada. As a young buck of 18, he had homesteaded a ranch in Boulder Valley, in southwestern Montana, 40 miles east of Butte. Anything outdoors was his dish. In addition to ranching, he hunted and trapped, having killed as many as 90 coyotes many winters. In all, he had liquidated 17 wolves, including nine that had come into the valley early one fall in a pack and started killing cattle. Before spring he had had the last one of them. He had knocked off so many bears that he couldn't remember the count. For years, however, he had specialized in hunting mountain lions, which were abundant in that section of Montana. In addition to the state bounty he received for his kills, Roy collected prize money from local stockmen who paid to keep the cats thinned down. His score was 40 in all, 11 of them taken in one winter. Perhaps the reason for Roy's success was that he never quit on a lion track. Whenever he got after one of those brutes he felt a grim urge to keep going until there was one less mountain lion to torture and kill deer and cattle in Montana.

It was that feeling, plus a persistent hunch that he was going to overtake the cat just over the next hill, that would bait him on during this hunt.

He left the ranch at sunup the morning after his brother called, riding a tough little horse, with his dog, Cougar, trotting behind. He had no inkling of what he was getting into and was carrying only his .30-30 Winchester snugged in a saddle boot, and four sandwiches. It seemed like it would be just a routine hunt. The weather was crisp and clear and there was plenty of snow to make tracking easy. Roy had never taken more than a couple of days to kill a lion, and this hunt would be no exception. He was sure he would be home at the latest by the next night.

Cougar was an airedale-collie cross, combining collie sense with airedale spunk. He would hunt anything his boss put him on, lions one day, ducks or prairie chickens the next. But on this hunt Roy had no intention of turning him loose until the cat was jumped, for he knew from experience that cold trailing a mountain lion with a dog is more likely to result in a dead dog than a dead lion.

They covered the 14 miles to the head of Johnny's Gulch before noon and found the track where the hunters had reported it. Roy decided it had been made two nights before, and was sure he would catch up by the next day. How wrong he was on both counts, Roy was to find out later. Clarence's report that the lion was a big bruiser was confirmed by the track, which looked almost as big as the horse's in the eight inches of soft, dry snow.

He had followed the trail less than an hour when he found the first kill—a fat little two-point buck. It was dressed out about as neatly as a man could have done, and nothing had been eaten but the tastier parts of the entrails. He cut a tenderloin out of the frozen carcass to take along for the dog.

He trailed the lion all that afternoon, pushing the horse at a steady clip. Darkness overtook them at the head of Crow Creek, miles from anywhere. Roy's camp that night was pretty cheerless, but he didn't mind. A man can stand one night of discomfort to do away with a lion, he reflected. He had no shelter, no blanket and no horse feed. He built a fire under an overhanging shelf of rimrock and spent the night dozing and waking up. After putting hobbles on its forelegs, Roy had turned the horse loose to crop browse around the makeshift camp. He and Cougar went without food. He still expected to kill the lion the next day, but at the same time something warned him to save his sandwiches and to wait until the next day to feed the dog.

It was a still, cold night, but even colder weather was on the way. He rode away from the dead fire at the first crack of daylight the next morning, eager to get the hunt over with. The lion had been traveling east. Now he looped back west and went through the head of Dry Creek, past Mud Springs, and on toward Leslie Lake. There, in late afternoon, Roy came on the lion's second kill—a big doe. The cat had again eaten only the liver and a few other odds and ends. After scratching a thin covering of snow and pine needles over the carcass, he had then pushed on. An hour after Roy left the doe it was dark. He rode into a stand of timber and made ready for another chilly night in the open. He figured he had ridden 50 miles in the two days, every mile uphill or down, and he no longer felt so sure about when he'd catch the cat. He realized now that the track at Johnny's Gulch might have been four nights old instead of two as he had first thought.

It went down below zero that night. Roy hunched in front of his fire, shivering, half asleep and half awake. He still had no real feed for the horse. It would have to make out another day on a bellyful of green twigs. Roy had not had anything to eat since riding away from the ranch. By now his sandwiches were frozen as hard as rocks, and he decided to hoard them as long as he could. He did break down, however, and whack off a piece of frozen tenderloin for the dog.

Chilled, stiff and hungry, Roy climbed into the saddle again as soon as there was light enough to ride. The lion was still traveling west. About noon the track came out on an open shelf above the ghost town of Elkhorn and Roy could see where the cat had stood and looked down on the empty mining camp. Then the lion had circled off through the old Elkhorn cemetery, and Roy could tell by the signs that he had climbed up on the biggest tombstone and sat for a while like a cat on a cushion, planning fresh devilment.

Roy crossed Elkhorn Creek that third afternoon, coming back toward Boulder Valley. It was at the head of Sloan's Canyon that he found the cougar's third kill. This one was a big six-point muledeer buck. Roy could tell it had given the big cat a bad time.

From the top of a little open park on a steep hillside Roy saw an odd snake track leading down the hill, as if a log had been dragged through the snow. Then he spotted the dead deer at the edge of the timber on the far side of the park. It was easy to put the story together. The snake track had been made by the lion stalking the buck, out in the open, belly to the ground. He had come up on his toes and started his rush when he was about 60 feet away. The tracks showed that he was on the deer before it had known he was coming. But the buck had fought back. The brush was trampled and the snow was torn up and bloodstained over a 20-foot swath that ran 50 feet down the hill. Handfuls of deer hair lay on the clean snow on both sides, raked out by the lion's hind feet as he rode the buck down.

He had landed on the deer's shoulders and, hanging there, had bitten into its neck, behind the ears, in an effort to crush the spine. All the time his hind feet had been working like power flails, ripping the buck's loins open and letting its guts trail out. The terrified deer had plunged and bucked and fallen and then staggered up again.

That's how a mountain lion kills. It's been said many times that if a cougar had nerve enough to tackle humans no man could ride safely through country where he ranges. Given courage to match his strength, a cougar would be as dangerous as the Indian tiger.

Roy treated himself to a sandwich at that point and Cougar ate a good meal of frozen venison from the deer's carcass. Again, the lion had eaten only the liver. As for the horse, it was grabbing a mouthful of browse at every chance. Roy would gladly have traded his other three sandwiches for a bucket of oats, but there was no chance of that.

He crossed Rawhide Creek late that afternoon and at dark rode up to an abandoned forest ranger's cabin on the headwaters of Muskrat Creek. At least he would have the shelter of four walls and a roof this third night, and a stove for his fire. It was a good thing, too, for the weather was turning steadily colder. He even found salt for the deer loin he had been saving. This meager supper was the nearest thing to a square meal he had eaten in three days.

A hunter of less determination would have been ready to quit by that time. Roy was putting in long, hard days, riding as soon as it was light enough to see each morning, staying in the saddle until he could no longer see at dusk. The country was rough and the weather was bitter. He had already trailed the lion some 70 miles and there was no knowing how far it was ahead now or how much longer he would have to follow it. But the idea of giving up never crossed his mind. Sooner or later, if he stayed on the track he would catch up with the cat. Nothing else counted.

The fourth morning the track again swung west, crossing first the main highway and then the Great Northern Railroad at the mouth of a tunnel, six or eight miles above the town of Boulder. Roy noted that old mining camps must hold a fascination for the lion. He had seemed to go out of his way to drop over on Comet Ridge where he had stood and looked down on the ghost town of Comet. The cougar hadn't been more than

a quarter mile above the camp where two or three families were still living. Probably there had been lights on in the houses, but that wouldn't have bothered the cat. Roy saw he had stayed and looked things over until he was satisfied. It was easy to picture him, crouching in the starlight on a snowy shelf of rock, sniffing and wrinkling his murderer's muzzle at the smells that drifted up from the houses.

Roy observed that the lion had gone south from Comet Ridge, across another road and up Galena Gulch. At the head of the gulch, late on the fourth afternoon, he rode onto the fourth kill. The cat had taken a big cow elk this time and, in doing so, had done a strange thing.

As Roy reconstructed the struggle, the cow had in tow a husky calf going on a year old, and the lion had climbed up on a big rock and lain in wait for them. When the cow was feeding close enough he had sprung from his perch, fifteen feet above, knocking her off her feet as he landed on her shoulders. The cow had floundered up and managed to run about 50 yards before going down for keeps. It was clear to him that at every futile jump the cow had made, the lion had clawed out big tufts of her hair.

By all the rules, what the lion should have done next was to kill the calf. But it hadn't. The perplexed calf, on the other hand, hadn't known enough to spook. Apparently it had stayed within sight while the snarling lion fed, and was still hanging around when Roy rode up over half a day later. He heard the calf bawling before he found the kill. The lion had stayed only long enough to eat the liver of the cow and then had gone off without molesting the youngster.

The trail went into high country after that. Roy followed it across Berry Meadows and on for eight or ten miles through the roughest, most heavily timbered places he had seen on the hunt—into canyons and gulches, up slopes as steep as a house roof, and down hills so sheer that the horse slid about as much as it walked.

Then Roy got his second break. At dusk he followed the cat out to another ghost town, at the old Shield and Ironside mine. No one was living there, but there was a good cabin that Roy used for a camp when he was herding cattle in summer. There were no supplies for him, but he did have hay and oats cached there and he was able to give the hungry pony its first real meal in four days. Roy broiled a couple of thick venison steaks for himself and the dog. After they had eaten, he felt that they were all in better shape now than they had been since the hunt began.

The fifth morning the lion kept to broken country almost as if he knew he was being followed, but Roy was sure that wasn't so. The lion crossed Little Boulder and Bigfoot Creeks, and along the Bigfoot made his fifth kill. This time it was a yearling cow elk. Once more he ate only his victim's liver and then went on. But now, for the first time since Roy had taken the track, the cougar wasn't satisfied with a single kill in a day. In late afternoon Roy trailed him out on the timbered slope of Bull Mountain above Whitehall Valley, and there, where a little spring creek trickled down an open hillside, the lion had found three or four cattle watering. He had crawled down on them, picked a yearling steer and killed him as easily as a cat knocks over a chipmunk. The terrified steer had run out onto a patch of ice, slipped and gone down, and the cat had ripped it open before it could get up again. Apparently beef liver suited the lion as well as deer or elk, for he had cleaned up that part and left without touching the rest of the carcass.

Roy was again in home territory. He had tracked the lion more than 100 miles in a trail that formed a sprawling letter S, through country he was familiar with every foot of the way, to within six miles of his own ranch. So at dusk, for the first time, he left the track. He didn't go home, however, not wanting to put extra miles on his horse. He owned an unoccupied place with a good house and barn down in the foothills on the Boulder River side of Bull Mountain. It was rented to a friend who used it as a fishing and hunting camp and kept it well stocked with supplies. Roy found everything he needed there. He, the pony and Cougar spent that fifth night in clover.

A skiff of snow had fallen just before dark. He picked up the lion track easily the next morning about where he expected to, in Mulvey Gulch, and an hour after daylight found a windfall under which the cat had bedded the previous day. There was snow in the track where it went into the windfall, but none in the track leading out! At last and for the first time Roy knew how much of a start the lion had. He was only one night ahead now.

By midmorning Roy was in Quinn's Canyon, less than a mile from his own place, but it was no time to think of home. He had business that he was hoping to finish before dark. He rode on and at the head of the canyon found what he had come to take for granted—the lion's daily kill.

It was a yearling mule deer, a doe, and, Roy could tell, the cougar had played with her and tormented her for a long time. The trampled snow was bloody and strewn with deer hair over a 100-foot area. From the tell-tale signs, Roy could see how the cougar had caught the deer, let her go, caught her again, pulled her down, let her up, mauled her and slashed her, until he had exhausted her or she had given up from pure terror. A greenhorn might have thought from the signs that the doe, which weighed under 100 pounds, had staged a battle royal with the cat. But for a seasoned hunter like Roy it was easy to see that the struggle had actually been deliberately prolonged as the cat played his horrible, bloody game before he killed his helpless prey.

The exercise must have sharpened the lion's appetite. For this time, he had eaten a good chunk of ham in addition to the liver. This was the only meat, aside from parts of entrails, that the cat had bothered with from any of the kills he had made while Roy was following him.

During the rest of the day Roy trailed the lion through McCauley Park, around the east slope of Bull Mountain and through Hadley Park, expecting to jump him every time he rode over a ridge. Roy knew that he couldn't stay ahead much longer. The track finally circled back to the place where the lion had killed the steer the day before. The track showed the cat had gone up to the carcass, smelled it, and then had turned and walked away without so much as touching any part of the cold beef.

At that point, with half an hour of daylight left, Roy quit the track for the second time. This track had taken six days so far, and Roy guessed he must be getting soft. But he would get Mr. Lion tomorrow, he prophetically promised himself as he rode away from the dead steer. He went down the Whitetail side of Bull Mountain to the Dave Connon ranch, where he was assured of a warm supper, a bed to spend the night in and plenty of feed for the horse.

The cat began the seventh morning by backtracking for a couple of miles. He had crossed the highway at the upper end of Whitetail Valley, gone up into the head of West Creek and there had made his first kill for the day—a calf elk. The lion was back in the groove again. He had eaten only the elk's liver, and then had struck out in the direction of the old Shield and Ironside mining camp, where Roy had trailed him three days earlier. They came together near there, late that seventh afternoon.

Riding down along the side of Little Boulder Canyon, in open country where the track was visible for a long way ahead,

Roy noticed his dog was beginning to work up steam for the first time. Cougar had trotted in the horse tracks for seven days, doing as he was told, biding his time. He had moved out in front only when they had come to bare ground where the wind had scoured the snow away. At these times, Roy had sent him ahead to smell out the track until it started in the snow again. But now they were getting warm and Cougar let his boss know it. His ears pricked up, he whined low in his throat, shivering with eagerness. He seemed to sense that the long ride was about finished and he could hardly wait to take on his end of the job.

Roy pulled up inside the edge of a belt of timber, quieted the dog, and had a long look at the track ahead. It went across the canyon and up a steep slope into a clump of young firs, 300 yards away. He knew the place well. The whole canyon was a natural lion hangout. On other hunts he had cornered two lions there but then lost them as they eluded the dog by taking refuge in the caves on the canyon wall.

The longer he studied the fir thicket, the surer he was that he could see signs of a fracas at the edge of it. The snow was trampled and torn up. The lion track went into the clump at that point but, so far as Roy could see, it didn't come out. If the cat was in the thicket, his going over there would probably spook him and drive him into the rocks. But alone, Cougar might be able to put him up a tree. Roy chewed on the situation for a couple of minutes and then waved the dog ahead on the track.

Cougar hit it like a steam calliope, bawling his lungs out. He streaked across the canyon and up the hill, not even hesitating at the edge of the thicket. He tore into the brush, chopping in gruff and angry tones. A big, tawny lion came out on the far side like a cannon shot. Roy had waited seven days to see that cat and he had never been happier about anything in his life!

There was no tree at hand big enough for the lion. He didn't dare turn and stand up to the dog, and Cougar was too close for him to make a run. The cat headed for the first place he could find, an outjutting slab of rock on the canyon wall 50 yards from the fir clump, springing up as if his heels were on fire. "This is the big, brave lion that has tortured deer and pulled down elk between two and three times his own weight," Roy murmured to himself as he watched the big cat.

The rock was too steep for Cougar. He danced around at the foot of it, fretting and swearing, while the lion crouched on the ledge watching him, growling in his chest, lips curled back. He loomed up like an alley cat on a pole and Roy could see a white patch under his chin, shining like a big silver medal in the afternoon sun.

The dog and cat were only about five yards apart, but about 250 yards from Roy. That's a long shot for a .30-30 with iron sights, but Roy didn't have much choice. If he tried to get any closer he was sure the cat would hightail it for those rimrock caves just the way the other two had. So he climbed off the horse, sat down in the snow and placed his elbows on his knees. Taking a very course bead, holding just over the top of the skull, Roy slapped a 150-grain dose of cat poison at the lion. It landed smack in that white breast patch, about a foot below where he had aimed. The cat fell dead instantly, and Roy reflected at that moment that it was a quicker end than the cat deserved, considering his tormenting, slow-death way of killing.

As the lion dropped off the rock, Cougar, all airedale now, nailed him. The two rolled down the hill, first with the dog on top and then the dead lion, until they lodged in a clump of brush. Cougar was still trying to convert 180 pounds of tough cat meat into hamburger when Roy rode up.

The first thing Roy did after tying up his horse was to look into the fir thicket to find out what the lion had been doing there and what had caused the fuss at the edge of it.

Inside, he found that the cat had been guarding a fresh kill—his second for that day. He had pulled down a two-year-old elk just outside the clump and dragged it in. Taken completely by surprise, the cougar had been lying on the newly killed carcass, eating a snack of liver, when Cougar had opened on his track, 300 yards down the canyon. Roy couldn't have timed the attack better.

After the week's ordeal, the horse should have been tired enough to have stood for anything, but Roy could neither get the pony up to the dead cat nor make it stand still in order to throw the carcass across the saddle. It hated lions as much as Roy did, only in a different way. There was fear mixed in the pony's aversion. Reluctantly Roy gave up the idea of packing the lion all in one chunk. Instead, he tied the horse a suitable distance away and went at the job of getting the pelt off. The green lion skin measured 9 feet, 2 inches, without stretching. He had certainly been a big cat and an insatiable killer. During the week Roy had followed him, the lion had made nine kills—four deer, four elk and a steer—from which he had eaten only a few pounds of choice parts. The rest had been left each time for the magpies and coyotes, as the cougar had moved on to make a fresh kill.

Roy had killed the cougar at four o'clock. It was dark, however, before he finished skinning the cat and was able to start the ten-mile ride to Boulder where the bounty office was.

He had another fifteen miles to ride after that before he could strip the saddle off the tired horse.

He was quite a sight when he got home. He hadn't shaved in a week and his face was streaked with the soot of open fires and smeared from eating half-cooked meat. His sleeves and pants legs were torn to shreds. But Roy felt fine. Nothing mattered except that he had killed another mountain lion— this one the most wicked killer he had ever trailed.

Arrow in the Night

BOB WARD was awakened out of a sound sleep and, not knowing what had disturbed him, sat up in his bag to listen. He heard a commotion about 150 yards off, which echoed loudly through the still night.

It was the last of May, 1955. Bob and his two companions, Clint Henry and Bill Davis, were camped in the open on that warm night, without a tent or shelter of any kind. For a few seconds it was quiet again, except for the heavy breathing of Bill and Clint, dead to the world in their bags on the ground beside him. Then, from up on the side of the cliff-like hill behind the camp, Bob caught the unmistakable sounds of a large animal moving through the brush, breaking twigs and rattling dry branches.

Bob's heart started to pound. He knew from the noise that it had to be either a moose or a bear. But it was unlikely that a moose would venture down such a steep, rocky hill. It must be what the three men had come to Canada for—bear.

They were camped in the Ontario bush about 45 miles northwest of Port Arthur. It was an unusual hunting party. None of the men carried a firearm, not even a handgun. Their only weapons were three hunting bows that lay strung and ready, with quivers of steel-tipped broadheads beside them, at the head of the sleeping bags.

Bob lived in Harbor Springs, Michigan, working as a ship's carpenter in a boatyard there. Both Bill and Clint were from

Midland, 150 miles to the south. Bob was Bill's brother-in-law and they had been hunting together for a dozen years. All three men shared a red-hot enthusiasm for bow hunting.

Bob had taken it up two years previously, for an unusual reason. He had served as a paratrooper in World War II and came home with injuries that caused several vertebrae in his back to slip out of place at the slightest twist of his body. This would happen if he just happened to turn his head quickly. Each time these dislocations occurred, the pain would knock him out. The condition had grown progressively worse. In casting around for a special exercise to strengthen the muscles of his back, he finally considered archery. His doctor was dubious about its therapeutic value.

"You can try it," he agreed skeptically, "but you better not spend money on a bow until we find out. Borrow one."

So Bob borrowed a battered yew, with a pull of 80 pounds, from a neighbor and started shooting. His back trouble ended then and there. But the archery bug bit him hard. After only a couple of weeks of preliminary practice, Bob took to the field for deer. He shot at two or three bucks that first season, but didn't hit anything. By the time the following season rolled around, however, he was better equipped and more practiced. In the interim, he had acquired a 50-pound-pull laminated bow, glass-backed, as fine as he could buy, and a supply of custom hunting arrows. He had also sharpened his eye by doing lots of roving and target shooting. Two weeks before the second season opened Bob burned his bridges by selling his favorite deer rifle, a .30-30. It would be the bow or nothing from that time on.

He hunted in the Upper Peninsula of Michigan for a few days, came home empty-handed only to go out the next afternoon and knock over a 140-pound doe on the Harbor Springs archery range. That settled things. Since then he had been committed to the bow, and his wife, who had never cared for guns, had taken up archery and found that she liked it about as much as Bob did. It was a sport they enjoyed together. Soon Bob sold his whole arsenal of seven rifles and shotguns.

With a deer to his credit, the next trophy he wanted was a bearskin rug. That was an ambition Bill and Clint also shared, so the three of them laid plans for a spring hunt in Canada. They had never hunted there, but decided on the Port Arthur area because friends who had made a trip into that country two years before reported that black bear was plentiful. The three hunters had no definite destination in mind and didn't plan to engage guides. Once they reached Port Arthur they would ask questions of local sportsmen, look things over and pick a spot.

They had left Harbor Springs four mornings earlier, crossing the Straits of Mackinac and heading for Port Arthur by way of Duluth and the International Highway along the north shore of Lake Superior. From Port Arthur they drove out 20 miles to Kakabeka Falls, where they found a woodsman who knew the country.

"Go on up to Jackpine," he advised. "You'll find as many bears around there as anywhere in this part of Canada."

It was 25 miles farther to Jackpine; the "town" turned out to be a general store plus a few cabins scattered in the woods. The Jackpiners, however, were helpful and the three men soon contacted a trapper who was willing to tell them where their chances would be best and how to get there. He told them to camp at a place called Silver Mountain, north of Jackpine and about four miles back from the road. To get there they would have to pack in, but the trip wouldn't be too tough, since there was an old logging road part of the way. He made it sound easier than it turned out to be.

Luckily, they had decided to do without a tent, since the weather was warm now, and had also pared their grub and equipment list to a bare minimum. All the same, their pack boards weighed between 70 and 80 pounds apiece when they were ready to start, a heavy load to carry over rough, rocky country grown up with thick brush and timber.

They had headed into the bush after breakfast on Memorial Day. Because of the tough going, however, it was half-past three in the afternoon before they reached Silver Mountain, tired and footsore. On the way, Clint had wrenched his back so badly that it would be three days before he would be able to draw his bow.

They picked a spot for camp at the foot of a sheer, 300-foot hill, with a little stream of clear, cold water 100 yards away. Making camp was a simple job. All they had to do was throw off their packs, unroll the sleeping bags and get a fire going for tea. After a quick snack, they went out to scout the country until dark.

It didn't take them long to decide that they had come to the right place. Although they saw no bears that afternoon, they did find, within 75 yards of camp, a used trail. Several times they saw tracks, dung and other fresh sign. They hunted hard the next day and again saw plenty of signs, but no bears. They turned in at dark, bone tired, and were asleep the instant they hit the sack. It was an hour past midnight when something jarred Bob awake. Sitting up, he heard brush breaking on the hill behind camp.

Stepping out of his bag, he pulled on his pants, slid his feet into his moccasins and bent over Bill to shake him awake.

The crackling of brush up on the hillside continued, and it was getting louder as the animal moved down toward the hunters.

"I hear something," Bob whispered urgently to Bill. "I think it's a bear."

But Davis was too sleep-drugged to grasp what his brother-in-law was saying. All Bob got from him was a grudging grunt, so he stepped over to prod Clint. Just then Clint's deep breathing rounded into a full-fledged snore. The noise out in the brush immediately stopped.

"Stop that snoring, Clint!" Bob growled in his ear. "There's a bear around. Get up!"

Clint must have had snoring troubles at home, for he mumbled quite agreeably, "All right, honey, I'll turn over." He did, the snore subsided, and brush broke again up on the hill. Bob wrote off his two partners. He had given them their chance. If they wouldn't wake up, he would go after the bear alone. It seemed like the logical thing to do at the time, but it wouldn't be many minutes before he realized the decision had been a rash one.

Before tiptoeing off in the direction of the noise, he picked up his bow, took two arrows out of his quiver, laying one on the string and holding the other in his left hand ready for instant use. The noise had been getting louder all the time as the animal moved down toward camp. Now it sounded no more than 100 yards off. But the animal was quieting down. Bob could hear brush being rattled softly, then a few seconds of complete silence, followed by another faint sound.

A half-moon had been overhead when the three had turned in, but it was now down behind the crest of the big hill back of camp. The sky was still radiant, however, and it shed enough light in the timber so that Bob could just about distinguish trees and logs. He was trying to move as quietly as a cat, but his moccasins were making little scuffing noises and, in spite of his stealth, he broke two or three twigs underfoot. After moving out about 50 yards, he decided he could walk more quietly without his moccasins, so he stepped out of them and went on in his stocking feet, sneaking along a step at a time. Ahead in the darkness, he could hear the animal move now and then, also carefully and quietly. It still seemed to be coming toward him and he began to wonder if he was stalking the animal, or if it were stalking him. Barely able to make out the shadowy shapes of stumps and trees and armed only with a bow and two arrows, Bob felt the skin start to prickle on the back of his neck.

Although the men had been in camp only a day and a night, they had started a small garbage heap, in a little brushy hollow near the creek, which they intended to bury before leaving. Bob realized from the direction of the sound that the animal was heading toward the dump. Then remembering that there were several empty sardine tins among the rubbish, and how much bears like fish, Bob was sure that he was dealing with a bear.

Now there was no more noise from the brush. Bob crept warily ahead to a low rise 25 yards from the dump, and stopped. There wasn't much light down in the hollow, so he stood stock still and stared into the brush, trying to sort out the shadowy shapes, straining his ears for the slightest sound. After what seemed like a quarter hour but was actually only a minute or so, his eyes grew accustomed to the blackness and he focused on a dark shape that didn't look quite like a stump. Then the shape moved. Bob heard a cautious step. The animal seemed careful not to rattle any of the cans. It just sniffed a couple of times

and moved again. In the darkness Bob could make out the outlines of a bulky black body, but he couldn't tell which end was
head and which was tail. There was no longer the slightest
doubt, however, that he was watching a bear, and a big one at
that.

The animal didn't know Bob was there, but seemed to be
moving stealthily just on general principles. Bob brought his
bow up and pulled the arrow back to half draw. Then he
stopped and eased the string down. Wasn't he taking a crazy,
foolhardy risk in shooting? If he drove an arrow into the bear,
what would happen? He knew he couldn't hope to kill the
bear in its tracks, and there was nobody to back him. It gave
him an uneasy feeling and he wished fervently that he had
dragged Bill out of his bag by force. He mulled the situation
over for a long minute, concluding that he couldn't go back
for help without spooking the bear and that he would never
get another chance like this. What had he come to Canada for?

So he brought the bowstring back until it rested alongside his jaw, where it belonged, and let go a blind shot in the
bear's direction. He didn't hear the arrow hit but almost at the
same time as the string snapped, the bear let out a horrible,
bawling roar that made Bob's hair stand on end.

Bob had just one idea then—to get the second arrow on
the string and pulled back to full draw. He stood holding it,
aiming at nothing, expecting the bear to swarm all over him
any second. But then he steadied down enough to listen, and
he heard the bear crashing through thick brush on the far side
of the creek. It was running straight away.

As soon as he was sure of its direction, Bob did some running of his own, back to camp. He burst in like a tornado and
this time he wasted no time shaking his partners awake.

"Roll out!" he yelled. "I've hit a bear!"

Bill raised up on one elbow, and Bob grabbed him by the shirt and yanked him to his feet. Even that commotion didn't arouse Clint, however. All in from two grueling days, he slept soundly on. Since his back was still too sore for him to draw a bow, Bill and Bob decided to leave him there in his sack, figuring that looking for a wounded bear in the dark was hardly sport for a man as good as unarmed.

Bill tumbled into his pants and shoes and both men buckled on their quivers, grabbed flashlights and headed for the spot where Bob had done the shooting. On the way he took time to retrieve his moccasins. Stopping at the top of the little knoll, they pointed their lights down into the hollow where the bear had stood. What he saw made Bob's heart sink all the way to his shoes. There was his arrow, sticking up out of the brush. That was a terrific letdown, but when Bob walked into the hollow to get it, he discovered all the arrow wasn't there, after all. What he picked up was only 19 inches of the feathered end, which was broken cleanly off. The business end, he figured, must be in the bear.

Remembering the bear's bloodcurdling roar as the arrow had punched home, Bob decided he didn't want any more of the bear that night. Bill agreed that the job of tracking would keep until daylight. They went back to camp and crawled into their bags, but were too excited to sleep much. At first light they were up and hurrying through breakfast. Clint, even with his wrenched back, wanted to come along, but Bill and Bob talked him out of it.

The two men picked up a blood trail at the place where the broken arrow had been found. There was not much blood but enough to follow, and they had trailed it only 40 yards when they came to a spot where the bear had stopped to vomit. Just beyond that they found a small mud hole he had wallowed in.

"He's your bear," Bill said confidently.

But their hopes soon took a tumble, for when the animal had moved on from the wallow, he had left no blood sign. The track turned down into a thick swamp where tracking was almost impossible.

But the men stayed on it, ferreting it out from broken weeds and brush, more wallows and vomit sign. Now and then there was a drop of blood where the bear had crawled out of the mud and water after wallowing. It took them two hour to trail 200 yards. Then they lost the track altogether.

They went back to camp, made coffee and sat around for an hour, talking things over. Bob was probably the most disappointed bear hunter in Canada. During a lull in the conversation, Clint noticed a pair of ravens circling over the swamp, croaking and making a big fuss.

"Suppose they've found your bear?" he asked.

"I don't know, but I'm going back and have one more try at that track," Bob said.

"I'll go along," Bill agreed.

It was then that the two trackers made a serious mistake, one that was going to come close to costing them their lives. The thick brush in which they had tracked the bear earlier had snagged their quivers so badly that they decided it would be easier not to take them this time. Without quivers they could carry only two arrows apiece, one on the string and one in the left hand; however, four arrows seemed plenty for a wounded bear.

Making a fresh start on the track at the place where Bob

hit the bear, they found sign they had missed on the first attempt. The bear had kept to the thickest stuff he could find, continuing to vomit a little froth now and then. There was no blood, however. The track led straight into a tangled cedar thicket with an open place in the center where a big tree had fallen. There was a puddle of water in the hollow formed by the upturned roots and the bear had wallowed there. They could see where mud and water had dripped from him when he had left. They circled the mud hole, searching for the next sign.

"He went this way," Bill said after a minute. "Here's a broken weed."

Then, a dozen feet in front, Bob saw an alerted bear's nose and ears projected above the top of a log.

"Look out, Bill!" he yelled.

They froze in their tracks. Nothing happened for a second. But then as Bill was taking a cautious step backward to get clear of the brush, the bear reared up on its hind feet and started for them. He wasn't running. Too sick for that, but standing straight up, he advanced in a lumbering walk. As he climbed over the log he reminded Bob of an awkward, thick-bodied man. It was obvious he was coming to kill. Plastered with mud and slime, eyes blazing like two coals, the attacking bear's teeth were bared in a blood-chilling snarl. Flecks of froth showed along his jaws, and he growled savagely.

Bob clawed free of the brush, brought his arrow back to full draw and slammed it at the bear. It hit a small branch, glanced off and whizzed past the fast-approaching target. Even in his terror and confusion, Bob heard Bill say clearly and distinctly, "Hell, you never touched him!" Then Bill's bowstring sang, and Bob saw the arrow sink head-deep into a cedar that lay in the bear's path.

"Things were happening pretty fast, but they stick in your mind at a time like that. I remember every detail," Bob told Clint later. "A four-inch green aspen stood in the bear's way, and he walloped it with a forepaw. It snapped clean a couple of feet above the ground, and he batted it aside before dropping to all fours."

Bob got his second arrow off then, and it found the target, knifing through the thick flesh of the bear's hind leg, high up near the body. Seconds later, Bill's other arrow buried itself half its length under the bear's shoulder blade and stayed there. The arrow's feathers, sticking up over the top of his head between his ears, looked like a small war bonnet. Bob cursed the fact that neither shot was the kind to slow the enraged bear down. Now they were both out of arrows.

The bear was almost on them. Bob found his hunting knife in his hand without knowing he had reached for it. He stole a quick glance across his shoulder at Bill who, with his feet apart and knife out, stood ready, too. He was dead white. Bob himself had never been more scared in his life, but it gave him a good feeling to know that his kid brother-in-law was there beside him. Whatever happens, he thought, it's two against the bear.

At the last minute the bear lost his nerve. Suddenly stopping exactly two paces away from them, he stood there swinging his head from side to side, snarling in their faces. Then just as suddenly, he turned and walked slowly into the thick brush. Just out of sight, he stopped, and the two terrified men could hear him growling and mumbling. When the bear quieted down, they screwed up enough courage to go after the two arrows that had missed him.

During the long moments while they were cutting Bill's arrow out of the tree with their knives, they kept an eye on the bear which was now lying, belly down, only 20 yards off. But he had been headed away from them when he fell; now he didn't even look in their direction.

"He's about done," Bob whispered to Bill.

When Bill's arrow was free, he laid it on the string, and covered Bob while the latter catfooted ahead another ten feet to where his arrow was sticking in the ground. Then, armed with an arrow apiece, they backed out of the thicket to wait for the bear's next move. After about a quarter of an hour, they heard him flounder to his feet and move farther off.

They gave him an hour before taking the track once more. They had never dreaded a job more in their lives, but it was one that had to be done. They had started the fracas; now it was up to them to finish it.

They had trailed the bear only 30 yards from where they had last seen him when they spotted him again, lying 50 feet ahead in the timber. They crept up, one on either side, arrows ready, keeping clear of brush and stopped four or five paces away. Was he still breathing? They couldn't see any movement, but it was no time to take chances. They had had enough close calls for one day.

Bill covered again, and Bob edged in until he was standing just back of the bear's shoulder. His bow was drawn, and his arrow was aimed at a spot behind an ear. The range was point blank. He meant to drive the steel broadhead clear through the brain if the bear so much as twitched. Bill moved up on the other side then.

"His nose is his tenderest spot," Bob suggested. "Prod him there. If there's a spark of life left in him, he'll show it."

He held his bow at full draw, while Bill reached cautiously around the trunk of a big tree and prodded the blackie's snout with an arrow. The bear didn't flinch.

As they dressed him out, it was hard to believe that the wounded bear had been able to live as long and travel as far as he had. Bob's first arrow had entered his side just back of his ribs, sliced through the bear's liver, stomach and belly wall. It had been stopped by the tough outer skin on the opposite side. They found a nine-inch section of arrow shaft as well as the arrowhead lying entirely inside the stomach. As the bear had grabbed the arrow in his teeth, he had apparently pulled it back several inches before his powerful jaws had broken off the major part of the shaft. They discovered that the liver wound had been a fatal one. The bear had actually died of hemorrhage, which kills most game shot with an arrow. The bear's belly had been full of blood when he died in the brush. Only his great natural vitality had kept him going for half a day after Bob's initial hit. They knew from experience that that type of strike would have downed a less rugged animal in an hour or two.

Standing over the lifeless, 300-pound carcass, Bill and Bob remembered how ferocious the bear had looked when they were facing him with only their knives in the cedar thicket an hour before. He had given them the scare of their lives, and now that he was dead they felt a curious mixture of satisfaction, excitement and letdown.

"Well, you got what you came after," Bill said, grinning feebly.

"Yeah, but the next time I come to Canada I'm going to hunt moose," Bob replied firmly. "This is all the bearskin rug I ever want."

Lost for Forty Days

BOB MULLIN and Ray Vanstone lowered the net over the side of their crude raft and watched anxiously as it sank down through the choppy water. It wasn't much of a net, only 20 feet of linen mesh weighted at the bottom, with a row of floats along the top to hold it upright. So far it had taken only one fish, a sucker less than a foot long. But to the seven men stranded in the wild bush country of northern Quebec, the net was an important link in their frail chain holding off starvation. They hadn't had a full meal in six days. Their best chance of eating at all that day or in the future rested with that net.

Bob had rigged a rope bridle for lifting it and attached a wooden buoy at the end of a line to mark its location. They saw the line tighten under water and then the cedar float went under and kept going, and too late they realized they had overshot the drop-off on the lake bottom. The lead weights were too much for the buoy and the net was sinking in deep water.

They lunged for it, but the wind had already carried their raft beyond reach. They grabbed up the paddles but the float was gone before they could even turn the cumbersome raft in the right direction. They hated to have to go ashore and tell the other five what had happened. The party's plight had been bad before; now it seemed hopeless.

The misadventure had begun simply enough, with no hint of danger, in late August, 1953. The seven men were on a routine bush flight from Fort Chimo, a lonely Eskimo settlement and trading post on the arctic rim of Quebec almost at the northeast tip of the continent, to Roberval on Lac St. John, 700 miles south.

Flying above unmapped country where the magnetic compass deviates as much as 37 degrees from true north, fighting shifting winds of gale strength, they strayed off course and missed their refueling station, a pinpoint in half a million square miles of uninhabited wilderness. Almost out of gas, they landed on a lonely lake, confident they would be found and soon be on their way again.

It wasn't a hunting or fishing trip. If it were they would have been far better prepared. Bob and his 19-year-old crewman, Dick Everitt, had flown the chartered Norseman, a single-engine pontoon plane, north to Chimo from Roberval to bring a group of miners and prospectors out of that iron-rich country before freeze-up. On the evening of August 24, with wet snow pelting down, they were told they would have to fly back to Roberval the next morning. A drilling boss whose face was abcessed needed medical attention. And since there was a waiting list of men whose summer work was finished and who were eager to get out of the arctic, they would have to take a full load.

The next morning dawned clear and crisp. After the men ate a hurried breakfast of toast and coffee—they later regretted eating so lightly—Bob gunned the Norseman off the water, loaded to capacity: seven men, their sleeping bags and other gear.

There were a few drums of gas cached, midway between Chimo and Roberval, at the weather station on Lake Nichicun. They would have to stop there and take on fuel.

The flight was uneventful. Bob was piloting the Norseman south at a little better than 100 miles an hour with the fuel mixture leaned out, over a jumbled, crazy-quilt country of lakes and rivers, mountains and tundra and bog, much of it not mapped at all. Save for the tiny weather station on Nichicun there was no human habitation ahead for nearly 700 miles.

Shortly after noon he flew over the sprawling watershed of Fort George River, a chain of big lakes linked together like misshapen beads on a crooked string. He recognized it from his maps and began to look for Nichicun. But a high wind, shifting from west to east, had blown the plane off course and he missed Nichicun which, he learned later, was about 35 miles to the west. When he had been in the air almost four hours he realized not only that he had missed the fueling station but that he was completely lost.

It's poor airmanship under those conditions to stay up until your fuel is gone, so Bob started looking for a lake, free of rocks and islands, big enough to land on. He spotted one that looked all right, and on the far shore made out a tiny clearing. When he came over it he could see the remnants of a tent. He didn't have much gas left by that time and figured he couldn't do any better, so he sat down. It was almost six weeks before the men learned that they had landed on Lake Emmanuel, on the upper tributaries of the Eastmain River. They gave it the name of Lake Aurora the second night, when the Northern Lights hung their flaring curtains of ghostly radiance across the sky.

Taxiing ashore they found the clearing had been made by Cree trappers who had built a shelter of log walls and covered it with a tarp. But it seemed to have been at least a year since anyone had used the place, maybe longer. The walls were sagging and the tarp had rotted and fallen in.

Nobody felt any real concern at first. The plane was radio equipped. Its signals would be heard, somebody would fly in a fresh supply of gas and they would be off again. A small chill of foreboding went through Bob later that afternoon, however, when he sat down and tapped out "Mayday," the international aircraft distress signal, adding the call letters of the Norseman and a request for fuel. After he sent his call, he heard all kinds of traffic, but none that answered his signals. He realized radio transmission was uncertain up there. He wasn't getting through, but he still wasn't really worried. Somebody would hear him tomorrow.

The men put up a 9 x 9 wall tent for overnight shelter, sorted their supplies and equipment, took inventory and made ready for an emergency, more to keep busy than because they thought they were in any danger.

They were fairly well equipped—for a short stay. They had two boxes of emergency rations, a kit of pots, pans, and dishes, the tent, a gun and a limited supply of ammunition, a casting rod, reel and half a dozen lures, the net, three axes and a small crosscut saw. Odds and ends included a roll of fine copper wire, three smoke flares, two hand-held veery cartridges for night signaling, and a first-aid kit that contained bandages, one bottle of an antifainting drug, sulpha ointment for burns—and very little else.

The gun was an over-and-under double, one barrel .22, the other .410. They had a box of cartridges for the .22, plus a few loose ones. Ammo for the .410 consisted of a box of fine shot and five slug loads.

The ration boxes contained enough food to last two men 14 days on an emergency basis. For seven men that meant a four-day supply. There was no sugar, no frying fat, very little salt, less than a pound each of tea and coffee, and only a little flour. The supplies were chiefly tinned meats, tinned fruit juices, powdered milk, beans, dehydrated soups and vegetables, and chocolate bars. There were also three packages of tobacco.

They didn't expect to be there four days, and everybody was hungry, so at supper time they broke out enough rations to treat themselves to a light meal. It proved to be the best they would have for many days to come. When their radio signals went unanswered the next day and the next, they tightened their belts and settled down to the grim business of trying to live off the land, eking out the rations, saving them for a possible last-ditch stand against starvation.

This was no hand-picked party of men used to the bush. They were seven ordinary men, strangers thrown together by accident. Bob Mullin had known Dick Everitt only a few days. The others, whom he had met only that morning, knew each other only a little better. Two were Europeans, totally unfamiliar with the country and situation in which they now found themselves. They were Dr. Rolphe Theinhaus, a geologist from Siegen, Germany, and Dr. Klaas Koeten, a Rotterdam mining engineer. They had come to Canada earlier in the summer and flown on to Fort Chimo to investigate iron deposits and mining properties there for German and Dutch mining interests. Victor Abel from Senneterre, Quebec, was the only experienced bush man in the party, except Bob. Suffering, however, from the huge lump on the side of his face, Abel was too ill to be of much help. The other two were Abel's helper, Marc Levesque of Rimouski, Quebec, and young Vanstone, a 20-year-old student at the University of Toronto.

They did not even have the bond of a common language. Levesque spoke only French, Vanstone and Bob only English,

Theinhaus German and a few English words. Dick spoke both English and French; Abel spoke French, English and Flemish. Koeten was the real linguist of the party, fluent in his native Dutch, English, French, German and two or three other languages.

They were an oddly assorted crew to face together the challenges, dangers, hardships and suffering that were coming. That they survived at all was due only to the unquenchable will of man to live, however great the odds against him, and to the fact that from the start they put the welfare of all ahead of the welfare of any individual.

Bob was a bush pilot with 6,000 air hours behind him, part of it in the RCAF and the RAF, where he flew from 1939 until the end of World War II, and much of the rest of it over the remote districts of Alaska and Canada. He had grown up in the town of Kenora at the north end of Lake of the Woods, where just about everybody hunts and fishes, and had married a girl whose family ran two fishing camps. The bush was nothing new to him. He had seen a lot of it, from the air and on the ground. Although this was the first time he had ever been forced down in it, stripped of wings and in a place where he could not get out, he knew what men had to do to stay alive in such a spot. Consequently, leadership of the party automatically fell to him.

Bob knew from the outset that they could not walk out. The distance to help in any direction was too great, the country too rough and laced with too much water. They had come down, he gauged, almost at the exact center of the great triangle of wilderness that lies north of the St. Lawrence and east of Hudson Bay. Somewhere, probably less than 50 miles away, was the Nichicun weather station, but they didn't know in which direction. The nearest settled country, around Lac St.

John, lay 300 miles to the south, with the Otish Mountains and innumerable lakes in between. Four hundred miles behind was Fort Chimo; eastward 500 miles the scattered settlements along the Labrador coast. The small trading posts on James Bay were 300 miles west. And it was all country slashed by white-water rivers and pocked with sprawling lakes that no man could travel through without a canoe.

Whatever happened, they would have to stay put and wait to be rescued. There were two possibilities of rescue; one—the chance that the Indians who had built the camp might return—was too slim to pin any real hope on. Empty canoe racks indicated they had come and gone by water, and the absence of a cache, pails, sleds or any other equipment seemed to indicate that they had abandoned the place permanently. There was little reason to expect them back.

The other hope of rescue lay in the air search that was certain to be made even though the party's radio signals were failing to get out. The difficulty was that there was so much country to cover and nothing was known of their location. Right away they set about doing what little they could to help searchers spot them. As soon as they had built a raft, they moved the Norseman out and anchored it in midlake where it could be seen readily from the air. They found an open place on a hill behind camp, gathered dry wood and green branches and made a fire ready, figuring that a smoke column there could be seen for a good 20 miles. They kept a man on watch, from daylight to dusk, ready to light that fire until the strongest could no longer climb the hill. Taking turns, they also stood a firewatch at camp at night, with a flare at hand ready for firing if a plane came over. The campfire was never allowed to go out until they had all become too weak to stay up and tend it.

In another attempt at signaling, Dick and Levesque paddled across the lake and tried in vain to set fire to the rain-soaked woods on the far shore. When that failed they attempted to burn an island in midlake, but it also was too wet. And every day as long as they had sufficient gas to run the plane's engine for electric power, Bob pounded out his SOS over and over, sending at the hours when he knew RCAF stations would be listening. After each transmission he held the key down for ten seconds to give ground stations and planes a chance to get a fix on his position. No reply ever came.

They had been down seven days when they heard the first aircraft, droning along behind a ridge to the west. Bob was out on the raft fishing. Back at camp the others set off a smoke bomb, but the plane didn't spot the signal. Two days later they caught the drone of a plane again, early in the morning, and that time saw it coming, due to pass within two or three miles. It was a bright day, the sky broken with fleecy clouds. They waited until the plane was almost abreast of camp and then touched off the second of their smoke bombs. At the instant the orange smoke was pouring out, the plane flew behind a cloud. When it came out, the pilot was already too far to the south to see the signal. The men cursed that cloud as if it had been a personal enemy.

But at least they knew that planes were looking for them. What they could not know was that their disappearance had triggered the biggest air search in the history of Canada. Their plight was one to stir the sympathy of all who heard it. A little band of men down in the vast reaches of the bush, lost, cold, hungry, perhaps hurt, awaiting help. All across Canada and the United States, and even in Europe, newspapers speculated about the fate of the seven men under black, scare headlines. Back home their families kept a tireless vigil, never far from a radio, jumping each time the phone rang, never losing hope.

RCAF and private planes, even planes of the USAF, flew together, covering more than 200,000 square miles of wilderness, looking with dogged determination for a thread of smoke,

a scar of broken timber on a mountainside, the wreckage of the Norseman, any sign at all. During the search as many as 40 aircraft were in the air at one time, directed by the RCAF Search and Rescue Command, and radio operators sat glued to their sets day and night, now and then picking up Bob's signals that were garbled and never strong enough to establish a fix on the location of the lost men. Planes specially equipped for tracking down the radio signals flew out of the base at Goose

Bay night after night, in pea-soup fog and rain and snow, but never heard the faint calls.

The day came finally, in the fourth week, when the last of the gas was gone and the radio was silenced. If the men were found now it would be by accident.

Things grew worse for them day by day. There is no autumn in that savage land. The summer rain changes to snow, the ground freezes and suddenly winter is at hand. That was happening now. The day they had landed they set up the tent amidst swarms of blackflies. Two days later the flies were gone, killed by the cold of a single August night. The men had no clothing for cold weather. Theinhaus' outfit consisted of a business suit and a light cotton fishing suit. He sat patiently for hours, sewing one inside the other for added warmth. Vanstone had no wind-breaker and no hat, and his boots were falling apart. Koeten's boots were also poor. Dick had one wool shirt and two pairs of light cotton pants, but no heavy coat. Among them they had three parkas and a leather jacket, but no heavy underwear and not enough gloves to go around.

The weather stayed wet for days on end, with rain and sleet and snow. The tent leaked and the sleeping bags were soaked night after night. There wasn't enough room in the tent for everyone to sleep comfortably, so at first two men paddled out on the raft and slept aboard the plane. Two or three times the wind was so bad when they awoke in the morning they couldn't make it back to shore. Twice Vanstone and Mullin were forced to huddle in the plane all day and through a second night, without heat or food. But it didn't matter much. There was nothing to eat in the plane, but there was next to nothing to eat at camp, either.

As the weather grew colder they had to have heat in the

tent, so Bob tackled the job of making a small stove from a ration box, using empty food cans for the door, draft and a short length of pipe. It worked, and after that they all slept in the tent, with the stove, a small pile of dry wood and the rations. It was crowded, but at least they were warm.

The days were not idle ones. Every minute was crowded with searching for food and performing other necessary tasks. But from dark to daylight there was little to do but try to sleep.

They had two or three crossword puzzle books and a couple of pocket books. Vanstone fashioned a deck of cards from cigarette cartons. The brief evenings were passed with these few amusements, or by just sitting around the fire for an hour or two, planning the things that needed to be done the next day or talking about homes and families, the favorite topics of conversation.

"I was married seven years ago on the second of October," Koeten said wistfully one night in September. "I hope I'm home by that date."

Of course, they also talked incessantly in the beginning about being found. Abel was reading a book about the search for the Franklin Expedition, which had failed. For a time they talked a lot about it, but after three or four weeks that subject was dropped. A few evenings they sang around the fire, Koeten and Theinhaus coming in with Dutch and German songs.

The discouraging hunt for food, which had begun the second day, was endless. One fish had been taken with the net before it was lost. They dragged for the net many hours with a grapnel rigged from big fishhooks, but never found it. Just before the net was lost, they had caught a second fish, a nine-inch trout, with the casting rod. Those were the only two fish they were able to catch during the entire ordeal. The men continued to cast along shore, around the islands and from the raft until the reel wore out, but never even got another strike. They had found a few dry fish heads on a shelf in the Indian camp and that had raised their hopes at first, but they soon concluded the fish had been carried there from another lake. Later they boiled and ate those shrunken heads.

It took only three or four days of hunting to convince them there was no big game in the country—no moose, deer, caribou, not even beaver. A few days after they landed, one of the men—bending over to do some work at the plane—let the .410 slug loads slip out of his pocket into deep water of the lake. Had there been big game around that would have been a major tragedy. As it was, it didn't matter. Bob reloaded a few of the fine-shot loads with homemade buckshot to replace the slug loads, melting lead sinkers in a pan and dropping the molten lead into water to form the big round pellets. But there was never any occasion to use the buckshot.

The food situation wasn't too bad the first week. They dipped sparingly into their little store of rations, and the third morning Bob had the good fortune to come on a flock of five spruce partridges, the fool hens of the north. He shot all five, and while they lasted, the partridges provided the best meals the party had since that good supper the first evening.

The men hunted partridges constantly, but the birds were limited to a small area around camp and were scarce even there. In all they killed about 30. From the copper wire, they made rabbit snares which were tended daily, but didn't yield much. The total take of rabbits was only five, and one of these was killed with the gun. The rabbits and partridges, the scanty allowances of tinned meat they doled out for themselves, and two red squirrels they shot—scrawny little animals that didn't yield a spoonful of meat per man—made up the entire meat supply for the seven men during the 40 days they were lost.

Vanstone and Dick came up to the tent one day from a trip out to the plane. "We're losing weight," Vanstone announced with a cheerful grin, as if he brought news none of the rest knew. "When we first built that raft Dick and I couldn't ride it without getting our feet wet. Now it floats the two of us high and dry!"

The men could see an old burn on a range of hills about three miles from camp. There would be blueberries there, so parties were sent out to pick them. At first the fruit was plentiful, but the freezing weather quickly finished it off. By the end of the second week the berrying parties were coming back from a whole day of patient search, tired, cold, drenched from the rain, carrying no more than a cupful of overripe, frozen fruit. As the supply of blueberries dwindled, they tried other berries, any kind they could find, red, black or green. Even cooked to a tasteless pulpy mush, they helped a little to fill the aching emptiness in the belly of each man. Sitting around the fire one night, Theinhaus made a quiet announcement.

"The mushrooms we see in the woods look like those I have eaten in Europe," he said. "I'm going to try them. If they don't poison me, we can all eat them."

The others had been also wondering about the mushrooms, but none had dared to take the risk. The next morning, Theinhaus gathered a mess and ate them. A day later the party added mushrooms to its skimpy menu.

After that the average meal consisted of half a cupful of berries and mushrooms boiled together, without sugar or salt. Both became harder to find as the weather grew colder, and many evenings there was only a spoonful for each man. But each got his share—if he was away hunting or on firewatch it was put aside for him—and nobody grumbled.

On red-letter days there was a rabbit or partridge to divide. The bones—head and all, even the beaks and feet of the grouse—and washed entrails were added to the pot. The meat was portioned out equally, a spoonful at a time. But the broth was never drunk at the same meal. It was saved over for breakfast.

Poor as they were, the meals became the big event the lost men looked forward to each day. They were out of tobacco, reduced to smoking leaves, bark and even coffee grounds. They had no sugar, but there were two small cans of peaches in the rations. One was opened on the second Sunday, the other on the fourth. They yielded half a peach apiece.

Abel had been lost in the Canadian bush twice before. The first time he had walked for two weeks before meeting a party of Indians. The second time had been in winter and he had been compelled to kill half of his team of sled dogs for food before being found.

"But this is worse," he declared.

Koeten agreed that they were in a desperate situation. He had spent most of World War II imprisoned by the Japanese in the Dutch East Indies, and he confessed he would rather go through the whole four years again than take what he was enduring now.

As the weather worsened with the onset of winter and it became more and more difficult to get mushrooms or berries, Bob realized that if they didn't find a substitute they would die of starvation before freeze-up. He had heard that caribou moss was edible, and there was plenty of it on the hill behind camp. On firewatch one day, he tried it.

There were three kinds of the moss: green, black, and gray. He learned later that the gray is the true caribou moss. He tried the wrong kind first and almost died from it. His stomach was tied in knots for two days. When he was better, he tested the gray moss next and it was all right, once they learned how to cook it. It had to be boiled to remove the acid, dried in a pan until it was brittle enough to be crumbled into a fine powder. After that the men made many meals on a spoonful of powdered moss, and Air Force doctors said later that in all likelihood it saved their lives.

Their hunger made them think of food all the time.

"You know what I dreamed last night?" Vanstone said one morning. "I dreamed about a harvest dinner, the kind we used to have on the farm. Chicken and potatoes and all the trimmings! Boy, oh boy!"

That day Bob used the last of the flour and a scanty supply of frozen berries to make a "blueberry pie." There was no sugar and the berries were not all blueberries, but it seemed to lift everybody's spirits. But their cramps and pain, dizziness and nausea grew worse each day. Bit by bit the seven healthy men were turning into gaunt, bearded skeletons. Their skin hung on them like wrinkled leather. During the 40 days, Bob lost 51 pounds, dropping from 184 to 133. The others fared no better, each losing in proportion to his weight. Any exertion became an agony. Cutting firewood was fast getting to be beyond their strength, and even walking was a fearful ordeal. They lay down more and more often, did the necessary camp chores in shorter and shorter shifts.

Abel walked to the edge of camp one morning to cut a small tree. He had only struck three or four feeble blows when the ax slipped from his hands and fell to the ground.

"I can't do it," he groaned as he turned back to the fire.

Bob knew from his experience in the RCAF that the search for them would be thorough and persistent. But he also knew that when they were not found and their signals were not heard, sooner or later the search would have to be called off. In his own mind he had set 30 days as the extreme limit of its duration, and the blackest hours for him came when the 30 days were up. Then he had to resign himself to the fact that in all probability they had been abandoned for dead. And that if they were to get out from now on it would have to be on their own. There was only the slimmest chance of that, they knew, but it was the one hope they clung to with the desperation of men who are aware that death is only a short time away.

They began the task of chinking the log walls of the old Indian camp, readying it for a winter shelter, meaning to move the tent there on the first fair day. But no fair day came and they never finished the chinking. It was too much for them.

Abel was in the worst shape. The others had been unable to do anything for his infected face except to bathe it with warm soda water and give him the aspirin from their personal kits. He was suffering terribly, and complained almost constantly of headaches and weakness. It was plain that he and one or two of the others could not survive more than a few days and Bob found himself haunted by a new and morbid worry. As each man died, how would the survivors dispose of his body?

None of the survivors would have the strength for a decent job of burial in the frozen, rocky soil. If they put the bodies in the lake, weighted down with stones, they would no longer want to drink the water. And if they laid them among the rocks behind camp, the simplest course, they would be there in plain sight, a horrible temptation to those who still lived to appease their hunger by indulging in cannibalism in the final extremes of hunger.

Bob finally decided that any corpses would have to be burned on the camp fire. He would do the job at night, with Theinhaus or Vanstone helping. He realized later that they could not have done it. It was a fantastic, hunger-wrought plan, but at the time it seemed plausible enough.

From the beginning and until they were too weak, the men organized and carried out one reconnaissance trip after another, in the hope of learning exactly where they were and finding a sign that would guide them to the weather station on Nichicun. If they only knew in which direction to travel, they reasoned, the stronger men of the party might still be able to reach it on foot and send help back for the others before winter finished them all.

They had explored all around the lake on which they were camped. The trips were rugged business. Whoever made one had invariably to climb endless hills, slog across bogs and tundra, wade waist deep in icy streams, sleep without a bag and with no shelter except a bough lean-to—and go without food until he was back at camp. No separate rations could be spared from the remaining store for the exploring parties. Each time a party went out it carried three tins of food, which was nearly half of the remaining canned food. It had been agreed that the party would open the tins only if it were unable to make it back to camp. Each time the cans were brought back unopened.

"I'll never cease to marvel at the courage and decency of the men with whom I shared those days," Bob related after their grueling experience was over.

Toward the end of September the reconnaissance trips were undertaken in a new spirit—one of desperation. Unless a way was found to reach Nichicun soon, all hope was gone. The last trip was made by Theinhaus and Vanstone. They trudged off to the northeast one morning in freezing rain, looking like mummies in their ragged clothes. They came back at dark the second night in terrible condition, cold and exhausted, and fell into their bags more dead than alive. It had been the most exhausting trip of all, but they brought word that sent hope rocketing up in the others.

From the top of a low mountain to the north they had sighted an arm of a big lake that they were sure was Nichicun. If Theinhaus and Vanstone were right, the men deduced from their maps that their camp was on Lake Patamisk. The outline of the lake, the lay of the country all around it, and the other lakes they had sighted to the north all supported this belief. And in that case they were less than ten miles south of the lower end of Nichicun—a distance that some of them could still manage to cover. But even if they reached Nichicun, 50 miles of rough country would still lie between them and the weather station—an impossible distance to walk for men in their condition. But that could be solved by building a raft and crossing the lake.

In desperation, they agreed to split the party and make the try. Abel and Koeten were beyond traveling now, and one man would have to stay behind with them. Since Levesque would be of little use without an interpreter, he and Everitt would have to be kept together. Ray's boots were about gone. That settled it. He would stay with Koeten and Abel. Theinhaus, Levesque, Everitt and Bob would try to get through to the big lake to the north. If they reached it and found it was not

Nichicun they agreed to return to the camp, but that was a promise that could never have been kept.

The weather was now so bad that the walking party would have to have shelter. They decided to take the tent, and to leave their bags. From the latter the three men left behind could rig a cover on the half-chinked walls of the Indian camp. The gun, for which only 12 shells remained, would be left at the camp, since without it the men there would have no means of hunting food until help came. That meant the four, without a gun, would have to take the bulk of the rations that were left, except for four tins of fruit juice. Actually all the four men would be taking was a handful of dry beans and three tins of beef. That would have to be their food supply while they lived. It was an almost hopeless scheme, but there was nothing to lose.

When morning came Bob sent Levesque, Dick and Vanstone ahead to hunt. Bob had planned it so that he and Theinhaus would meet them at the north end of the lake. There Vanstone would leave them and go back to camp with the gun.

It was a bleak, cold morning. Rain and snow were falling. Theinhaus and Bob took down the tent and rolled it up, shook hands with Abel and Koeten and trudged away, not looking back. It was a solemn, almost wordless parting, both groups of men quieted by the belief that neither would see the members of the other alive again.

Bob and Theinhaus had walked less than a quarter mile when they realized that in their weakened condition they could not carry the wet tent. Without it they would face shelterless nights. It was a grim prospect, but they had no choice. They left the tent in an open place where Vanstone could find it easily, and went wearily on.

They reached the north end of the lake shortly after noon

and found Dick and Levesque and Vanstone waiting. They had a fire going and they had good news. They had shot a partridge.

The five discussed the disposition of the bird at length. It was desperately needed back at camp, but to the men who were going to march north the nourishment might make the difference between reaching or not reaching Nichicun, and all of their lives depended on their making it. So it was agreed the walking party should take the partridge.

The four said good-by to Vanstone. From the start he had been one of the best members of the team, carrying out every order cheerfully, and volunteering for the hardest of the extra work. There were tears in Bob's eyes as they parted.

After the rain of the morning, the weather had turned windy and gloomy. The four walked steadily until dark. By that time the light load divided among them—an ax, two paddles, two flare cartridges, 30 feet of rope for the raft they hoped to build, and the three precious tins of beef—had become an almost unbearable burden. They stopped for the night at the spot where Theinhaus and Vanstone had camped on their last trip, built a fire and laid up a bough shelter. They cooked and ate the partridge that evening. Even though the portions were small, it was the best meal they had had in many days, and it renewed a spark of life in all of them.

They needed that because it snowed all night, and the wind blew a gale. The men lay huddled in the open lean-to, half-frozen in their wet clothes, sleepless and terribly discouraged. It seemed as if morning would never come.

At daylight they warmed up and spooned out the broth from the partridge and then started slogging north once more, stumbling along like drunken men. That forenoon Levesque's legs started to give out. He could no longer carry his share of the supplies. Dick called up some final reserve of his own strength and took Levesque's load, and they plodded painfully on.

They hoped that day's march would take them to the lower end of Nichicun. There, Bob realized, the party would have to be split again. This would be Levesque's last day on his feet. He'd have to be left on the shore of the lake with Dick while Theinhaus and Bob attempted to cross Nichicun on a raft. The lake was 20 miles long.

The day was endless. The four stumbled through deep gullies, crawled up hills, waded streams, staggered across one muskeg after another. Levesque complained more and more often that his hands were cold and finally had to pull on a pair of socks over his gloves. The end seemed to be not far away for him.

Shortly after noon they reached the hill from which Theinhaus and Vanstone had sighted what they believed to be Lake Nichicun. They could see the distant lake, gloomy and forbidding under gray storm clouds. It looked right for Nichicun, but no one could be sure.

"We'll know tomorrow," Bob said.

Levesque could no longer keep up and they had to stop more and more often for brief rests. About three o'clock they suddenly heard the hum of a plane off to the north. It grew louder and louder.

"My God, he's coming over us!" someone cried.

They could see the plane, a big RCAF Lancaster, bearing down no more than 200 feet above the trees. Bob fumbled in his pack for the flares and as the plane boomed toward them fired one directly in front of it. The star shell streaked skyward, a faint spark in the daylight, as the plane passed over them and thundered on. The men waited numbly while its drone died out in the south, and no one said anything. None of them had ever known another minute of heartbreak and despair like that one.

Less than 15 minutes later the impossible happened. They heard the Lancaster coming back. Again he roared by, almost overhead, and again they sent up a veery flare. Once again the pilot didn't notice it. But somehow it wasn't quite so bad that time. They had hardly expected to draw his attention.

They heard aircraft again to the south toward dark, but did not believe they could be search planes. But they were. Things had turned in their favor at last. The Search and Rescue Command had called off the hunt once, resumed it at the pleading of families and friends, and then abandoned it again after Bob's faint radio signals had stopped. Then, toward the end of September, Canada's Minister of Mines, George Prudham, had paid a chance visit to the iron properties at Fort Chimo where mining men had urged that another attempt be made.

"We know from the radio's signals that they came down alive," one of them pointed out. "They're in there somewhere, on one of the lakes, and the freeze-up will finish them."

Convinced then that one more try ought to be made, Prudham had put the wheels in motion and on October 1, the morning the four left the camp on Lake Emmanuel, the search planes had taken to the air again.

Before reaching the shore of the big lake, darkness halted the march late the second afternoon. The men dragged themselves up a long slope to a shelf which should have overlooked the water, but a range of hills ahead cut off the view. They still could not be sure they were approaching Nichicun. Morning would tell the story.

Reluctantly they opened and ate one of their three small tins of beef that night, knowing they could go no farther without some food. The night was a repetition of the one before. They kept a fire going and lay under a flimsy bough shelter, lashed by snow and a bitter wind. Nobody slept at all. There was no breakfast the next morning, not even partridge broth. Theinhaus and Bob left the camp at daybreak, without loads, leaving Levesque behind with Dick. They planned to climb the hills in front of them to find out whether the lake on the other side actually was Nichicun.

They staggered up to the crest of the last hill about 8 o'clock that morning and looked down on a large, empty lake which according to their map was not big enough or dotted with sufficient islands to be Nichicun. They stood staring at each other, stunned and wordless, each knowing that this was the end. There was nothing to do but go back to Dick and Levesque, tell them the truth, and then make ready for the march back to the three they had left.

They could never have made it, of course. Levesque could not walk now and the others would not have abandoned him while he lived. By the time he no longer needed them another would have been too far gone to travel, and eventually all four of them would have died there on the barren hill. By that time the three back at camp would have died too, and the bush might have kept forever the secret of what had happened, for when the ice went out of Lake Emmanuel in the spring the Norseman's waterlogged floats almost certainly would have caused the plane to sink.

Theinhaus and Bob broke the news to Levesque and Dick,

and it was decided first of all to try to scrape together a meal of frozen berries and reindeer moss. The four men were crawling around on hands and knees on the snowy hillside when they heard a plane coming from the south.

It was low, almost at treetop height, and it set them wild. There on the open hillside, with the fire still burning from the night before, they had a good chance of being seen. Theinhaus stumbled toward the fire to build a smudge; Dick and Bob ran, slipping and staggering, for the crest of the hill where Bob whipped off his shirt to make a signal flag. Even Levesque managed to get to his feet and tottering, stood waving his arms like a grotesque human windmill.

As the plane got closer, Bob identified it as an RCAF Canso amphibian. It roared over the brink of the hill, barely clearing the trees. They kept on waving and Theinhaus frantically piled the evergreen branches of the night lean-to onto the fire.

The plane went over and lumbered on a quarter of a mile while they waited in an agony of suspense. Then it came around in a wide turn and headed back, straight at them. They were found. It was October 3, their fortieth day in the bush.

As the plane passed over the second time, they heard a message from the loud-hailer in the belly of the Canso: "Stand by for a parachute drop!" A parcel came away; then an orange chute blossomed and floated down. They ran and picked up a metal cannister which had hit a rock. The lid was jammed. There was an ax back at the fire and they stumbled that way. While they were beating and prying at the cover, the plane came back and the loud-hailer called again. "Stay by your fire," the voice instructed. "We'll land on the lake and send a walking party in."

They finally succeeded in opening the cannister. Inside were chocolate and biscuits, dehydrated meat and salt, mittens, socks and moccasins. They ate the salt first of all.

When the food was gone Bob started out slowly north to meet the walking party. The man in charge, Flying Officer Gary Williamson of Vancouver, was a short distance ahead of the others. He and the lost pilot met on an open hillside and Williamson was within hailing distance before Bob saw him. He realized then that his eyes were giving out.

Williamson was the first human Bob had seen in 40 days except the members of his own party. The meeting was quietly dramatic. The two men shook hands and said hello. Neither seemed able to think of anything else to say. Bob asked for a cigarette, and then remembered Abel and Koeten and Vanstone.

"What about the others?" he mumbled. "There are three more of us, back at our camp."

"They were found yesterday afternoon," Williamson replied. "They're on the way out now."

The Lancaster that had missed the four earlier had made the find, spotting the Norseman on Lake Emmanuel about an hour after it had flown over the walking party. Unable to land on water, the plane had radioed for a Canso. Vanstone, Koeten and Abel had spent their last night in the bush warm, fed and safe. Rescue had come for Koeten on his seventh wedding anniversary. While Theinhaus and Bob had been making their short march across the hills the next morning, nine planes had been winging north from the RCAF base at Bagotville to search for the four others in the country around Lake Emmanuel until they were found.

Levesque had to be carried down to the plane. The crew

had a steaming meal ready, milk, soup and steaks. Real food was too rich for Bob and his came up about as fast as it went down. But that didn't matter. He'd have plenty of time to get used to eating again, he reminded himself. Ahead for all of them were soft beds, medical care, showers, shaves, smokes, any kind of food they wanted, families, home—all the things they had dreamed and talked about for so long.

Soon afterward the Canso lifted for the return flight and in minutes the miles that Bob, Dick, Theinhaus and Levesque had found so painful to trudge in those two final days were behind them and they were over Lake Emmanuel. The Norseman was already gone. Gas had been brought in and it had been flown out. The four caught a last glimpse of their little clearing, empty, covered with new snow, no sign of life around it. Feeling so much better already, they found it hard to believe that those terrible weeks down there had not been a dream.

There was a reception waiting at Bagotville such as a movie queen might have expected: a hushed crowd of about 200 clustered around the air station, including reporters, press and television photographers and radio technicians. Flashbulbs started popping and microphones were shoved in front of them the minute they stepped out of the Canso. It took them by surprise; they hadn't realized that their rescue was big news to the world that had waited 40 days for word of them. There was an ambulance waiting, too, but only Levesque needed it. Theinhaus even managed a little jig on the landing platform as he stepped out, just to show everyone he was all right.

It was quite a surprise to Bob to find that the Air Force doctors at the base hospital rated him in about as bad shape as Levesque. They ordered that the two men be hospitalized and be put on a special diet, but, after only three days, pronounced

Bob well and he was released. Levesque was hospitalized only a little longer. Dick also spent the week-end in the base hospital, but as a walking patient.

One thing that made all the men happy was that the doctors said flatly that none of the men was "bushed." Canadians don't use that term as it is used in the United States to indicate that a man is played out, completely exhausted. When a Canadian says someone is bushed, he means bush-queer, off his rocker from living too long alone in the woods, overwhelmed mentally by the immensity and loneliness of the country. That had not happened to any of the lost seven.

Vanstone, Abel, Koeten and Theinhaus flew on to Montreal that same Saturday afternoon, on the first leg of the trip home. Newspapermen who made the flight with them said it was easy to pick them out among the 47 passengers on the big airliner. They unwrapped sandwiches and peeled oranges all the way to Montreal.

In the end none of the men showed any lasting effects from the ordeal. Theinhaus and Koeten were home in Europe in a few days. Vanstone headed back to Toronto and school and his girl. Abel went home at once, and Dick, Levesque and Bob as soon as they were well enough.

In a few months all seven of them were back once more at their normal pursuits—the ordeal merely a memory. At Bagotville, however, Bob summed up their common feelings about the experience.

"The bush will never look the same to any of us again, and none of us will ever wonder again how a condemned man feels when he is reprieved at the last minute!"

The Desperate Search

"HEY, THERE!"

The shout was loud and clear, and Bill Metsala spun around, astonished.

He saw a thin, frail figure hunkered down on a log by a beaver pond about 40 yards away. So this was the man, Bill thought to himself, that he and more than 50 other volunteers had been searching for during the last three days. Was the man really alive? He looked more like a scarecrow.

His gray cotton pants and blue-jean wampus were both just rags and tatters. He wasn't wearing any gloves or hat, and his thin white hair framed a hunger-sunken face, which was stubbled with gray beard and seamed with scratches. When Bill started for him at a run, the gaunt figure pulled itself up from the log.

"I'm all right. Take your time," he croaked in a fatigue-broken voice.

That was the scene of Ed Downs' rescue. The 77-year-old sportsman had been lost for four cold days and three colder nights, without food or fire, in the tangled Michigan wilderness along the south shore of Lake Superior.

The near-tragedy had begun on the morning of October 11, 1953. It was cool and cloudy as Downs walked away from his cabin in the Whitefish River valley near the hamlet of Kiva, 25 miles southeast of Marquette, to spend a few hours that Sunday hunting for grouse.

He knew the country well, but, as he was to discover, not quite as well as he thought. Ed Downs made the mistake, a near fatal one in this case, of being over-confident. It's not hard to understand why he would feel more than adequately experienced to handle himself in the woods. Ed had hunted and fished nearly all his life, ever since his parents brought him to the town of Hastings, in southwestern Michigan, at the age of eight. He still lived in the town, where for many years he had worked as court bailiff. Much of his free time, however, had always been spent out in the woods hunting. All told, Ed had hunted deer in the Upper Peninsula of the state more than 40 years, and he had owned his cabin at Kiva, which he used as a base camp when hunting birds and deer, for seven or eight years.

The Whitefish River country is a sizable chunk of roadless forest, mixed swamp and hardwood ridges. Here and there one finds an abandoned clearing or old brush-grown logging road running through the timber. But all in all, it's an easy place to get lost in, especially on an overcast and windless day.

When Ed trudged into the woods that morning, he walked west from his cabin and the highway. He was carrying his 12-gauge Remington pumpgun, and his pipe, tobacco, a pocket full of matches and not much else. His compass was pinned to his hunting coat, which he left hanging on a peg in the cabin. He didn't need the coat on such a warm day; he never gave the compass a thought.

He was wearing a pair of old, patched, rubber-bottom pacs that he kept for hunting in dry weather, light cotton clothing over light underwear, and carrying a pair of cotton gloves. He had about a dozen shells for the Remington with him. That was Ed's complete inventory of clothing and equipment with which he would have to make do for the next 80 hours.

During the forenoon, he saw no grouse and didn't fire a shot. He had told his wife he would be back for dinner shortly after noon. When he looked at his watch and discovered it was already one, he turned and headed, so he thought, in the direction of the cabin. He knew he would be quite late.

For a couple of hours he tramped steadily, up one ridge and down another, and through narrow tongues of alder and cedar swamp. He knew something was wrong, but even then he felt no real concern. He was confident that if he walked steadily on in one direction he would come out of the timber before dark. His own place lay to the east, south was an old clearing where he had hunted many times, and north the brush-bordered fields of a neighboring farm. He knew he had to be traveling in the right direction; he couldn't be going toward the west. In the west there were only woods and swamps, and streams flooded by beaver dams. He had hunted all day in dry country. Not finding any water fit to drink was really the only thing that bothered him; he was beginning to suffer from thirst.

Late in the afternoon he heard a distant shot, off in what he thought was the north. He turned toward it, hoping that by walking in that direction he would find a hunter who could set him straight. Half an hour later he heard a second shot from the opposite direction. This time he fired an answer and then hurried that way. Nothing good came of those two attempts to make contact with other hunters. His sense of direction became even further confused, and he was diverted from the straight course he had been walking.

It was close to dark when Ed finally admitted to himself that he was hopelessly lost and would have to spend the night in the woods.

During the day he had lighted his pipe repeatedly. Now he

was down to two matches. He still had all of his shells but one. Those 11 shells represented just about all of his resources for helping himself to be found. He fired two signal shots. When they brought no reply, he set about the job of collecting dry firewood; however, he had waited too long. Daylight was fading; in the dusk he tripped time after time over logs and undergrowth in frost-killed thickets. The exertion aggravated his thirst, which now was a real torment.

When it was almost dark, Ed found a big pine stump that had a snug, cave-like hollow between its exposed roots. He decided he wouldn't find a better spot before dark for his night camp. Now for a fire. He hadn't been able to find any birch, pitch-fat pine twigs, or anything that was suitable for kindling. He didn't have his knife either, so he couldn't whittle shavings. By that time, Ed was beginning to panic. At least his next actions seem to indicate that. Breaking off a handful of small stuff from a dead tree, he piled it beside the stump and struck one of his two remaining matches. The wind caught the meager flame and it flickered out. Really worried now, Ed hurried as he scratched the second match. The yellow flame licked up among the twigs. They caught, smoldered, and a wisp of blue smoke curled up into Ed's face as he hovered over the beginnings of a fire. First the match flame died. The twigs continued to burn on, half-heartedly, for a minute or two. Then the tiny fire guttered and went out. Around him the silent woods were darker than before. Ed stayed on his knees a long time in front of the dead fire, stunned as the realization that he had to face a night without warmth sank in.

Standing up again at last, he fired a string of signal shots, one after the other. The search for him, however, had not yet been launched and no one answered the shots. He stopped shooting when he was down to three shells. Two of those, he discovered, wouldn't chamber in the pump gun. He realized then that they must be two ancient black-powder hulls that had been in his gear for more years than he could remember. He decided to hang onto the only usable shell he had left.

He didn't try to make a bed for himself, but he did scoop out some of the leaves and the trash from between the roots of the stump, which helped to shelter his head and shoulders a little. He broke off some big slabs of bark, sat down and covered his legs with them. The night wasn't too cold. He didn't mind the hunger and, now that he wasn't moving around, his thirst abated somewhat. He slept fitfully, nevertheless, waking, moving his arms and legs to work the chill out of them, and then drifting off to sleep again.

Sometime toward morning it started to rain. Ed awoke. He saw that the stump was protecting his head and face, and the bark was keeping the rest of his body reasonably dry. It turned out to be a brief shower. He awoke again at first light, feeling unrested, stiff and sore. The sky was so heavily overcast that he couldn't see at which point on the horizon the sun was rising. This didn't discourage Ed too much; glad it was light again, he rubbed the stiffness out of his legs. Then he struck off toward what he believed to be east, confident that within an hour or so he would come to an old logging road that led back to his cabin.

About midmorning he found water—the first since becoming lost. It was only a little shallow pool in an alder bog. It was filled with dead leaves, stagnant and roily, but by that time he was too thirsty to care. He got down and put his face into it and drank. The water was cold and tasted pretty good. An hour or so later he found a beaver pond on a small creek, and after that he was careful not to wander far from a stream. Ed had learned that water is the one thing a man who is lost can't do without. As he continued to walk, he crossed quite a few creeks by walking across beaver dams. Each time he was careful not to fall in, aware that if he got wet he would be in real trouble. He was also careful to circle big cedar swamps, knowing that it would be exhausting to try to force his way through them.

It was sometime Monday afternoon that he saw a squirrel, the first living creature to cross his path since he had become lost. He didn't consider shooting it for food. Ed didn't have any salt and no way to make a fire; he just wasn't hungry enough at that point to tackle raw squirrel meat.

He still believed during the day that he would at any moment find his way out of the woods. He walked steadily all that day, stopping now and then to rest briefly, and then forcing himself to his feet and slogging on again. By late afternoon— even though it was full daylight—he was beginning to trip over brush and logs. He fell heavily several times before calling it a day at dusk.

When the failing light of the cold, raw autumn evening made further walking impossible. Ed resigned himself to a second night in the woods and went about fixing a bed. He had to sleep in the open, since there wasn't even the inadequate shelter of a stump around. With fresh evergreen branches, he fashioned a crude bed. Some of the boughs he used to cover himself with.

The temperature fell to nine degrees below freezing during the night, silvering the ground with frost. It was much worse than the night before. Ed lay on his rough bed, shivering and miserable, as the hours of the long night slowly slipped away. His feet were aching with cold, but he was too exhausted to get up to tromp some warmth into them. Yet he was only able to sleep a little. Despite the misery of the night, in the morning Ed was in good spirits. Still confident that he would find his way out, he felt no fear over the outcome of this ordeal.

Possibly Ed was optimistic because he felt he had to be; he never believed that his disappearance would trigger any sort of search. Besides, he told himself, that wasn't necessary. He would do it on his own. As a result, although he had heard aircraft two or three times on Monday, he never thought they might be search planes. He would have been amazed to learn that his name was in front-page headlines halfway across the country by that time, and that his disappearance had touched off the full search machinery of a state that spares no effort when the cry "Lost hunter!" goes out.

Ed Downs might have thought his being lost wouldn't make news, but actually his story was one to stir the imagination and sympathy of all who read it. Here was a man close to 80 years of age, suffering from hunger and cold as he wandered helplessly through a maze of roadless woods. People in cities as far away as 500 miles, well-fed and warm, pondered the fate of Ed Downs, trying to answer the questions his story caused to leap into their minds. Where was he in that tangle of country south of Lake Superior? How was he protecting himself against the cold of the October night? Would he ever be found? When? In time?

Although he didn't know it, a desperate search was under way for Ed Downs in the area where he had become lost. Keeping his advanced age in mind, the searchers weren't wasting a minute.

When Ed had failed to return to the cabin on time for dinner that Sunday, his wife wasn't alarmed. She was used to having him come home an hour or two late when he had been out hunting. When he hadn't showed up by dark, however, Mrs. Downs knew something was wrong. Ed must have either become lost or have suffered a mishap of some kind. Without further delay she notified the Michigan State Police that Ed was missing and asked them for help.

A detail from the Marquette post reached the cabin promptly, but there was little the police could do that night. They drove along the roads in the vicinity of the woods until after midnight, flashing a spotlight against the cloudy sky in the hope of attracting the lost man's attention. That brought no results, so they returned to the post to organize a full-scale search for the next morning.

The police search party was back shortly after daylight, reinforced by other men who knew the area well: state conservation officers, sheriff's deputies and a posse of trappers and woodsmen recruited from around Marquette. A state police plane was assigned to fly a low-altitude grid pattern over the wooded country in which the lost man was believed to be wandering. And at the same time, anxious to overlook no means for rescuing Ed, the searchers fell back on one of the oldest tools of the trade—tracking. A trained bloodhound was sent for from Wisconsin, 150 miles away.

On Monday the efforts of the manhunt proved fruitless. Ground searchers and those in the plane saw nothing. The dog, which only arrived after dark, was unable to pick up the track, since the ground had frosted by that time. At dark the search ground to a halt to await daylight. By then fear had spread among the tired men that Ed Downs, lost now for two days and a night, would not be found alive.

Ed himself said later that there was little to tell about his experiences on Tuesday; however, if one has spent much time in the woods, it is easy to piece the details of his day together. Ed was up at daylight, chilled and unrested after another almost sleepless night. Although he felt surprisingly little discomfort from hunger, the lack of food was causing him to grow steadily weaker. He plodded on all day. He fell frequently, and, in doing so, scratched and bruised himself from head to foot. Sometime during the day, in an effort to curb the growing number of falls, he started using his gun as a cane.

It was also on Tuesday that Ed started losing things. Hungry for the comfort of his pipe, which he had no way of lighting, he took a pinch of tobacco out of his pouch and chewed it. That helped to relieve the craving. When he reached for the pouch later on, however, it was gone. He never did know what happened to it.

"I guess I must have dropped it instead of putting it back in my pocket," he admitted later with a dry grin.

During Tuesday he also lost his glasses, his cap and one of his gloves. By this time the legs of his pants and the sleeves of his jacket were in shreds, and his pacs were falling apart. Although he didn't realize it at the time, by the end of Tuesday his ordeal had caused him to become confused mentally as well as depleted physically. That afternoon he wandered back and forth, unable to concentrate on maintaining a straight course. He heard the sound of deer and other animals in the timber around him. Looking back on it later, he was certain the noises had been imaginary. His bed Tuesday night was the same as the night before: a scanty armful of evergreen branches to fend off the sharp, still cold.

Without letup the search party combed the woods again on Tuesday, in the face of fading hope. The bloodhound was started at the door of the Downs' cabin that morning and was led off in the direction Ed had gone. The searchers hoped the hound might strike the track, but it was 48 hours old. The melting frosts of two nights had washed out the scent. The dog bayed a few times near the cabin, but whatever trail he found was too faint to follow.

On Tuesday afternoon the searchers came across the crude bed of dry leaves and balsam branches on which the lost man had slept Monday night. They found no ashes, no sign at all of a fire. Now they had the answer to two big questions. They knew that they were looking for a hunter who was still alive, lost and wandering in the woods, not for the body of a dead man. Many had feared Ed might have been fatally stricken by a heart attack. They also knew that Ed was without fire, with which he could have signaled and kept himself warm.

On Wednesday morning a helicopter from the U.S. Coast Guard station at Traverse City joined the search in a last desperate bid to locate the lost man from the air. Hope was waning fast now. Even Ed's distraught wife agreed if he wasn't found that day, he would never be found alive. Everyone voiced the same opinion: three days and three nights in Michigan's northern woods without food or fire to ward off the chill of fall are about all a man of 77 can endure.

But Ed Downs could take more than that and proved it. On Wednesday morning he saw the sun for the first time since becoming lost. It rose in a cloudless sky. When he started off that morning, he was at least certain which direction was east. He was hobbling on blistered feet and tired old legs that would hardly bear his weight; however, he was confident that if he could push on for an hour or two more he would find the old logging road he had been looking for in vain for more than two discouraging days of wandering.

The Desperate Search

The trouble now, however, was that walking had really become too much for him. He was tripping so often that he finally broke a dry branch to use as a second cane. He could make only a few yards at a time, and his rest periods grew longer and longer. Ed was very close to the end of his endurance. He shuffled along all morning until noon. It was around then that he decided he had bypassed the logging road; he hadn't seen a familiar landmark since Sunday morning. His resolution to find his way out failed at that point. It no longer seemed to matter which way he walked. Thereafter, Ed wandered aimlessly.

He was following a deer runway because it was easier going, when he came to a fallen log. Clambering over it, he broke off a small dead tree that leaned in his way. After a while Ed was back at the same place. There was the log and the broken snag. He knew then he had been circling but couldn't straighten himself out. Anyway, it didn't seem to make a great deal of difference. A little later he crossed the log again. This time he wasn't even able to decide whether he had been circling again or merely back-tracking. It troubled him, but once more he decided it didn't make much difference.

Rescue came heartbreakingly close on Wednesday, only to pass him by. He had heard aircraft several times on Tuesday and again that morning, and guessed they were looking for him. About noon, resting in thick stuff along a creek, he heard a plane thundering straight at him. It pounded over so close that he could see the two men in it peering down over the side. He jumped to his feet and waved his arms frantically, but the plane droned on.

He sank down on a log, exhausted and disheartened, and was still sitting there when he heard the plane, making a wide turn in the distance, head back. As it swept over again, not quite so near, he crammed his one good shell into the chamber of the pumpgun and fired it. The roar of the engine, however, drowned out the noise of the shot. The plane flew on. Twice after that it passed within sight, each time a little farther away.

Shortly after noon on Wednesday ground searchers found a second bed—the one in which Ed had spent Tuesday night. It told them only that he was still alive at that time and still without fire. The helicopter went back to its base late that afternoon. This was no longer a job for aircraft, even for such good search craft. If Ed were found now, it would be by men on foot, plodding through the thickets, and looking behind logs and under the low branches of evergreens. Plans were laid to build up the ranks of the posse to 300 men by the next morning. It takes more searchers to find a dead man than a live one.

Later Ed could not remember much about Wednesday afternoon, except that the plane had flown over him four times. He had little or no sense of direction left, and he moved very slowly, taking a few tottering steps only to sink down, and then staggering on once more.

An hour or so before sunset he started to make a bed for his fourth night in the woods. He broke off a few evergreen branches but his exhaustion was so great that he slumped on a log to rest. Hunched there with his chin in his hands, nearly unconscious from the results of being lost for 80 terrible hours, he heard a noise in the brush near by. Ed looked up and saw Bill Metsala, a trapper who lived not far from his cabin, peering this way and that as he walked along a low ridge.

Bill had not yet seen him. Ed pulled together what strength he had left and let out a loud yell. Startled, the trapper whirled around and then started for him at a run.

"He came lickity toot!" Downs recalled with a chuckle.

Bill fired three shots into the air—the prearranged signal that meant Ed had been found. More searchers arrived on the scene in a very few minutes. Two of them supported Ed while getting him out of the woods. Ed could hardly believe he had been found. For supper that night he ate hot soup, while warming up under woolen blankets in a Marquette hospital. It was a wonderful change after the long days and nights of cold and hunger.

Despite the severity of the ordeal for a man of his age, Ed Downs came through in remarkably good condition. His weight had dropped from 125 to 109, the broken pacs had galled his feet, and he was scratched and pummeled from many falls; however, he suffered no serious or permanent effects. Four days in the hospital fixed him up about as good as new.

Whenever he spoke about his experience, Ed would always mention a couple of simple rules that would keep other hunters out of the kind of trouble he had known. First, he would warn, never go into the woods, even if you know the country, without a compass, a knife and a reserve supply of matches. No matter what happens, keep those matches for an emergency. If one does become lost and realizes he can't get out of the woods before dark, he should get a fire going and stay in one place until help arrives. Ed's experience proves the soundness of that last one.

He got the surprise of his life when Bill explained that at no time had Ed ever been four miles away from his cabin. If he had remained by the stump where he spent Sunday night, he would undoubtedly have been rescued the next day.

"Wandering won't get you anywhere," he would say, remembering. "It's no use to travel unless you are sure of your directions and know where you are going. Don't ever count on your judgment to take the place of a compass, either, and don't be cocky about getting out by yourself. I'll tell you something. Being lost is a terrible experience, and four days of it is plenty long enough."

The Bad Actors of Africa

THE RHINO was a big cow, weighing around 3,500 pounds, with a snub-nosed calf in tow. That's a bad combination with dangerous game of any kind, and Berry Brooks scented trouble the instant he saw them. She couldn't fail to get his wind, and when she did, he was certain she'd come for him.

He had been photographing birds along the edge of a big papyrus swamp on the Tsavo River in Kenya when he heard the two animals floundering through the dry reeds. He wasn't sure what they were at first, but a couple of hundred yards farther on he came across their tracks where they had gone down into the swamp to water.

If not disturbed, rhinos often leave a thickly grown place of that kind at the same spot where they go in. The cow-and-calf team promised something unusual in pictures, so Brooks set his cameras up near by and got ready.

They didn't keep him waiting. He heard them breaking through to the edge of the papyrus, and then the old lady came into the open with the calf beside her. Both were coated with grayish swamp mud, and looked whiter than any rhinos he had ever seen.

As they started across a strip of marshy plain, he tripped the shutter on his movie camera. The cow heard the whirring noise, stopped and, in the same instant, got his scent. Her big square head went down and her ridiculous little tail went up. She whipped to the left and plowed three or four times her own length, charging blindly, until she ran out of the scent ribbon. She changed ends then and went tearing to the right. When that failed to pay off she came back to the spot where she had first smelled the man and stopped to take inventory.

A second later the vicious, two-horned head went down again. She had the scent and was charging squarely on the beam at last.

There are few things in Africa more businesslike and determined than the charge of an enraged rhino. A lion charges with far more dash and speed, a buffalo is more vindictive, and an elephant more upsetting. But a rhino settles down and comes on as if nothing could turn him aside or stop him, and by the time he gets close he has a man half convinced that nothing can. An experienced and cool-headed hunter, however, has one advantage: the rhino's poor eyesight. No other dangerous animal in Africa has such poor vision. Veteran hunters say a rhino can't spot a man in the open if he is more than 75 yards away, and at times the animal is not likely to see him clearly at all until he's almost on top of his target.

Berry's Awemba gunbearer, Siede, was standing beside him, ready to put a .470 double express rifle in his hands, but the hunter had no intention of killing the cow if he could avoid it, and he was sure he could. Before setting up the camera he had studied the surroundings carefully. He knew exactly where he and Siede were going to do their dodging and running when the showdown came.

But they didn't have to dodge. When the cow was a dozen yards away, Brooks realized she had failed to locate them. She was charging blindly on a course that would take her past him just to his right, unless she changed direction.

He kept the movie camera going until her head and shoulders filled and overflowed the view finder. When he looked up she was pounding past no more than three paces from him, head down and tail stiffly erect, with the calf lumbering at her heels.

Berry swung the camera and picked her up again as she went away, half expecting her to turn and come thundering back when she discovered she had lost the scent. But she kept going instead, and he was still exposing film as the two animals disappeared into thick bush. He turned to look at Siede. The gunbearer hadn't moved out of his tracks. He was watching his *bwana* with an exultant grin, and Brooks knew he had a man he could count on.

This was a dream safari. Berry, a cotton merchant from Memphis, Tennessee, was allowing himself seven months in Africa to collect the trophies and make the pictures he wanted.

He had made his first African hunt two years earlier, in 1947, spending two months in the bush and returning home with trophies of 32 species of game, the kind most successful safaris take, including good elephant, rhino and lion.

This time he had planned a far more ambitious undertaking. Before this safari returned to its starting point of Nairobi, it would cover 18,000 miles, doubling back and forth through Kenya and Tanganyika, north through the Belgian Congo, down the Nile in the Anglo-Egyptian Sudan and then far south to the game paradise of Northern Rhodesia. The party would travel through country that almost no white hunters had penetrated, winching their cars out of mud, ferrying over crocodile-infested rivers on rafts made by lashing native dugouts together, tramping through 2,000 miles of forest and veldt on foot, and wallowing through swamps where mire and water were armpit deep.

The effort and hardships would be terrific. There would

be black bees and mosquitoes, tsetse flies and ants and scorpions, scorching heat in the jungle and numbing cold on the mountains, thirst and malaria, blistered feet and dysentery, and bone-deep fatigue. But the rewards would be correspondingly great. There would be pictures and trophies of a kind few men had seen, adventures to be remembered forever.

Unique game pictures, both movies and stills, were Berry's foremost objective. Although he loved hunting above all other sports and prized good trophies as highly as any sportsman, he had shot enough African game for his personal gratification on his earlier safari. This time he wanted primarily to share the fruits of his trip with others. Whatever trophies he took would be turned over to establish an African hall in the Memphis Public Museum. That had been a dream of his for a long time. Even more, he hoped for the kind of game pictures few sportsmen ever have had a chance to make, including an outstanding movie that would bring pleasure to people who might never see firsthand the vast, teeming treasure house of bird and animal and reptile life that is Africa. Throughout this safari the camera would be used more than the gun.

Among the rare animals he hoped to photograph and collect were the maneless zebra from the almost impenetrable swamps along the Sudan Nile, a species not known until 1947 to exist; the rare black lechwe, an antelope found in the treacherous papyrus swamps of Northern Rhodesia; the red lechwe; the sassaby, a large dark purplish red antelope; the sitatunga, which, although allied to the harnessed antelopes, is not striped with white except when young; and above all, the Nile lechwe, a big antelope living only in the unvisited swamps that border the Nile in the Sudan, a trophy not more than a handful of American sportsmen had ever heard of.

He knew he was taking on a tough assignment. The mane-less zebra, for example, had been hunted by only one white man, a Dane. The Nile lechwe had never been photographed and had been shot by an American only once, in 1936, when Bill Campbell collected one for the American Museum of Natural History. Berry was prepared, however, for whatever lay ahead; he had engaged one of the best professional white hunters in Africa, Don Ker of the Nairobi outfitting firm of Ker and Downy. Don Ker was as interested as Berry in the objectives of the safari.

They had rare luck. The safari left Nairobi on January 29, 1949, and returned on August 26. In those 210 days there was not one, save for a brief spell in April while Berry battled malaria, when he did not see wildlife of some kind within camera or gun range. He collected 37 species of game he had not taken previously, including some of the rarest and most difficult to get in Africa. He came home with 18,000 feet of 16 mm. motion picture color film, and 4,800 still pictures, more than 4,000 of wildlife. The price he paid for these films was more than one close brush with danger, more than one show-down with wounded animals or those he crowded too hard. He had close and hair-raising dealings with all of Africa's big five—elephant, rhino, buffalo, lion and leopard.

The morning he wandered onto the cow and calf rhino the safari was only two days out of Nairobi, but already Berry had stalked and filmed two bull rhinos, a herd of 100 elephants, a big zebra herd, a bull elephant with 40-pound tusks and a good black-maned lion. The safari was off to a lively start.

Following the rhino spisode they drove south through Kenya and into Tanganyika; the game seemed to get more and more abundant. On the Serengeti plains they traveled through a herd of Thompson gazelles that was 30 miles long and 20 wide—the biggest Don had ever seen. From the rim of the extinct crater of Ngorongoro they looked down on the fantastic spectacle of countless thousands of game animals. They watched hyenas and leopards make kills, saw a ten-foot python attack a big lizard within five paces of their breakfast table, heard lions roar outside their tents night after night, saw a single herd of wildebeest which Don estimated to contain 300,000 head, and from only a few steps away filmed a pack of wild dogs. In March they moved into the Belgian Congo, where in one day Berry was charged by a bull elephant, nine buffaloes, and an enraged hippo.

The buffalo herd came first. The animals were grazing in dry, open country dotted with patches of low scrub, when Berry turned his camera on them from behind a clump of brush at 100 yards. Then, not satisfied with the range, he moved 25 yards nearer, stepping into the open. They saw him, lined up, and advanced at a trot.

Berry was in a tight spot. Siede was at his elbow with the .470 and Don was backing him, but Berry knew that even these reinforcements would not have the slightest chance of stopping all nine bulls if they really meant business. But for some reason, maybe because the buffaloes had never smelled man before, they stopped 35 yards away from the men and finally backed off, pawing the ground and swinging their heads. It was one of the closest shaves Berry had in Africa.

Less than three hours later he took on the enraged hippo. The river pig is not generally considered dangerous; however, if cornered or surprised at close range, he can be decidedly mean. There are places in Africa where the hippo regularly waylays and kills the natives' cattle at waterholes, and charges dugouts on sight. This one was a big, surly-looking bull, feeding along the Rutchuru River. Berry moved in with his movie camera to within 25 feet. The hippo's temper exploded at that point, and he broke into a lumbering charge.

There was only one thing for Brooks to do and he did it. He abandoned his camera and ran. The soles of his feet were covered with blisters, the result of long hard days on the game trails in punishing equatorial heat, but in his flight Berry forgot the blisters and left the hippo so far behind that it gave up.

The brush with the elephant came that same afternoon. He was a big bull with good ivory; they spotted him feeding in the open. Berry stalked to within 50 yards, and set his movie camera going from the shelter of the thicket. Then the wind shifted.

It all happened in a clock tick. One second the bull was browsing peaceably, breaking off leafy branches and curling them into his mouth. The next second he smelled man and was charging, trunk lifted high, ears spread out like giant bat wings. Don yelled to run, but Berry wanted a film record of the charge and stuck to his camera until the elephant's head filled the view finder. When he looked up he saw he had let the bull get closer than he intended.

He left the camera, dodged to the right, and for the second time that day called on his blistered feet to save his skin. A second later looking back over his shoulder, he saw that the elephant was still coming. He remembered that Don had told him to throw his hat on the ground if ever charged by elephant. Sometimes a maddened brute will stop to trample a hat, giving a hunter a chance to get away, Don had explained. Berry flung his hat off with a backward sweep of one arm and kept on running. When he looked back again, the elephant had stopped just short of the hat and was standing, shuffling his feet, trunk still lifted. Barry had shaken him off.

A couple of days after that, while filming a big herd of hippos (126 in sight at one time) on a mud bar in the Rutchuru, he witnessed one of the most exciting episodes of the entire safari; a battle to the death between two bull hippos that were tangling over the affections of a lumbering cow.

As Berry watched, they slashed and tore at each other savagely, coming together with their huge, tusk-studded jaws gaping wide, churning the river to muddy foam, breaking apart, resting a few minutes, then rushing each other again. The battle continued hour after hour, and the other river pigs gathered around like ringside spectators at a heavyweight bout. They were still fighting when Berry left at dark, five hours after the battle began. When he went back the next morning one bull lay dead on shore, its throat ripped wide open. Berry noticed the victor was sidling coyly up to the cow that was the cause of it all.

From the Belgian Congo the safari crossed into the Anglo-Egyptian Sudan, pushed into the great roadless Loweli Swamp, where no vehicles had ever turned a wheel before, and collected two maneless zebra stallions in a single day—the second and third ever taken by a white man.

From there they went on to the country of the Dinkas, a tall, thin, long-legged people who live in the great papyrus swamps along the Nile. The most primitive blacks in Africa, the Dinkas outrank even the pigmies of the Ituri rain forest in their aboriginal way of life. Only the married women of the tribe wear clothing of any kind, and that merely consists of two very abbreviated aprons of goatskin, worn front and back, from a waist cord. The men and unmarried women go around stark naked at all times, except for a string or two of beads or ivory ornaments worn around the waist or chest.

Although Berry was in the Dinka country for almost a month, he never did get used to seeing the six-foot black belles walking around nude, equally innocent of clothes and shame.

Both sexes dress their bodies with the gray ash of burned cowdung to keep off the swarming hordes of flies and mosquitoes that infest the swamps where they live, and plaster their hair down with fresh cowdung, rinsed out with cow urine, which produces an odd yellowish-brown bleach.

Here in the Dinka swamps, wallowing hip-deep in mud, Brooks killed a situtunga—a strange, long-haired, twisted-horned antelope—the first, so far as he could learn, ever taken by an American sportsman. Then the safari set up base camp on the shore of a big lake along the Nile and made ready for the most important quest of all: the search for the animal that Berry wanted to photograph and collect more than any other in Africa—the extremely rare Nile lechwe.

At the camp a Dinka said he knew where there were many lechwe, so the next morning Berry and Don crossed the lake in Dinka dugouts—the strangest craft they had ever seen. Each was made of two palm trunks laid butt to butt and lashed together. Tapering enough to keep bow and stern above the water, the trunks were left open at each end.

Beyond the lake lay an open, half-flooded, treeless swamp, in which grass alternated with big beds of reed. The men pushed on afoot, wallowing across flooded areas on mats of dead reeds, and breaking through to plunge shoulder-deep into mud and water.

Two hours of wretched toil took them two miles. Suddenly their tracker swept an arm off to the right. Half a mile away, silhouetted on the flat, empty skyline, was a herd of game. Berry and Don lifted their glasses to look at a band of close to 150 Nile lechwe. Probably no other white man had ever seen such a sight. They stood speechless, glassing the herd carefully, studying the curving, backswept horns, the saddle of white across the necks, the curious antelope tails that never stopped switching, and most of all, the strange posture of the animals as they walk and feed: shoulders low and rump high.

With his glasses Berry could pick out not fewer than 30 old bulls, which are distinguishable by their black hides. The young bulls are rich chestnut-brown, the cows lighter brown. Berry and Don took their time studying the herd with the binoculars, trying to locate the biggest of the bulls. Then they began a slow stalk across the open marsh, wading, slipping and floundering. At 300 yards the herd grew restless, at 200 it was evident the hunters could get no nearer.

Berry was up to his belt in water and mud. Although he had made clean kills with his last 12 consecutive shots, now, with the blue chips of the long hunt lying on the table, he didn't feel too confident. But when his scope-sighted .300 Magnum sounded its thunderclap, they heard, clear and loud, the 180-grain open-point bullet smack home.

The bull stumbled, ran into the middle of the milling herd and went down. A smaller bull rushed at him and raked him as he lay dying on the ground. He staggered to his feet, made one savage counterlunge, and fell dead.

The herd ran 50 yards, then stopped for another look. Berry dropped his second bull with a shoulder shot. The second shot caused the rest of the herd to stampede; however, after 400 yards, it stopped and resumed grazing.

The two bulls Berry had taken represented his full quota

of Nile lechwe—for a lifetime. Under Sudan game regulations then, a sportsman was entitled to only one license during his lifetime to hunt this rare antelope. But Berry wasn't disappointed; both trophies were good ones. The horns of the first measured 33 inches, the second 30½. The world record at the time was 34¼.

Don and Berry spent the rest of the day following the herd with cameras, taking pictures that Brooks later prized almost as highly as the two lechwe trophies.

Still in the Sudan, Berry next went after buffalo along the White Nile, tramping through forests of thick bush and low trees in burning heat that caused his toes to swell and blister until each step he took was agony. But there were rewards. He killed a fine bull, with wide-spreading, heavy horns, which were as sharp tipped as stilettos, with one shot from the .470. The first kill precipitated a lively brush with a second bull that was lying beside the first, a mangy old outlaw with blunt stubs of horns. At the crack of the rifle, it came for him and Don, but at 15 paces, when Berry had his sights lined on its chest and was starting to squeeze the trigger, the buffalo changed its mind. It swerved so abruptly that its hoofs gouged out small clods of turf.

Later that same day, on the way back to the safari car, Berry's black tracker, N'Yamu, stopped suddenly and pointed out a third bull, as good as the one they had killed, lying under a scrubby tree 50 yards away.

This one boiled to his feet and started for them at a fast trot, but not in a real charge. He seemed to want to look them over at close range. He was hostile but not deadly, yet. He trotted to within ten paces, while Berry kept his movie camera grinding. Then, just as Berry was reaching back to take the

.470 from Siede, the bull stopped, head high, facing the intruders with a hard, defiant stare of sullen hatred.

This was the closest Berry had ever been to a live African buffalo. He braced himself and got the rifle ready for the shot. But the charge never came. The hulking black brute suddenly wheeled and galloped off. At 30 yards he stopped, turned and had another look. Then he lurched around and left at a steady trot.

There was a day, after the safari left the Sudan and returned to the game riches of Kenya, when Berry could have killed elephant, rhino, buffalo, lion and leopard between breakfast and lunch, and taken respectable trophies of all five. He shot only the leopard, however, and it gave Berry and Don a tense few minutes following it into tall grass after a 220-grain Silvertip from Berry's .300 Magnum had failed to do a clean job. But the leopard was done for; when they caught up with it, the cat was flailing the ground under a fallen tree, in its death flurry.

Then Brooks went after a lion in the Masai country. He was not willing to kill a trophy over bait, but he had no scruples against using bait to promote his camera hunting. Therefore, he shot zebra, kongoni, topi and wildebeest and pegged the carcasses out as lion lure, building thornbush blinds near by.

The baits drew hyenas first; however, as they began to ripen, lions went to work on them. Berry drove out near a zebra carcass before dawn one morning and crept into the blind from which he could hear something tearing at the bait. When the light brightened he made out four lionesses and a small male. They had pulled the zebra out of the tree where it had hung and were tearing it apart. Berry took a few pictures, but the lions were not spectacular enough to suit him, so he backed out of

the blind and drove to the next bait. There he found as handsome and regal a pair of maned lions as he had ever seen. They
too had managed to drag the bait out of the tree and had eaten
their fill. The pair were lying now in a patch of shade, guarding
what was left.

They proved superb models, eying the approaching hunters with aloof disdain, refusing to leave their shade, watching
with a cold expression in their yellow eyes that said plainly nobody better force the issue. Berry was challenged afterward
on the pictures he took of the pair. The shots looked too posed
and perfect to be true, and a few skeptics accused him of filming park lions. Actually, never once on the entire safari did he
trip his shutter on game in a reserve. His camera hunting was
done without exception in the same places where he took his
trophies, in territory where the camera and the gun were both
legal.

The next morning he tangled with the most cantankerous
lion he saw on the hunt. At one of the blinds he found seven
lionesses and a fairly good lion on the bait, and crawled into the
blind for close-ups. A little later he happened to look behind
him—and there strolling arrogantly in was a fine maned lion.

Simba hadn't spotted the man in the thorn blind; Berry
waited for him to walk in front of the cameras, but he never
made it. All of a sudden three of the lionesses left the carcass
and went streaking for the intruding male. He turned tail and
they ran him into the bush 500 yards away.

Half an hour later he showed up again, angling in from the
side. The three females, apparently protecting the young lion
in their group, rushed him again. This time, however, he stood
his ground, and they backed down. Then he singled out the
cause of all the trouble, the young male, and went for him like

an avenging thunderbolt. Junior took his cue and ran; the old man chased him far enough to make the lesson stick, then turned and started back for lunch.

Berry had stepped out of the blind to record the action with his movie camera. When the big lion was 100 feet away he picked up man scent, which he was in no mood to tolerate. He stopped short, growling, his black-tipped tail twitching. Then he pivoted around and came for Berry in long bounds.

The charge of a wounded or cornered lion in thick cover is a deadly serious affair. He comes with one idea in mind—to close the gap and maul and kill. But a lion charging in the open, for no better reason than that he has been crowded too close or that his regal dignity has been disturbed, or because he has had family troubles, is more showy than dangerous. All he wants is to run off the source of his annoyance; the rush is half bluff.

Siede was standing by with the .470, but Berry did not want to kill the lion if he could help it. He and the gun bearer ran behind the blind, circled a thorn clump and sprinted off to one side. The lion lost their scent and stopped, stood for a minute, snarling and muttering, and then stalked over to the bait and lay down. Berry decided to take the hint, and left the area.

On the way back to the camp that noon he ran into so big a pride of lions that he could not get them all in his viewfinder at once. There were a dozen in the lot, six males and six females, lying in the thin shade of a leaning acacia tree. Full fed on a kill of their own, they impressed Berry as being as contented as indulged house cats; he spent an exciting hour photographing them at close range. It provided him with everything he had hoped for in lion pictures.

Now he wanted a lion trophy.

He had made it a rule of the safari not to kill any animal he photographed, except in self-defense. If a lion or a rhino or an elephant posed for him, he felt the beast was entitled to walk off unharmed. As for lions, he had decided he wouldn't use bait in order to shoot one. So he went looking in the open for a heavy-maned male.

It took him only two days there in the Masai country to find what he wanted. Driving along in the safari car, he and Don spotted a big lion with a very heavy mane, walking slowly along the crest of a low ridge 400 yards away. Silhouetted against the sunrise, it was one of the most majestic and beautiful specimens they had seen on the safari.

During the months they had been on the hunt, Berry had had opportunities in non-game-reserve areas to kill at least 25 male lions, not to mention countless females and youngsters. None of them, however, had quite met his requirements. This one did. The hunters sat tight until the lion disappeared over the hill, then Berry grabbed his .300 Magnum out of the gun rack of the hunting car, jumped down and ran for the ridge at a half crouch.

They were on an open plain with little cover, but the low rise of ground would hide him until he reached the top. He dropped down on his belly and crawled the last 10 yards, poking his head up cautiously behind a fringe of short grass. The lion was walking away from him, 200 paces off.

The scope on the rifle confirmed his exceptional size, thick mane and good color. Berry rammed a shot home at the roots of his tail.

The lion lunged forward and went down in a ball, but was up again almost instantly, running for a patch of thick cover. Berry put a second shot in the shoulder, and the lion dropped and rolled into the grass. Brooks could see the movement from his thrashing around, so he went in very cautiously. If the big cat had life enough left to manage a charge, he would come out murder-bent, an altogether different lion than the one that had blustered at the bait a couple of days before. This fellow would have to be stopped at very close range, stopped cold with the first shot.

Berry walked up to the grass as if he were treading on eggs, and not until he had circled it at a distance of only four or five yards without provoking a growl did he venture in. The lion was dead.

With Berry's acquisition of the extraordinary lion trophy, the safari left the Masai country, heading for Mount Kenya and setting its sights on black rhinos. The hunters made camp in an open grove at an altitude of 8,000 feet, which happened to be square on the equator. Nevertheless, they shivered at night, even under four blankets.

Some Kikuyus, natives from a nearby village, told them there was a very good rhino that used the natural salt licks on Kihali Hill, three miles away. The rhino was old, the blacks reported, and would be hard to hunt, but he was big and his horn was long.

The almost impenetrable tangle of bush in this area proved to be an effective cover for rhinos. The hunters could get through only by following rhino trails, virtual tunnels angling through the thickets, which were interlaced with brush overhead. The bush semed especially bad on Kihali Hill, so Don advised they skip it. For days Berry managed to average 18 to 20 miles on foot, but the going was the worst imaginable. Poisonous nettles stung him. He suffered continuously from the altitude, becoming drenched with sweat while walking and shivering in the thin air each time he stopped to rest. The hunters traveled uphill and down, alert at every turn against blundering into a rhino unexpectedly. He and Don saw bushbucks, buffalo, elephants, monkeys and forest boars, plus plenty of rhino tracks but nothing of Mr. Horns himself. The Kikuyus still insisted that the big bull was somewhere on Kihali Hill. Then one morning while Berry and Don were at breakfast, a native boy came into camp to report that he had seen the big rhino near the top of the hill on the previous afternoon and believed he was frequenting a salt lick there.

After hurrying through their meal, they followed the boy all the way to the top of the hill, where they had not gone before. The boy did his best, but could produce no sign of the rhino. It had rained the evening before; if there had been tracks, they had washed away. After an hour of hunting in dense cover around the rim of an ancient crater, they gave up and started back.

Halfway down the hill, they came to a clearing from which they could see their safari car below. A native left to guard it spotted them and signaled frantically. They realized he had spotted a rhino, maybe the one they were looking for, so they turned and labored up the hill once more.

A hundred yards below the crater rim, Berry broke out of the dense bush on the edge of a ravine, and found himself face to face with the biggest rhino he had ever seen. It was standing 60 paces away on the far side of the ravine.

The bull had made himself a wallow on a knoll there. Having heard or scented the hunters, the rhino was waiting for them with angry truculence written all over him. Berry saw at once that this was the trophy for which he had been hunting a week. This was a monster rhino; the horn looked longer than a man's arm.

The situation wasn't to the hunter's liking. The brute, facing head-on, offered him a frontal shot—a poor one on a rhino. A rhino's horn will stop or deflect the heaviest bullet, so it's useless to try for the head in such a case. Berry reminded himself, however, that if he just hadn't happened to have come out the bush where he did, there might be much less than 60 yards between him and the bull. This bull, facing the man squarely, didn't show much shoulder for a target. His actions, however, warned he was ready to charge; Berry's best chance was to try to get in an effective shot before he moved.

Picking a spot on the front of the shoulder, Berry drove home a 500-grain solid bullet from the right barrel of the .470, hoping it would rake the entire length of the rhino's body, perhaps smashing both shoulder and hip. The impact of the heavy bullet, driven by 100 grains of Cordite, turned the bull's tremendous body halfway around. At the same instant, Berry poured a 500-grain softpoint from the other barrel into the rhino's side, just back of the shoulder.

The two bullets knocked all notion of charging out of the rhino. He lunged headlong into the bush and went crashing down the steep hillside in blind flight, breaking through the thickets like a runaway bulldozer.

Berry and Siede picked up the track and found blood at once. The spoor led down through dense bush through which they had to crawl on all fours. At times they crossed deep-shaded rhino paths only to be led off into the thickets again. In some places there was profuse blood sign, in others very little.

This kind of tracking is dangerous. A wounded rhino in such cover is pure poison. Berry thought of the position they were in as he clawed through the tangles, crawled along the wild-game tunnels, tried to avoid thorns and nettles, fully expecting that at any second two tons of insane fury would turn on him at point-blank range.

At the end of an hour the peak of Mount Kenya, far above them, vanished in sullen clouds as a misty rain began to fall on the hillside. Berry was thoroughly discouraged; he knew the rain would quickly wash out both blood and track. But Siede predicted the trail would last long enough for them to find the rhino. They had continued on less than 200 yards in the rain when there was a sudden hair-raising crash from the bush ahead, and Berry saw the big black shape of the rhino loom up, only 15 yards off. It paused, as if trying to locate them, and then charged. Berry made out the outline of a bulky shoulder. He assumed the head was pointed toward him. Not waiting any longer, he hammered both shots into the shoulder, first the right barrel, then the left.

Nothing happened. There was neither sound nor movement from the rhino and he realized, even while he fed fresh cases into the breech, that the shots had not been needed. The bull was dead before they were fired. He had died coming for them, midway in his headlong rush, in bush so thick that it supported his weight and kept the carcass from falling to the ground.

The bull measured five feet four inches tall at the shoulder and ten feet ten inches from nose to base of tail. He weighed well over 4,000 pounds. His horn measured 30¼ inches in length and more than 25 inches around at the base; the second horn stood 12 inches above the skull.

Although the Kikuyus were known to exaggerate their

reports of game, they had not embroidered the truth about the old monster rhino of Kihali Hill.

Now Berry was ready for the biggest adventure of the entire safari—getting some good elephant pictures and a trophy bull. From the time he had started to map his plans for getting the trophies he wanted, an outstanding elephant had loomed above everything else, except the Nile lechwe. He also wanted just as much to make the kind of elephant pictures no sportsman had gotten before. The fulfillment of these objectives was to involve him in the greatest difficulties, the severest hardships and the gravest danger he faced while in Africa, but their realization also was to bring him the ultimate in thrills and satisfaction.

Berry, contrary to common reference to the lion as king of the beasts, felt that the elephant stood unchallenged as monarch of African game. He also considered the elephant to be the most dangerous trophy animal on the face of the earth, ranking ahead of lion, rhino or buffalo. When enraged, the elephant strikes fear into all living creatures, animal and human alike.

During his 1947 safari, Berry had killed a bull with tusks weighing 95 pounds apiece. He was out to break his own record; unless he could better it, he would not shoot this time. That meant he must find at least a 100-pounder. He was setting his sights very high. The average tusker killed by safari parties nowadays carries ivory weighing not more than 60 pounds to a side. An 80-pounder is considered very good; anything bigger exceptional. An elephant with 100-pound tusks is an almost unheard-of rarity today.

Don thought their chances would be best on the Voi River in Kenya, where two very large elephants had been taken within the last decade or so. At a Walangulo village in that district the native chief told them of an exceptional bull that was raiding the local corn patch. All who had seen this elephant agreed that he had ivory four arms out, the chief said.

Among the blacks, that is the standard way of measuring tusks. An "arm" is 18 inches, a measure determined from the average span between finger tips and elbow. Four arms would mean six feet of tusk protruding from the jaw; another two feet or more would be imbedded in the skull.

Berry and Don were at the patch at first light the following morning. They found the garden completely trampled. With N'Yamu, their tracker, and the chief, they followed the spoor into a mat of bush, grass and vines, which was ten feet high. They trailed the elephant through that hellish tangle and got themselves charged point-blank at 15 yards, only to find the elephant was no better than a 60- or 70-pounder. Luckily, however, at the last second he lost them in the thick bush. Berry and the others cautiously backed away.

That was the disappointing beginning of an elephant hunt that was to last 25 days and would take them over much of Kenya, from the seacoast to the mountains, into swamps and over dry plains, and through jungles so thick that campsites had to be hacked out of them with knives. Deliberately they invaded the most remote and inaccessible areas, knowing that their prizes would not be found in country where hunters penetrated regularly. The suffering they endured during this expedition, and the roughness of the terrain, were the greatest of the whole safari.

In the Athi River country, they tramped 30 miles a day in blinding sun with the thermometer registering 130 degrees at noon, tracking down a bull that Wacomba natives said carried tusks five arms out, only to find he was no better than an 85-pounder. Not far from the Athi they located a waterhole where more than 100 elephants came to drink in the course of an hour. The location provided Berry with actors for one of the finest film sequences of the hunt, but not a good tusker. There wasn't a large one in the herd.

At last they found what they wanted on the Tana River. An hour after daylight one morning, they discovered a huge track crossing the trail their truck had made the day before. When Berry set his booted feet in it, one directly ahead of the other, the two of them did not quite span the giant footprint.

They took the track across open arid country toward the dense jungle that paralleled the river. Siede and a local tracker were sent ahead to try to get a look at the ivory. Three hours later Siede sprinted back to report that they had overtaken the bull halfway to the Tana, and that the long search was over.

"He has bwana's ivory, and it is more than four arms out," the gunbearer explained.

The track led into a belt of dense bush and grass. The cover meant Berry would have only one chance. In all likelihood, he would have to make a brain shot at very close range. A six-ton elephant can move through tangles as silently as a ghost if he chooses; however, if undisturbed, he's likely to reveal his whereabouts by breaking branches as he feeds or flapping his huge ears, or by the rumbling of his giant belly. Berry and Don wormed along, avoiding the dry bush and the thickest grass, hoping to hear the bull before he heard them.

They didn't quite make it.

A couple of steps ahead of Berry, the native tracker, without time to dodge or run, suddenly went down on his knees to give his bwana a clear shot. Just then Berry saw the head of the biggest elephant he had ever seen burst through the bush 40 feet away. His ears were outstretched, tusks lifted high, trunk coiled and ready to flick out like a great whiplash. He did not trumpet and made little noise, but he was coming to kill.

In one lightning glance, Berry took in all of him: the wrinkled, dusty skin, the open mouth that looked like a small red cave under the upcurled trunk. He even measured the tusks with his eyes and gave Siede a flick of mental credit for making a close estimate. Then he shot.

It was a forehead shot, which meant that there was no chance of the bullet reaching the bull's brain, but Berry had no choice. Unless he stopped the tusker in its tracks, he or the native or both of them would be trampled to a bloody pulp.

From a distance of only ten paces, Berry's 500-grain solid bullet delivered a deadly battering-ram blow, squarely in the center of the elephant's head. It stopped the bull as a blow on the point of the chin stops an oncoming boxer. The elephant swung halfway around. Then Berry, trying for the brain, poured the solid from the left barrel into his ear.

The great, gray hindquarters sagged momentarily, but then the elephant, maddened by pain, whirled away and went crashing blindly into the bush. The bull was no longer running quietly. The small trees in his path cracked and broke as if a tornado were knocking them down.

Berry raced after him, feeding fresh cartridges into the breech of the .470. After a hundred yards, he overtook the bull, which was still lumbering straight away. Berry tried for a spine shot, but the bullet was too low to break him down. It spun him sidewise, however, and Berry had one more chance to try for the brain. He laced the heavy bullet into the ear opening. The bull's hindquarters failed, his knees buckled, and he slumped forward on his belly and lay quietly, apparently dead. Berry shot twice more to make sure, once in the brain and once in the heart region. As the huge head settled, its tusks were resting on the trunk of a broken tree. Berry's elephant hunt was over.

Berry and Don put a tape on the bull; it showed that he stood 11 feet 6 inches at the shoulder and his outspread ears had a span of 10 feet 4 inches. His rear foot measured 26 inches in length, the front 24. He was an inch over 29 feet from tip of trunk to tip of tail, and his tusks were 6 feet 5 inches out, 9 feet overall. They measured 23 inches in circumference at the gums, and weighed almost 140 pounds each.

Although Berry had taken a much better trophy than he had hoped for, before leaving Africa he was to see an elephant far bigger.

From the time of his first safari, he had believed that in some remote place where white hunters had not penetrated— and he knew there were still a few such spots in Africa—elephants bigger than any believed to exist still lived. He was convinced that bulls with tusks six arms out still roamed the jungle. Now he wanted to find such a place and photograph a gigantic elephant, a tusker so old and so huge that Berry could feel reasonably certain there was none older or bigger on earth.

He did not want to kill it. He would be satisfied with pictures. For the climax of his long African hunt, he was willing to put his guns aside, although Siede would always be beside him with the .470 in case of trouble.

Berry never revealed where he went for this grandfather of elephants, but he did find what he had been looking for. The breathtaking pictures he brought back proved it. Berry knew that if the home country of such a bull were made known ivory hunters or trophy seekers would be on the trail the next day. He did not want that to happen. He would only say that after the safari left the Tana it invaded country that had never been tracked before—the most inaccessible and impossible territory of the entire hunt.

The hunters followed overgrown, forgotten roads. They came to a bridge so decayed that in order to use it they had to rebuild it first with rope bark and other available materials. When all trace of old wheel tracks vanished from their route, they sent a dozen safari boys on ahead to cut away the vines and thorns so that there would be some kind of a path for the hunting car and the truck to follow. The terrain chewed their tires to ribbons, and the vehicles forded rivers on sandbars that had never known a wheel before. Each time the path ended, they had to hack their way through jungle and grass and swamp. Africa grudgingly yielded, inch by inch, but fought back by inflicting the tortures of heat and thirst. In addition, the men were bedeviled by flies and mosquitoes and black bees, as well as thorns and nettles and bearded grasses that set human skin on fire.

Their endurance, however, paid off. At last the safari penetrated the lost world that Berry had believed existed. The natives of this African Shangri-La had never seen a truck or held a rifle in their hands. Many of them had never seen a white man before. For hunting and defense, they used bows and poison-tipped arrows; their hunters claimed that an elephant shot with one of these arrows would die within half an hour, a man within three minutes. Even a rhino would vomit, rear up, and fall dead, they declared.

They said, too, that there were elephants in their country with tusks six arms out. That was worth looking into.

Almost at once Berry and Don tracked down a bull bigger than Berry's trophy. It was apparently an outcast from a herd, since it was traveling with a younger *askari* bull, or bodyguard. Such strange teams are commonplace when an old elephant leaves the herd. Nine times out of ten the bull being guarded is a one-tusker, past his prime and no longer able to defend himself.

That was the case this time. The old bull's one tusk was a long, curving, magnificent crescent, the other a broken stub that jutted out bluntly from his jaw. This was not what Berry wanted, even for pictures. When he tried to back away, however, the askari got his scent and blasted out a shrill squeal of rage. He started for the men at a shuffling trot, his feet kicking up puffs of dust in the dry sand. The hunters scattered like a covey of quail and shook him off. After trumpeting a few times, he walked slowly into the bush after the broken-tusked giant he had undertaken to protect.

Many days later at a water hole, Berry and Don picked up a huge elephant track and followed it for hours across dry plains in the broiling heat. They finally overtook the elephant at the edge of a strip of forest. When he came in sight he was walking toward them, about 400 yards off.

Berry Brooks' breath caught in his throat. He could hardly believe there was such a bull left in Africa. The gray bulk stood close to 12 feet at the shoulders and could not have weighed less than seven tons. The aged skin hung in loose folds; the gleaming, perfectly matched tusks were very heavy, and they curved down so much that they almost touched the ground as the great head bobbed with each majestic step. Those tusks would weigh 165 pounds each. The natives had come close to the truth when they bragged they knew of an elephant with ivory six arms out. Here, indeed, was a patriarch bull, an ancient giant older and bigger than Berry had ever hoped to see; it must have been living for at least a century on these parched plains in the secret heart of Africa.

Berry went to meet him with the cameras. Siede went along, carrying the .470, but they had no need of the rifle. The wind was right, the light good. With the calm dignity of royalty, the great tusker marched past them and entered the forest 50 yards away. Berry kept the cameras trained on him until the thick timber swallowed up the magnificent beast.

"I hope no hunter ever lays eyes on you again," he said softly to himself.

SPECIAL OFFER FOR BOOK CLUB MEMBERS

Save $10 on these versatile Stellar 7 X 35 Binoculars

They're ideal all-purpose binoculars — good for a wide range of outdoor activities from football games to bird watching.

Look at these features:

☐ **Fully coated optics.** Both lenses and prisms are coated to give them maximum light-gathering power and to insure bright, clear, sharp images.

☐ **Quick, accurate focusing.** A right-eye adjustment compensates for differences in vision of the two eyes. A center focusing wheel permits fast adjustment.

☐ **Magnification.** "7 X" refers to the magnifying power of the binoculars. It means an object 700 feet away will appear to be only 100 feet away. "35" refers to the diameter in millimeters of the objective lenses, which determines the amount of light admitted. The larger the lenses, the greater the amount of light and the later in the evening you can use the binoculars.

☐ **Field of View.** The Stellar Binoculars provide a 393-foot field of view at 1000 yards.

☐ **Weight.** 21½ ounces.

The binoculars come in a soft vinyl case with carrying strap. You also get a shoulder strap and four lens covers.

Suggested Retail Price $49.95. Your Club Price only

$39.95

plus delivery and handling

Stellar 7 X 35 Binoculars are fully guaranteed against any defects in workmanship.

TO GET YOUR BINOCULARS, JUST SEND YOUR ORDER TO:
BOOK CLUB P.O. BOX 2044, LATHAM, N.Y. 12111

Ask for STELLAR BINOCULARS, NO. 7000, and enclose your check or money order for $39.95 plus $3.10 for delivery and handling and we'll send you your binoculars right away.